Be A Better Reader

Level D

Seventh Edition

Nila Banton Smith

GLOBE FEARON EDUCATIONAL PUBLISHERS
A Division of Simon & Schuster
Upper Saddle River, New Jersey

Pronunciation Key

Symbol	Key Word	Respelling
a	act	(akt)
ah	star	(stahr)
ai	dare	(dair)
aw	also	(awl soh)
ay	flavor	(flay vər)
e	end	(end)
ee	eat	(eet)
er	learn	(lern)
	sir	(ser)
	fur	(fer)
i	hit	(hit)
eye	idea	(eye dee ə)
y	like	(lyk)
ir	deer	(dir)
	fear	(fir)
oh	open	(oh pen)
oi	foil	(foil)
	boy	(boi)
or	horn	(horn)
ou	out	(out)
	flower	(flou ər)
oo	hoot	(hoot)
	rule	(rool)
yoo	few	(fyoo)
	use	(yooz)

Symbol	Key Word	Respelling
u	book	(buk)
	put	(put)
uh	cup	(kuhp)
ə	a as in along	(ə lawng)
	e as in moment	(moh mənt)
	i as in modify	(mahd ə fy)
	o as in protect	(prə tekt)
	u as in circus	(ser kəs)
ch	chill	(chil)
g	go	(goh)
j	joke	(johk)
	bridge	(brij)
k	kite	(kyt)
	cart	(kahrt)
ng	bring	(bring)
s	sum	(suhm)
	cent	(sent)
sh	sharp	(shahrp)
th	thin	(thin)
z	zebra	(zee brə)
	pose	(pohz)
zh	treasure	(treszh ər)

Be A Better Reader, Level D, Seventh Edition
Nila Banton Smith

Copyright © 1997 by Globe Fearon Educational Publisher. One Lake Street, Upper Saddle River, New Jersey 07458. All rights reserved. No part of this book may be kept in any information storage or retrieval system, transmitted or reproduced in any form or by any means without the prior written permission of the publisher.

Printed in the United States of America
9 10   99 00 01

C12
ISBN 0-8359-1926-9

Acknowledgments
We wish to express our appreciation for permission to use and adapt copyrighted materials.

The dictionary definitions in this book are reprinted with permission of Macmillan General Reference USA, a Division of Simon & Schuster Inc., from WEBSTER'S NEW WORLD DICTIONARY, Basic School Edition. Copyright © 1983 by Simon & Schuster Inc.

G.P. Putnam's Sons for the adaptation of "Incident at Exeter." Adapted by permission of G.P. Putnam's Sons from INCIDENT AT EXETER by John Fuller. Copyright © 1966 by John Fuller.

Photo Credits
p. 11: *(left)* George Gerster/Photo Researchers, *(right)* Jerry Frank/DPI; **p. 13:** George Holton/Photo Researchers; **p. 14:** The Bettmann Archive; **p. 18:** Rex USA; **p. 19:** Rex USA; **p. 41:** Wide World Photos; **p. 42:** Leonard Lee Rue III/Monkmeyer; **p. 46:** Animals, Animals/Oxford Scientific Films; **p. 47:** *(left)* © R.F. Head/DPI, *(top right)* Lewis Watson/Monkmeyer, *(bottom right)* Zig Leszczynski/Animals, Animals; **p. 48:** *(left)* Leonard Lee Rue III/Animals, Animals, *(top right)* Leonard Lee Rue III/DPI, *(bottom right)* Sydney Thomson/Animals, Animals (cat), Paula Wright/Animals, Animals (dog); **p. 58:** Jen and Des Bartlett/Bruce Coleman; **p. 63:** Baseball Hall of Fame; **p. 70:** *(in order of appearance)* The Bettmann Archive, Gamma Liaison, AP/Wide World, Gamma Liaison, AP/Wide World; **p. 77:** The Bettmann Archive; **p.86:** *(left)* Esty Epstein/DPI, *(right)* Wide World Photos; **p. 100:** DPI; **p. 104:** Shelley Grossman/Woodfin Camp and Associates; **p. 105:** *(left)* M. Mickey Gibson/Animals, Animals, *(top right)* Clem Haagner/Bruce Coleman, *(bottom right)* George H.H. Huey; **p. 115:** UPI; **p. 117:** Wide World Photos; **p. 158:** *(left)* Art Resources/EPA, *(right)* The Bettmann Archive; **p. 159:** *(right)* The Bettmann Archive, *(right)* NASA.

Contents

Unit Four Egypt and the Nile 92

Unit Five Forces of Nature 122

Unit Six Communications 152

How to Use *Be A Better Reader*

For more than thirty years, *Be A Better Reader* has helped students improve their reading skills. *Be A Better Reader* teaches the comprehension and study skills that you need to read and enjoy all types of materials—from library books to the different textbooks that you will encounter in school.

To get the most from *Be A Better Reader*, you should know how the lessons are organized. As you read the following explanations, it will be helpful to look at some of the lessons.

In each of the first four lessons of a unit, you will apply an important skill to a reading selection in literature, social studies, science, or mathematics. Each of these lessons includes the following seven sections.

Skill Focus

This section teaches you a specific skill. You should read the Skill Focus carefully, paying special attention to words that are printed in boldface type. The Skill Focus tells you about a skill that you will use when you read the selection.

Word Clues

This section teaches you how to recognize and use different types of context clues. These clues will help you with the meanings of the underlined words in the selection.

Reading a Literature, Social Studies, Science, or Mathematics Selection

This section introduces the selection that you will read and gives you suggestions about what to look for as you read. The suggestions will help you understand the selection.

Selection

The selections in the literature lessons are similar to those in a literature anthology, library book, newspaper, or magazine. The social studies selec- tions are like chapters in a social studies textbook or encyclopedia. They often include maps and tables. The science selections, like a science textbook, include special words in boldface type and sometimes diagrams. The mathematics selections will help you acquire skill in reading mathematics textbooks.

Recalling Facts

Answers to the questions in this section—the first of three activity sections—can be found in the selection. You will sometimes have to reread parts of the selection to do this activity.

Interpreting Facts

The second activity includes questions whose answers are not directly stated in the selection. For these questions, you must combine the information in the selection with what you already know in order to *infer* the answers.

Skill Focus Activity

In the last activity, you will use the skill that you learned in the Skill Focus section at the beginning of the lesson to answer questions about the selection. If you have difficulty completing this activity, reread the Skill Focus section.

The remaining lessons in each unit give you practice with such skills as using a dictionary, an encyclopedia, and other reference materials; using phonics and syllabication aids in recognizing new words; locating and organizing information; and adjusting reading rate. Other reading skills that are necessary in everyday experience are also covered, such as reading a bus schedule and a menu.

Each time that you learn a new skill in *Be A Better Reader*, look for opportunities to use the skill in your other reading at school and at home. Your reading ability will improve the more you practice reading!

Lesson 1

Point of View

Reading a Literature Selection

▶ **Background Information**

People and scientists have observed UFOs, or unidentified flying objects, for many years. Some think that UFOs are spaceships from other planets; others believe that UFOs are really airplanes or are strange occurrences of nature.

The following story, based on a news report of an actual event, took place in a small New England town. Did the UFO carry beings from other planets? The people of Exeter thought so.

▶ **Skill Focus**

Before writing, an author must decide who is going to tell the story. The story can be told by one of the characters who participated in the events or by an outsider who observed the events. The **point of view** an author chooses determines the information that is given in a story and how it is presented.

When a story's events are reported by an outsider who witnessed or knew about the events but did not participate in them, the author is using the **third person objective point of view.** Like a newspaper reporter, the narrator does not tell what he or she is thinking or feeling. Also, because the narrator does not enter the minds of the story characters, the narrator cannot tell the reader what they are thinking or feeling. The narrator tells only the facts of the events.

When you try to determine the point of view in a story, think about these questions.

1. Is the narrator an outsider or a participant in the event?
2. Do you know what the narrator is thinking or feeling?
3. Do you know what the characters in the story are thinking or feeling?

▶ **Word Clues**

When you read a word that you do not know, look for context clues to help you. Context clues are nearby words and phrases that help make the meaning clearer. Read the following sentences.

Officer Toland listened suspiciously to Norman's story. Afterward, the officer admitted that he had reacted skeptically.

If you don't know the meaning of the word *skeptically,* the word *suspiciously* in the first sentence can help you. The words *skeptically* and *suspiciously* are synonyms. *Skeptically* means "suspiciously."

Use **synonym** context clues to find the meaning of the three underlined words in the selection.

▶ **Strategy Tip**

"The Thing at Exeter," is written from the third person objective point of view. As you read the selection, pay special attention to the information that the narrator gives you about the events that took place in Exeter.

The Thing at Exeter

Are there visitors from outer space? Nobody has proved anything one way or the other. But people around Exeter, New Hampshire, haven't stopped talking about the "thing" that appeared the night of September 3, 1965.

That night, eighteen-year-old Norman Muscarello arrived at the Exeter police station. He was pale and trembling. Officer Reginald Toland, who was on desk duty, got Muscarello to calm down a bit. Then Muscarello told him an incredible story.

Muscarello said he had been hitchhiking home along Route 150, just outside Exeter. Suddenly, in the moonless night sky, a huge, silent, glowing object glided toward him across an open field.

Muscarello leaped from the road into a shallow ditch and watched. He later admitted that he was terror-stricken. The object drifted and circled over a nearby house. Muscarello estimated that the dome-shaped, saucer-like object was about eighty feet wide. He noticed that it had flashing red lights and made no noise. When it seemed to back away, Muscarello

jumped up and ran to another house. He banged with his fists on the door, but the people inside would not open it. He then ran to the road and waved down a car. A middle-aged couple drove him to the police station.

Officer Toland listened suspiciously to Muscarello's story. Afterward, the officer admitted that he had reacted skeptically. He didn't think that Muscarello had seen anything extraordinary. Officer Toland thought that Muscarello had probably spotted a low-flying plane or helicopter. But when Muscarello insisted that he'd seen something very strange, Toland called in another officer from patrol.

On arriving at the police station, Officer Eugene Bertrand reported an odd coincidence. He had stopped on a <u>bypass</u> of Route 101 to check a parked car. The driver told him that even after she had taken the detour from the main road, a silent object with flashing red lights continued to follow her. It glided above her for about nine miles and at times came within a few feet of her car.

When he heard this report, Toland turned to Muscarello and said, "Does this sound like the 'thing' you saw?" Muscarello said it did.

Officer Toland asked Bertrand to escort Muscarello back to the open field where he had sighted the strange object. At 3:00 A.M., Officer Bertrand and Norman Muscarello got out of the car at the field along Route 150.

The sky was clear. It was <u>crystalline</u>. Visibility was unlimited and there was no wind. The stars were like bright pinpoints against the dark.

The two walked down the sloping field. Bertrand took out his flashlight and shined it on the shrubs and distant trees. About a hundred yards from the roadside was the barn in which Carl Dining kept his horses. Bertrand and Muscarello reached the fence and still saw nothing.

Bertrand told Muscarello that he must have seen a helicopter. The youth insisted that, because he was familiar with all types of aircraft, he would have recognized a helicopter.

Muscarello walked away into the field. Bertrand turned his back to the barn and shined his light toward the trees. Suddenly, the horses in the barn began to kick and whinny. The dogs penned up nearby began to whimper and howl.

Muscarello shouted, "I see it! I see it!" Bertrand wheeled around and looked at the trees beyond the barn. He reported that a bright, rounded object rose slowly into the air from behind two tall pine trees. Making no sound, it moved toward them in a seesawing motion, like a leaf fluttering in the air. The entire area was bathed in brilliant red light. The white sides of Carl Dining's house turned blood red.

Officer Bertrand reached for his .38, hesitated, then shoved the gun back into its holster. Looking again at the red light, he shouted at Muscarello, "It might be radioactive! Run for cover!" He grabbed Muscarello and yanked him toward the cruiser. Bertrand called Toland, back at the station, on his car radio. "I see the thing myself!" he screamed.

Just then, another officer, David Hunt, sped up to the farm in his police car. He had heard Bertrand and Toland talking on the radio and rushed to see what was going on.

As he jumped out of his patrol car, he could see the "thing." It was <u>hovering</u> about a hundred feet in the air. Suspended noiselessly, it slowly started to move east. The three men stared in surprise at the UFO. If it were a plane or a helicopter, it was like no other they had ever seen. It didn't move like an airplane or a helicopter. It could speed away, stop in a second, and then hover. It could change direction instantly. Lights along its bottom rim flashed in a left-to-right and then right-to-left pattern. The two officers and Muscarello said that it didn't seem like anything of this world.

After the "thing" disappeared over the

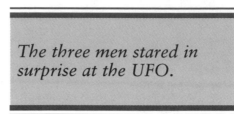

The three men stared in surprise at the UFO.

horizon, the three men headed back to town and filled out a police report. Although Officer Hunt filled out a long report about the sighting, he no longer discusses the case.

Officer Bertrand later said that his fellow officers didn't make fun of him for reporting seeing a UFO. "We saw something out in that field," he said. "I think there is probably some explanation. I don't say it was from outer space. But I know there was some sort of flying craft. I was in the Air Force, and I know aircraft make noise. This one didn't. It was silent; no hum. . . . Just moving through the air silently. And the light, so bright it lighted up the whole field. There was something there. We weren't all seeing something that wasn't there!"

During the 1960s, the U.S. Air Force was in charge of looking into UFO sightings. What was the Air Force's opinion of the "thing" at Exeter? The Air Force said that the Eighth Air Force was carrying out an operation known as Big Blast in New England that night. Air Force officials stressed that the "general description of flashing lights is somewhat like reports of aircraft during refueling or when taking low-level pictures."

However, Air Force officials insisted that Operation Big Blast had ended by the time of the sightings. None of the aircraft from the exercise were in the area after 1:35 A.M. The Air Force report simply stated that "since no aircraft can be placed in the area at 2:00 A.M., the case is listed as unidentified."

RECALLING FACTS

Write the answers to the following questions on the lines provided. You may go back to the selection to find an answer.

1. In the story, how many people saw the "thing"? Who were they?

_____

_____

_____

2. When and where did the story take place?

_____

_____

3. Describe the "thing."

_____

_____

_____

4. Why did Norman Muscarello rush to the police station?

_____

_____

5. How did Officers Bertrand and Hunt react when they saw the "thing"?

_____

_____

6. How did the Air Force list this case in its final report?

_____

7. Draw a line to match each word with its correct meaning.

hovering   transparent

bypass   floating

crystalline   auxiliary road

INTERPRETING FACTS

Not all the questions about a selection are answered directly in the selection. For the following questions, you will have to figure out answers not directly stated in the selection. Write the answers to the questions on the lines provided.

1. Why do you think that Officer Bertrand stopped to help a woman parked on a bypass?

_____

_____

_____

_____

2. Why did Carl Dining's farm animals become upset and agitated?

_____

_____

_____

3. How did the UFO differ from an airplane or helicopter?

_____

_____

_____

_____

_____

4. Why might Officer Hunt have decided not to talk about the sighting?

_____

_____

_____

5. Why did the Air Force list the sighting as unidentified?

_____

_____

_____

_____

6. What do you think the "thing" was? Support your opinion with details from the story.

_____

_____

_____

_____

_____

Write the answers to the following questions on the lines provided. You may go back to the selection to find an answer.

1. a. Does the author tell you who the narrator is? _____

    b. Is the narrator an outsider or a participant in the event? _____

    c. Does the reader know the narrator's thoughts and feelings about the UFO? Explain.

_____

_____

2. In the story, does the reader know what Norman Muscarello was thinking or feeling when he saw the UFO? Explain.

_____

_____

_____

3. In the story, does the reader know what the police officers were thinking or feeling when they saw the UFO? Explain.

_____

_____

_____

4. Why is the third person objective a good point of view for this story?

_____

_____

_____

5. Imagine that you are a reporter. Write the first paragraph of a newspaper article describing the event that occurred on September 3, 1965, in Exeter, New Hampshire. Using third person objective point of view, answer the questions *who, what, when, where,* and *why.*

_____

_____

_____

_____

_____

_____

▶ **Real Life Connections** Write the first paragraph of a newspaper article from a reporter's point of view describing a UFO event in your community.

Fact and Opinion

— Reading a Social Studies Selection —

▶ Background Information

Before you read this selection, preview it. Previewing will give you an idea of what is in the selection. First read the title and the headings. Then study the photographs; be sure to read their captions. This information will give you an overview of the topics in the selection.

When reading textbooks, you may find words that are difficult to pronounce. These words are usually respelled to help you pronounce them. In this selection, the word Nazca is respelled (NAHZ kah). The pronunciation key on page 2 will help you pronounce the respelled words.

▶ Skill Focus

When you read books, newspapers, and magazines, you should try to recognize which statements are **facts** and which are **opinions**.

A fact is information that can be proven. You can check a statement of fact to be sure that it is right. The following sentences are statements of fact.

> The Nazca Desert is in Perú.

> The statues are carved from volcanic rock.

An opinion is a belief or feeling based on what seems to be true or valid. An opinion cannot be proven. People can hold different opinions about the same topic. Following are two different opinions on the same topic.

> Intelligent life probably exists in other galaxies.

> I believe Earth is the only planet to have intelligent life.

Because none of the planets in outer space has been explored, the existence of life on another planet has not been proven or disproven. Therefore, both statements are opinions.

Sometimes authors do not draw conclusions about what they write. When authors do not draw conclusions, the reader must do so. While facts and opinions are both important, conclusions based on fact are always stronger than those based on opinion.

▶ Word Clues

Read the sentence below. Look for context clues that explain the underlined word.

> In addition, people who are not scientists have come up with some startling underlined theories, or ideas, of their own.

If you don't know the meaning of the word *theories*, the word following the word *or* can help you. Theories are ideas that explain how something is done or came to be. The word *theories* is explained in the appositive phrase set off by commas and the word *or*.

Use **appositive phrases** set off by commas or dashes, and the word *or* to find the meaning of the three underlined words in the selection.

▶ Strategy Tip

As you read about the archaeological finds in "Ancient Visitors?" try to sort out the facts from the opinions. Remember that whatever conclusions you draw will be stronger if they are based on facts.

Ancient Visitors?

The earliest civilizations on Earth stretch far back in time toward the unknown past. Yet we do have knowledge about the way earlier human beings lived. People have always left their marks on the earth. Their marks, or remains, include buildings, tools, weapons, and cave wall drawings. All these remains help us to create a picture of the past.

Some ancient peoples, however, left remains that are mysterious to us. Several of these remains have become famous. In the Nazca (NAHZ kah) Desert in Peru, there are huge drawings that can be seen only from the sky. Easter Island in the Pacific Ocean has giant statues of strange-looking people. In Egypt, pyramids loom over an empty desert.

Although there are many different opinions about these ancient remains, no one explanation so far is complete. Scientists, using observable facts and hard evidence, have attempted to explain the ancient remains in many ways. In addition, people who are not scientists have come up with some startling theories, or ideas, of their own. Some theories suggest that such remains prove that <u>extraterrestrials</u>—visitors from outer space—came to Earth long ago.

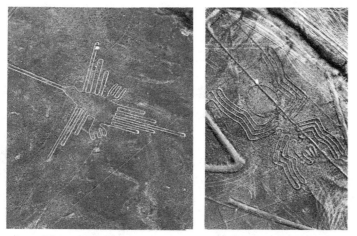

These drawings found in the Nazca Desert can be seen only from the air.

The Nazca Desert Drawings

The Nazca Desert is on a high plateau. On this plateau, huge figures and patterns are scratched into the ground. The drawings are clear only when seen from the sky.

In 1939, when planes began to fly over the desert plain of southern Peru, pilots recognized huge figures on the ground. These figures included giant birds, fish, lizards, and other animals. One eight-legged spider measures over 150 feet in length.

Other drawings are of geometric shapes. There are angles, triangles, and lines. Some lines, running straight for five miles, were laid out straighter than if they had been measured with modern air-survey techniques.

The drawings were made by scratching away the thin top layer of dark stones. The light-colored soil underneath formed the patterns. Although the Nazca drawings are over one thousand years old, they have not been affected by time, because the climate of the area creates little soil erosion. Scientists know how the drawings were made, but there is little information about who made them and why.

Many scientists believe that the drawings were made by the Nazca Indians. The Nazcas lived in this area of Peru long ago, but little else is known about them. Some people think the Nazcas were able to make the drawings by doing them first on a small scale and then on a large scale on the desert surface. The perfectly straight lines were probably the most difficult to create. Logs may have been erected as sighting posts to help the Nazcas lay the lines straight.

Why were the drawings made? Some scientists think that the Nazcas studied a kind of astronomy. The drawings may have shown the positions of the stars and the sun. Other people believe the drawings were part of the Nazca's religion. They were messages to the sky gods who could see them from above.

Another explanation for the strange drawings connects them with extraterrestrial visitors. One man, Erich Von Daniken, suggested that the patterns served as landing strips for ancient astronauts. Because the drawings can be seen only from the air, he claimed that they must have been made by beings who were capable of flight. Daniken believed that visitors from outer space used their higher technology to create the Nazca drawings.

The Easter Island Giants

Easter Island, or Rapa Nui, a remote island in the South Pacific Ocean, is famous for the giant statues that have stood on its soil for centuries. These statues were carved from the volcanic rock of a crater on the island. First, more than three hundred statues were discovered in various places on the island. Later, about four hundred more were found inside the crater; these statues were unfinished or waiting to be moved.

✗ The Easter Island statues are large, heavy, and strange-looking. Some of the statues weigh as much as 30 tons and stand 12 feet high. One giant statue, found inside the crater, weighed 50 tons. The appearance of the statues is unusual. They look like human beings, but they have long earlobes and squared-off heads.

Many mysteries surrounded the statues after their discovery. Who carved them? How were they moved out of the crater? How were they raised into an upright position? What was their purpose? Who were the ancient people of Easter Island?

Many researchers have visited Easter Island to try to <u>unravel</u>, or figure out, the secrets of its mysterious past. Thor Heyerdahl (HY ə r dahl), a famous writer and explorer, visited the island in 1956. With the help of the native people, he tried to duplicate how the statues may have been carved and moved. Using stone tools, the workers carved out the general shape of one statue in three days. Then, with ropes tied around the statue, 150 people dragged it a short distance.

Since Heyerdahl's experiments, many other researchers have investigated how the huge statues could have been moved. Searching for evidence, they found stone posts used to secure ropes and wear marks in statues from ropes that were wrapped around them. Researchers also found that the bases of some statues were chipped, indicating that the stone had rubbed against something. In addition, some statues that were found along the transport route lie

Much about the gigantic statues on Easter Island remains a mystery.

broken into separate pieces—something that would happen only if they had fallen from an upright position. Based on this evidence and their own experiments, researchers concluded that the statues were moved while standing upright on wooden platforms dragged over rollers cut from tree trunks.

There are no trees on Easter Island today. However, scientists have found evidence that at least some parts of the island were once covered with thick forests of palm trees. The evidence for these forests includes ancient palm nuts, fossilized roots of palm trees, and thick layers of palm pollen in the mud at the bottom of a lake.

Heyerdahl believed that the original settlers of Easter Island sailed there from South America to the east. However, recent analysis of skeletal remains shows that the islanders' ancestors came from the Polynesian Islands to the west. Many of the words in the Rapa Nui language spoken by some people on Easter Island today are the same as words in languages spoken in the Polynesian Islands.

Erich Von Daniken and others believed that the Easter Island statues are further proof of ancient visitors from outer space. Daniken argued that the statues are too large and heavy to have been moved by ordinary people. He believed that the statues were erected by ancient astronauts visiting Earth from distant planets. He also believed that these extraterrestrials carved the statues in their own likeness.

The Great Pyramid of Egypt

The Great Pyramid of Egypt has long been one of the wonders of the world. Built over five thousand years ago, it is the largest and most impressive of the many pyramids that dot the Egyptian desert.

✔ The Great Pyramid covers 13 acres of land. It stands almost 500 feet high, as tall as a 42-story building. The pyramid is made of more than two million stones, each weighing about 2.5 tons.

The pyramid is not only very large but also precisely made. Its corners are almost perfect right angles. The four sides face exactly north, south, east, and west. The stones are so perfectly shaped that they fit snugly together without <u>mortar</u>, a mixture of cement, water, and sand used to hold stones together. Not even a knife blade can be put between them.

How were the ancient Egyptians able to move and raise such huge stones? How did they acquire their knowledge of geometry and architecture? Most experts believe that the Egyptians knew enough about geometry and astronomy to build and position the pyramid. History books explain that thousands of laborers worked over six hundred years to construct the pyramid. They pulled the stones over the desert with ropes or on wooden rollers. They used ramps to pull the stones to the top of the pyramid.

Some people, however, doubt that the Egyptians could have built the pyramid on their own. These people believe that more advanced beings from outer space told the Egyptians how to build the pyramid. They think that these visitors to Earth gave the Egyptians a special power source or special machines to raise the heavy stones. In the opinion of these people, the Great Pyramid is more evidence that extraterrestrial visitors once came to Earth.

There is no proof that extraterrestrials have ever visited Earth. Many people would like to believe that the theory is true. Yet, until it is proven, it is simply a fascinating explanation for the mysteries of Earth's past.

An ancient engineering marvel, the Great Pyramid rises into the sky like a solitary mountain.

Write the answers to the following questions on the lines provided. You may go back to the selection to find an answer.

1. Match the details listed below with the ancient remains that they describe.
   a. Nazca Desert drawings
   b. Easter Island statues
   c. Great Pyramid of Egypt

   _____ as tall as a 42-story building

   _____ portrays figures of animals

   _____ some found in a crater

2. Write the cause for the effect below.

   Cause _____

   _____

   _____

   Effect The drawings in the Nazca Desert have not been affected by time.

3. Reread the paragraph with an X next to it. Then underline the sentence that best states its main idea.

4. Fill in the circle next to the word that correctly completes each sentence.

   a. The detective tried to _____ the mystery of the disappearing cats.
      ○ recognize   ○ unravel   ○ scratch

   b. A mason works with stone, brick, and

      _____.
      ○ mortar   ○ lava   ○ technology

   c. Some people believe that there are

      _____ living on other planets.
      ○ scientists ○ craters ○ extraterrestrials

Not all the questions about a selection are answered directly in the selection. For the following questions, you will have to figure out answers not directly stated in the selection. Write the answers to the questions on the lines provided.

1. Write the effect for the cause below.

   Cause The Nazca drawings are only clear when seen from the air.

   Effect _____

   _____

2. What could happen that would help solve the mystery of why the Easter Island statues were erected?

   _____

   _____

   _____

   _____

3. Reread the paragraph in the selection with a check mark next to it. Write a sentence describing its main idea.

   _____

   _____

4. Look at the photographs of the drawings scratched on the surface of the Nazca Desert.
   a. What does the first figure resemble?

   _____

   b. What does the second figure resemble?

   _____

   c. How have some people explained the significance of all the Nazca figures and shapes?

   _____

   _____

   _____

Reread the selection to find the statements of fact and opinion asked for in the following questions.

1. List two facts about the Nazca Desert drawings.

   a. _____

   b. _____

2. List two opinions about why the drawings were made.

   a. _____

   b. _____

3. List two facts about the Easter Island statues.

   a. _____

   b. _____

4. List two opinions about the statues.

   a. _____

   b. _____

5. List two facts about the Great Pyramid of Egypt.

   a. _____

   b. _____

6. List two opinions about how the Great Pyramid was constructed.

   a. _____

   b. _____

7. a. Choose one of the mysteries in the selection. Explain how you think it came to be.

   _____

   _____

   b. On what information did you base your explanation? _____

   _____

8. What conclusions can you draw about these ancient mysteries and the extraterrestrial visitor theory?

   _____

   _____

▶ **Real Life Connections** Would you be surprised to run into an extraterrestrial being? Why or why not?

Inferences

__ Reading a Science Selection __

▶ Background Information

Many people believe that Earth is regularly visited by extraterrestrials, or alien beings, from another planet. Many believe that unexplained things are evidence of space visitors. For example, some people believe that alien beings built the Egyptian pyramids; others believe that petroglyphs, or writings on stone, were messages from alien visitors. This selection describes another mysterious occurrence—crop circles—that some believe are markings of extraterrestrials.

▶ Skill Focus

Sometimes you can **infer**, or figure out, information that is not stated directly in a selection. Read the following paragraph. Try to infer the period of time during which the crop circle was created in the farmer's field.

Crop circles always appear suddenly. . . . In Ashcombe, England, a farmer who discovered a crop circle in his cornfield one morning said, "I have a good view of this field from where I live, and the circle is not something I would have missed if it had been there earlier."

The following clues from the paragraph can help you infer when the crop circle was created: Crop circles always appear suddenly. The farmer discovered the crop circle one morning. He said that it was "not something I would have missed if it had been there earlier" because he had a good view of the field from his house.

Using these three clues, you can infer that the entire crop circle was created during the previous night. If it had been in the farmer's field the day before or even earlier, he would have noticed it. He also would have seen it if it had formed over a period of several days.

If you go through the following steps, you will find it easier to infer information.

1. Read carefully.
2. Think about what you've read. Be sure that you understand all the information.
3. Read again and look for clues to information not stated in the reading.
4. Put together the information stated in the selection with information that you already know. Use clues to help you make inferences.

▶ Word Clues

Read the sentences below. Look for context clues that explain the underlined word.

Many people think that crop circles are merely a hoax. A hoax is something that is done to trick or mislead other people.

If you do not know the meaning of the word *hoax*, the second sentence states what the word means. A word meaning that is stated directly can often be found before or after a new word.

Use **definition** context clues to find the meanings of the three underlined words in the selection.

▶ Strategy Tip

Before you read "The Mystery of Crop Circles," preview the selection's headings to see how the information is organized. As you read, pay close attention to the facts and theories. Use them to infer information that is not directly stated.

The Mystery of Crop Circles

A natural phenomenon or a message from alien beings, crop circles, such as these shown here, have baffled scientists for years.

Since the early 1980s, about 2,000 strange patterns have appeared in grainfields in southern England and, less often, in other countries throughout the world, including Canada, Japan, and the United States. The patterns, known as **crop circles,** are made of flattened plants that are all bent down in the same direction. Crop circles range in size from less than 1 meter (39 inches) across to as large as 90 meters (295 feet) long. The flattened areas can be seen by someone standing on the ground, but the patterns are most clear when viewed from a hill or a low-flying airplane.

Some people believe that crop circles are created by a natural <u>phenomenon</u> that we still do not understand. A phenomenon is an event or process that can be observed with the senses. Other people believe that crop circles are the work of extraterrestrial visitors. Many people think that crop circles are merely a hoax. A hoax is something that is done to trick or mislead other people.

Simple to Complex Patterns

The first crop circles to be discovered were single circles in which all the plants were flattened in a clockwise or counterclockwise direction. Over the years, however, the patterns have become more complicated. Some crop circles discovered in recent years have incorporated squares and other angular shapes,

loops and curls, keylike shapes, straight lines to connect shapes, and sets of <u>concentric</u> rings. *Concentric* means "having a common center," like the rings in a bull's-eye target. Some unusual patterns look like strange animals or humanlike figures.

Sudden Discoveries

Crop circles always appear suddenly, usually when the weather is calm. In Ashcombe, England, a farmer who found a crop circle in his cornfield one morning said, "I have a good view of this field from where I live, and the circle is not something I would have missed if it had been there earlier."

Another puzzling fact about crop circles is that there is no evidence of a trail made by anyone entering or leaving the field. "It's two hundred yards from the nearest gate and a long way from the road," the Ashcombe farmer said. "I'm sure a prankster would not have bothered to walk so far." The farmer was even more puzzled when the field was harvested. "We tried to lift the flattened corn but it was impossible, even by machine. That is something I have never known before." The farmer concluded, "While I am still keeping an open mind, I am convinced it was not made by human hand."

A Natural Phenomenon?

Terence Meaden, a retired physics professor in England, has investigated about 1,000 crop circles. He has observed that they often appear when the atmosphere is calm near the ground but windy above. Meaden concluded that crop circles are caused by a <u>vortex</u> in the atmosphere. A vortex is a mass of rapidly spinning air or liquid. Meaden's vortex theory would explain the circles and rings often found in crop circles but not the straight lines and angular shapes. Meaden believes that the angular patterns are simply a hoax.

Japanese physicist Yoshi-Hiko Ohtsuki thinks that crop circles are caused by ball lightning. Ball lightning most often appears as a grapefruit-size fireball that hovers above the ground and moves in bizarre ways, such as against the wind or through walls. Ohtsuki has created some miniature crop circles in the laboratory using a small blob of ball lightning and aluminum dust. "It creates very beautiful circles," Ohtsuki said, "including the double rings sometimes seen in fields." However, the only natural phenomenon known to produce ball lightning is a thunderstorm, and that is not the type of weather in which crop circles have appeared.

Messages from Extraterrestrials?

"This is without a doubt the most wonderful moment of my research," said Pat Delgado as he viewed a new crop circle in Sevenoaks, England. "No human could have done this." A retired engineer, Delgado makes a career of investigating and writing about crop circles. He believes that the patterns are created by a "superior intelligence," most likely extraterrestrials.

Perhaps crop circles are the landing sites of UFOs, say some of Delgado's supporters. Delgado himself thinks that the circles may be coded messages from space visitors. He and his supporters claim that the circles radiate mysterious energy forces. Delgado contends that he can distinguish between a "true" crop circle and a hoax by testing the soil with probes to see whether the circle produces electromagnetic noises.

An Elaborate Hoax?

In 1991 two Englishmen, David Chorley and Douglas Bower, stepped forward to confess that for 13 years, they had been sneaking around southern England at night creating crop circles. The two men claimed to have made 25 to 30 new circles every growing season. They showed reporters how they had used a ball of string and a sighting device made from a wire attached to a baseball cap to lay out the designs and wooden planks to flatten the crops.

The men told reporters that they began making crop circles in 1978 as a joke. They had heard news reports about supposed UFO landings and about crop circles that Australian farmers had created with tractors several years earlier. "Wondering what we could do for a bit of a laugh," the men said, they decided to flatten some corn to make it appear that a UFO had landed.

David Chorley and Douglas Bower show the device that they used to create crop circles around southern England as part of a 13-year hoax.

For three years, their creations went unnoticed. Then, in 1981, one of their circles was discovered and reported in the news as a possible landing site of a UFO. "We laughed so much that time," recalled Chorley, "we had to stop the car because Doug was in stitches so much he couldn't drive." The two men finally decided to admit to their hoax when circle investigators began seeking government funding for their research.

The Research Continues

Not everyone believes that the mystery of the crop circles has been solved. Pat Delgado points out that Chorley and Bower could not possibly have made all the circles that have been discovered in England, not to mention those found in other countries worldwide. "These two gents may have hoaxed some of the circles," Delgado said, "but the phenomenon is still there, and we will carry on research."

One of Delgado's supporters, Joan Creighton of the British newsletter *Flying Saucer Review*, explains why the research continues: "We all have an inner sense that there is a mystery behind the universe. We like mysteries. It's great fun."

Write the answers to the following questions on the lines provided. You may go back to the selection to find an answer.

1. What is a crop circle?

_____

_____

_____

2. From which position are crop circles most easily seen?

_____

_____

3. How have crop circle patterns changed over the years since they were first discovered?

_____

_____

4. What inspired David Chorley and Douglas Bower to decide on crop circles as their practical joke?

_____

_____

_____

5. Complete each sentence with the correct word below.

   phenomenon   concentric   vortex

   a. A _____ of churning water spun the rubber raft as it passed through the rapids.

   b. Hailstones the size of baseballs are a rare weather _____.

   c. The orbits of the planets form _____ paths around the sun.

INTERPRETING FACTS

Not all questions about a selection are answered directly. For the following questions, you will have to figure out answers not directly stated in the selection. Circle the letter next to the words that complete each sentence.

1. David Chorley and Douglas Bower had to use string and a sighting device to lay out a crop circle because
   a. they could not see the entire pattern from the ground.
   b. precise measurements could not be made at night.
   c. The crop circles were created on steep hillsides.

2. Pat Delgado believes that crop circles produce electromagnetic noises because
   a. the circles are hoaxes.
   b. a vortex creates energy forces.
   c. the circles are made with extraterrestrial technology.

3. Chorley and Bower admitted their hoax because
   a. they wanted to encourage people to copy their techniques.
   b. they didn't want the government to spend taxpayers' money on crop circle research.
   c. Pat Delgado found out that they had been making crop circles.

4. What do you think causes crop circles? Support your answer with facts from the selection.

_____

_____

_____

1. Read the clues listed below. Then, on the lines provided, write an inference that can be made based on those clues.

   Clues   Crop circles most often appear in calm weather.

   A vortex can occur when the atmosphere is calm near the ground but windy above.

   A Japanese physicist created miniature crop circles in a laboratory using ball lightning and aluminum dust.

   Ball lightning hovers above the ground and moves in bizarre ways.

   Inference _____

   _____

2. Read the inference stated below. Then, on the lines provided, list two clues in the selection that support that inference.

   Inference   Ball lightning or a vortex could not have created all the crop circles that have been discovered.

   Clues   a. _____

   _____

   b. _____

   _____

3. List two clues contained in the selection that support Pat Delgado's inference: *Crop circles are created by extraterrestrials.* Explain how each clue supports Delgado's inference.

   Clue 1 _____

   _____

   Explanation _____

   _____

   Clue 2 _____

   _____

   Explanation _____

   _____

4. Delgado pointed out that Chorley and Bower could not have made all the crop circles that have been discovered and inferred that the others were made by extraterrestrials. What is another reasonable inference that could be made?

   _____

   _____

▶ **Real Life Connections**   In what ways can a practical joke be harmful?

Exponential Notation

— Reading a Mathematics Selection

▶ **Background Information**

Mathematics is the use of numbers to describe and explain the world. In Africa, where most scientists believe the first people lived, there is evidence of people's use of math. Early, or prehistoric, people developed a variety of ways to count. In addition to using their fingers, they also used pebbles, knots in a rope, or marks on wood, bone, or stone. A fossil bone was discovered in Zaire at a place that is now called Ishango in Africa. This bone is about 25,000 years old. It has many tallies, or marks, that represent number counts. Although the exact meaning and use of the Ishango bone is unknown, scientists agree that it shows mathematical thinking.

As you can probably guess, counting and recording numbers with tallies, pebbles, and knots in a rope is only useful if you are using small numbers. Recording large numbers with tallies is not practical. It takes too much time, and tallies are difficult to read. So people came up with a new way to record numbers.

Around 3,000 B.C.E., mathematicians of ancient Egypt used a decimal system without place values. A decimal system is a system of counting in groups of 10. These Egyptian mathematicians still used tallies for numbers one through nine. But they used a different symbol to stand for ten tallies. They invented more symbols to write numbers up to 1,000,000. This invention made it easy to use larger numbers.

The number system that we use today is based on 10. However, because of modern science and mathematics, the numbers that we use can be quite large. Therefore, another system of notation had to be developed.

In the following selection, you will read about the base 10 number system and exponential notation.

▶ **Skill Focus**

Exponential, or scientific, notation is a special method for writing very large numbers in an abbreviated form. Exponential notation is useful in many fields, such as mathematics, astronomy, and chemistry, where extremely large numbers are frequently used.

An **exponent** is a small number written above and to the right of a number. It signifies the number of times that the lower number, the **base number**, is being multiplied by itself.

In the following mathematical expression, 10 is the base number and 2 is the exponent.

$$10^2$$

In our number system, which is based on 10, exponential notation is an easy way to write large numbers.

▶ **Word Clues**

When reading the following selection, look for these important words: *exponent*, *base number*, and *factor*. They will help you understand more about exponential notation.

▶ **Strategy Tip**

The selection that follows explains how to read and write numbers with exponents. Read the explanations carefully. Reread any sections that you have difficulty understanding.

Exponential Notation

In the number 10^2, the numeral 2 is the **exponent.** It is written above and to the right of the **base number,** which is 10. The exponent tells how many times the base number is used as a **factor.** Factors are numbers that form a product when multiplied together. Thus, the mathematical expression 10^2 means that 10 is used as a factor twice, or 10×10. The expression 10^2 is read ten to the second power, or ten squared.

$$10^2 = 10 \times 10 = 100$$

Look at the following powers of ten. The dots between the tens stand for multiplication, just as the symbol $\times$ does.

$$10^3 = 10 \cdot 10 \cdot 10 \qquad\qquad = 1,000$$
$$10^4 = 10 \cdot 10 \cdot 10 \cdot 10 \qquad = 10,000$$
$$10^5 = 10 \cdot 10 \cdot 10 \cdot 10 \cdot 10 \qquad = 100,000$$
$$10^6 = 10 \cdot 10 \cdot 10 \cdot 10 \cdot 10 \cdot 10 = 1,000,000$$

The mathematical expressions 10^3, 10^4, 10^5, and 10^6 are read ten to the third power, or ten *cubed*, ten to the fourth power, ten to the fifth power, and ten to the sixth power, respectively.

For each of these examples, look at the exponent and then count the number of zeros in the product. What do you notice? In each case, the exponent and the number of zeros in the product are the same. The exponent shows how many zeros are in the product. Ten to the seventh power, or 10^7, has a product with seven zeros, which is 10,000,000, or ten million. Ten to the twelfth power, or 10^{12}, has a product with twelve zeros, which is 1,000,000,000,000, or one trillion.

The number 10 is represented as 10^1.

The number 1 is represented as 10^0.

Any number can be written using exponential notation. However, exponential notation is most useful with extremely large or extremely small numbers. It is easier and quicker to write a very large number using exponential notation than it is to write the number with all its zeros. For this reason, scientists find exponential notation useful in their work. For example, instead of writing sixty billion as 60,000,000,000, they write $6 \cdot 10^{10}$. This expression is read as six times ten to the tenth power, which is $6 \cdot (10 \cdot 10 \cdot 10 \cdot 10 \cdot 10 \cdot 10 \cdot 10 \cdot 10 \cdot 10 \cdot 10)$. The parentheses indicate that the mathematical process inside them must be completed before the result can be used in another mathematical process. Therefore, the tens must be multiplied before their product can be multiplied by the number 6.

Eight hundred thousand, 800,000, is written $8 \cdot 10^5$, or eight times ten to the fifth power.

Three hundred trillion, 300,000,000,000,000, is written $3 \cdot 10^{14}$, or three times ten to the fourteenth power.

Look at the diagram below. You can see that the average distance of Mars from the sun is 228,000,000 kilometers. The number of kilometers can be written as $228 \cdot 1,000,000$, or $228 \cdot 10^6$. Scientists prefer to express the number before the multiplication sign as a value between 1 and 10. Instead of writing $228 \cdot 10^6$, they express the number as $2.28 \cdot 10^8$. The whole number 228 is changed to the decimal 2.28 by moving the decimal point two places to the left. To make up for the two

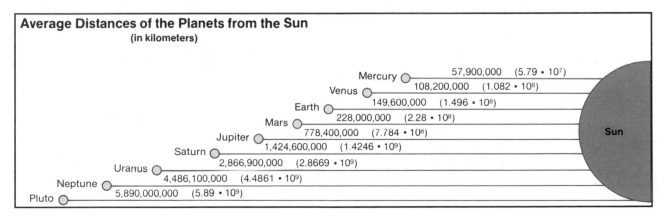

Average Distances of the Planets from the Sun
(in kilometers)

Mercury — 57,900,000 (5.79 · 10^7)
Venus — 108,200,000 (1.082 · 10^8)
Earth — 149,600,000 (1.496 · 10^8)
Mars — 228,000,000 (2.28 · 10^8)
Jupiter — 778,400,000 (7.784 · 10^8)
Saturn — 1,424,600,000 (1.4246 · 10^9)
Uranus — 2,866,900,000 (2.8669 · 10^9)
Neptune — 4,486,100,000 (4.4861 · 10^9)
Pluto — 5,890,000,000 (5.89 · 10^9)

Sun

decimal places, the exponent is increased by 2, from 6 to 8. Both $228 \cdot 10^6$ and $2.28 \cdot 10^8$ equal 228,000,000.

It is not necessarily easier and quicker to write moderately large numbers using exponential notation. For numbers other than 10, each digit of the number is written in terms of its place value. In the number 245, the 2 is in the hundreds place and can be written as $2 \cdot 100$. The 4 is in the tens place and can be written as $4 \cdot 10$. The 5, in the ones place, is simply written as 5.

$$245 = (2 \cdot 100) + (4 \cdot 10) + 5.$$

This can be further simplified using exponents.

$$245 = 2 \cdot (10^2) + (4 \cdot 10) + 5$$

Following are two more examples of writing numbers using exponential notation.

$$
\begin{aligned}
92,476 &= (9 \cdot 10,000) + (2 \cdot 1,000) + (4 \cdot 100) + (7 \cdot 10) + 6 \\
&= 9\,(10^4) + 2 \cdot (10^3) + 4\,(10^2) + (7 \cdot 10) + 6 \\
236,512 &= (2 \cdot 100,000) + (3 \cdot 10,000) + (6 \cdot 1,000) + (5 \cdot 100) + (1 \cdot 10) + 2 \\
&= 2 \cdot (10^5) + 3 \cdot (10^4) + 6 \cdot (10^3) + 5 \cdot (10^2) + (1 \cdot 10) + 2
\end{aligned}
$$

RECALLING FACTS

Write the answers to the following questions on the lines provided. You may go back to the selection to find an answer.

1. In the mathematical expression 10^8, 8 is the _____.

2. In the mathematical expression 10^4, 10 is the _____.

3. In the exponential notation, the _____ tells how many times the _____ is used as a _____.

4. In exponential notation, the exponent equals the number of zeros in the _____.

5. The mathematical expression 10^2 is read _____, or ten _____.

6. The mathematical expression 10^3 is read _____, or ten _____.

7. The mathematical expression 10^6 has _____ zeros in the product.

8. Exponential notation is most useful with _____.

9. In exponential notation, scientists prefer to express the number before the multiplication sign as a value between _____.

INTERPRETING FACTS

Not all the questions about a selection are answered directly in the selection. For the following questions, you will have to figure out answers not directly stated in the selection. Circle the letter next to the correct answer(s).

1. If $10^4 = 10 \cdot 10 \cdot 10 \cdot 10$, what does 6^4 equal?
   a. $6 \cdot 6 \cdot 6 \cdot 6$
   b. $10 \cdot 10 \cdot 10 \cdot 10 \cdot 10 \cdot 10$
   c. $4 \cdot 4 \cdot 4 \cdot 4 \cdot 4 \cdot 4$

2. In which two situations below would exponential notation be most useful?

  a. to show the distance from here to the moon

  b. to show the height of a person

  c. to show the speed of a moving car

3. What effect does lowering the value of the exponent have on the product?

  a. It increases.

  b. It decreases.

  c. It equals zero.

4. What effect does raising the value of the exponent have on the product?

  a. It increases.

  b. It decreases.

  c. It equals zero.

5. In the expression 10^0, the exponent shows that the numeral this expression equals has _____.

  a. no zeros

  b. no tens

  c. no ones

SKILL FOCUS

A. Write the standard numerals for the following mathematical expressions.

1. 10^5 = _____

2. 10^0 = _____

3. 10^9 = _____

4. 10^1 = _____

5. 10^{11} = _____

6. $8 \cdot (10^3)$ = _____

7. $3 \cdot (10^2) + (2 \cdot 10) + 3$

= _____ + _____ + _____ = _____

8. $7 \cdot (10^4) + 6 \cdot (10^3) + 9 \cdot (10^2) + (1 \cdot 10) + 6$

= _____ + _____ + _____ + _____ + 6 = _____

B. Write the following numbers using exponential notation. The first one is done for you.

1. 40 ___$4 \cdot (10^1)$___

2. 600 _____

3. 16,200,000 _____

4. 8,000 _____

C. Write the following numbers using exponential notation. The first one is done for you.

1. 3,764 = $\dfrac{(3 \cdot 1,000) + (7 \cdot 100) + (6 \cdot 10) + 4}{3 \cdot (10^3) + 7 \cdot (10^2) + (6 \cdot 10) + 4}$

2. 84,652 = _____

= _____

3. 777,559 = _____

= _____

▶ **Real Life Connections** Name two daily situations in which exponential notation would be useful.

Syllables

To help you pronounce long words, divide the words into syllables. Then pronounce each syllable until you can say the whole word. There are several different ways of deciding how a word should be divided.

Guide 1: Compound Words

One of the easiest guides to use in dividing words is the one for a compound word. Because a compound is made up of two words, it must have at least two syllables. Always divide a compound word into syllables by separating it between the two smaller words first. If one or even both of the smaller words in a compound word has more than one syllable, it may be necessary to use another guide. However, you can pronounce most compound words if you divide them into two words.

sailboat   sail boat

Read each of the following compound words. Divide the word into two syllables, writing each of the two smaller words separately on the line to the right of the compound word.

1. windstorm _____
2. driveway _____
3. northwest _____
4. goldfinch _____
5. drugstore _____
6. textbook _____
7. limestone _____
8. seashore _____
9. campfire _____
10. pigskin _____

11. moonlight _____
12. bookcase _____
13. earthworm _____
14. sandpile _____
15. footstep _____
16. landlord _____
17. cardboard _____
18. campground _____
19. spaceship _____
20. drawbridge _____

Guide 2: Words with Double Consonants

Another guide that you may use is for words with double consonants. Divide the word into two syllables between the two consonants and read each syllable.

ribbon   rib bon

Divide the following two-syllable words into syllables. Write each syllable separately on the line to the right of the word.

1. dinner _____
2. account _____
3. swimmer _____
4. bottom _____

5. muffin _____
6. message _____
7. narrow _____
8. scrimmage _____

9. summon _____   15. allow _____

10. mammal _____   16. raccoon _____

11. blossom _____   17. plummet _____

12. passage _____   18. effort _____

13. blizzard _____   19. ballad _____

14. correct _____   20. command _____

Guide 3: Words with a Prefix or Suffix

A prefix or a suffix always has at least one sounded vowel. Therefore, a prefix or a suffix always contains at least one syllable. You can divide a word that has a prefix or a suffix between the prefix or suffix and the root word.

restring   re string

pitcher   pitch er

Divide each of the words below into two syllables between the prefix or suffix and the root word. Write each syllable separately on the line to the right of the word.

1. harmless _____   11. subway _____

2. useful _____   12. kindness _____

3. western _____   13. react _____

4. breakage _____   14. weaken _____

5. singer _____   15. prejudge _____

6. nonsense _____   16. actor _____

7. refill _____   17. insight _____

8. swiftly _____   18. foolish _____

9. mistake _____   19. dislike _____

10. untie _____   20. healthy _____

Divide each of the words below into syllables. Write the syllables separately on the line to the right of the word. Then, on the line to the left of the word, write the number of the guide or guides that you used to divide the word. Some words have three syllables. The first one is done for you.

<u>3, 2</u> rearrange ___re ar range___   ____ unhappy _____

____ careful _____   ____ roadside _____

____ Tennessee _____   ____ cunning _____

____ quarrelsome _____   ____ buttermilk _____

____ homemade _____   ____ reappear _____

____ transplant _____   ____ teapot _____

____ doorway _____   ____ misstatement _____

____ gossip _____   ____ unfruitful _____

____ postwar _____   ____ correctly _____

Stated or Unstated Main Idea

When you read a chapter in a textbook, the main idea of each paragraph will often be stated in a sentence. The sentences in the remainder of the paragraph contain the supporting details that give additional information about the main idea.

Often the main idea of a paragraph is not stated in one of the sentences. You need to use the information in the paragraph to **infer**, or figure out, the main idea. To do this, you need to ask yourself what the paragraph is about. Then think of a sentence that summarizes this idea.

Read the following selection to become familiar with the content. Then reread it and look for the main idea of each paragraph. Is the main idea stated or unstated?

The War of the Worlds

1. On October 30, 1938, the Earth was invaded by creatures from Mars! Or at least that's what thousands of radio listeners believed in the United States. Actually, on that evening a man named Orson Welles directed and starred in a radio broadcast entitled *The War of the Worlds*. The radio play was based on a book of the same title by H.G. Wells, an English writer. The performance described a fictional attack on New Jersey by invaders from Mars. The broadcast was not of a real event—but it seemed so real that it caused a national panic.

2. In the 1930s, radio had a great influence on life in the United States. Television sets were not yet available for home use, so there were no live TV broadcasts to show people events as they happened. It was therefore not totally surprising that so many radio listeners believed what they heard on *The War of the Worlds*.

3. The Martians' invasion, only a small part of the original story of *The War of the Worlds*, was used for the radio program. Playwright Howard Koch, who rewrote the story for radio, had picked up a map at a New Jersey gas station to find a location in the United States for the Martians' landing. He opened the map, closed his eyes, and pointed his pencil. The pencil landed on the town of Grovers Mill, New Jersey.

4. The radio play was presented like a regular radio broadcast—with music, a weather report, and then a series of special news bulletins. Most listeners missed or did not listen to the introduction of the program: "The Columbia Broadcasting System and its affiliated stations present Orson Welles and the Mercury Theatre on the Air in *The War of the Worlds* by H.G. Wells." The newspaper listing for the show also identified the title of the program. In addition, three announcements during the program stated that the broadcast was fiction.

5. The first "news bulletins" and "eyewitness accounts" during the broadcast described a meteor that was supposed to have landed near Princeton, New Jersey. Later "reports" changed the meteor to a metal cylinder containing creatures from Mars armed with death rays. The creatures finally burst into flames, and the whole field where they had landed caught fire, spreading destruction.

6. Because radio listeners were used to interruptions in broadcasts during the recent war scare in Europe, the program seemed real and caused fright and panic. Some families

grabbed their personal belongings and fled into the streets. Traffic came to a standstill. Outraged citizens flooded radio stations, newspapers, and police headquarters with telephone calls. For days afterward, the broadcast was the topic of newspaper headlines.

7. Following the broadcast, a Grovers Mill farmer collected a fifty-cent parking charge from each of the hundreds of carloads of people who wanted to see where the invaders attacked. Even thirty years later, land in Grovers Mill was being sold at high prices because it was advertised as the site of the Martians' landing. The choice of Grovers Mill, New Jersey, as the town where the Martians landed helped to create new business opportunities there.

8. One New Jersey woman summed up many people's feelings when she said, "I thought it was all up with us. I grabbed my boy and just sat and cried." Believing that the entire human race faced death, many a person reached for someone nearby, for few people wanted to die alone. Others merely accepted their fate. A woman who had some leftover chicken in her icebox said to her nephew, "We may as well eat this chicken—we won't be here in the morning." Her remark was her attempt at making life go on as usual.

9. One woman said, "My only thought was delight that if the Martians came, I wouldn't have to pay the butcher's bill." A man who enjoyed spreading news said, "It was the most exciting thing that ever happened to me. I ran all through my apartment building telling everybody the Martians were here."

10. Close to one-quarter of the estimated six million listeners believed that the broadcast was fact. Surprisingly, many listeners failed to change to another station to check whether the broadcast was true. Why were so many people ready to believe this outrageous fantasy, and why did they react in panic? As one person remarked, "Being in a troublesome world, anything is liable to happen. . . . So many things we hear are unbelievable." If we can learn anything from the public reaction to the broadcast of *The War of the Worlds*, it is that we should not be too quick to believe everything that we hear and see over the air waves and read in print.

For each paragraph in the selection, if the main idea is stated, write stated on the line provided. If the main idea of a paragraph is unstated, choose a main idea from the sentences below and write the letter on the line provided.

a. Many people believed that they were going to die.

b. The broadcast described how the Martians landed and caused destruction.

c. People thought that a radio program about invaders from Mars was real.

d. Listeners reacted to the broadcast with mixed feelings.

e. The producers of the broadcast took many measures to ensure that people would know the show was not about a real event.

f. The broadcast appeared in the newspapers the next day.

g. The original English story needed to be rewritten with a location in the United States.

h. Some listeners reacted to the broadcast with delight.

i. The inhabitants of Grovers Mill were thrilled that their dull lives were changing.

j. Music and comedy helped people forget about the Great Depression.

Paragraph 1 _____   *Paragraph 6* _____

Paragraph 2 _____   *Paragraph 7* _____

Paragraph 3 _____   *Paragraph 8* _____

Paragraph 4 _____   *Paragraph 9* _____

Paragraph 5 _____   *Paragraph 10* _____

Now go back to each paragraph that has a stated main idea, and underline the sentence that expresses the main idea.

Table of Contents

Using the table of contents saves you time when you want to find out what kind of information is in a book. The table of contents gives you a quick overview of the topics in the book. This is especially true if you are interested in reading about a general subject.

The **table of contents** lists the titles of the chapters, along with the page on which each chapter begins. Sometimes a table of contents gives the most important topics included in each chapter. It may also give the page on which each topic begins.

To use a table of contents, glance through the chapter titles and topics until you find your subject. Then turn to the page number given next to the chapter title or topic. Skim this section until you find the information that you need on your subject.

Below is a table of contents from a book on transportation. To answer the questions that follow it, use two steps.

1. Look at the chapter titles to find the chapter in which you might find the information asked for.
2. Read through the topics under the title to find the page on which the particular information is given.

Contents

1. You need to find information about road travel used by the colonists.
   a. Under which chapter title would you look? _____
   b. Under which topic would you look?

   _____
   c. On which page would you start to read? _____

2. You need to find information about the first transcontinental railroad.
   a. Under which chapter title would you look? _____
   b. Under which topic would you look?

   _____
   c. On which page would you start to read? _____

3. You need to find information about space travel.
   a. Under which chapter title would you look? _____
   b. Under which topic would you look?

   _____
   c. On which page would you start to read? _____

4. You need to find information about the use of trucks.
   a. Under which chapter title would you look? _____
   b. Under which topic would you look?

   _____
   c. On which page would you start to read? _____

5. You need to find information about how early explorers used the compass.
   a. Under which chapter title would you look? _____
   b. Under which topic would you look?

   _____
   c. On which page would you start to read? _____

6. You need to find information about the first balloon flight.
   a. Under which chapter title would you look? _____
   b. Under which topic would you look?

   _____
   c. On which page would you start to read? _____

7. You need to find information about Peter Cooper's "Teakettle on Wheels."
   a. Under which chapter title would you look? _____
   b. Under which topic would you look?

   _____
   c. On which page would you start to read? _____

8. You need to find information about the effects of the automobile on family life.
   a. Under which chapter title would you look? _____
   b. Under which topic would you look?

   _____
   c. On which page would you start to read? _____

Reading a Paycheck Stub

An employee, or worker, earns a fixed amount of money—a salary. Yet the money that is taken home is usually not the whole salary. Money is deducted, or taken out, from most paychecks for taxes and other things. **Gross pay** is the amount of money earned before any money is deducted. **Net pay** is the amount of take-home pay after deductions.

Most paychecks have two parts. One part, the actual check, can be cashed for the amount of take-home pay. The other part, the stub, contains a statement of earnings for the person's records. Information on the stub tells how much of a person's salary has been deducted. If all the deductions are added together and then subtracted from the gross pay, the amount left equals the net pay.

The paycheck stub below shows how much money has been deducted from Linda Wong's paycheck. The federal, state, and local taxes that she pays are used for defense, education, welfare and other services and programs. Employers also may deduct money from the salary of each employee for retirement funds, health insurance, and any professional or union dues.

The deduction for the FICA, or Federal Income Contribution Act, tax goes to the federal government for Social Security payments. When an employee either retires or becomes unable to work due to injury, he or she receives money from Social Security. The amount of FICA tax on the earnings statement is half the total amount that is due. The employer pays the other half.

ACE SPACECRAFT MECHANICS
Wong, Linda

CHECK # **616545**

AMT. OF CHECK ▶ 913.00

PAY DATE	PAY PERIOD	SOCIAL SECURITY NO.
1/31/96	1/16/96-1/31/96	341-06-1596

GROSS PAY		TAXES		DEDUCTIONS		NET PAY
1400 00	-	441 00	-	46 00	=	913 00
2800 00	-	882 00	-	92 00	=	1826 00

DEDUCTIONS	THIS CHECK	YEAR TO DATE
FEDERAL TAX	238 00	476 00
FICA TAX	105 00	210 00
STATE TAXES	70 00	140 00
LOCAL TAXES	28 00	56 00
HEALTH INSURANCE	40 00	80 00
UNION DUES	6 00	12 00

OTHER EARNINGS		AMOUNT

OTHER EARNINGS		AMOUNT

STATEMENT OF EARNINGS AND DEDUCTIONS • DETACH AND RETAIN FOR YOUR RECORDS

A. Fill in the circle next to the answer to each question.

    1. How much money did Linda Wong earn before deductions in this pay period?

      ○ $913.00   ○ $1400.00   ○ $441.00   ○ $476.00

2. Which is the largest deduction?
   ○ FICA tax   ○ state tax   ○ federal tax   ○ health insurance

3. Which is the smallest deduction?
   ○ local tax   ○ union dues   ○ health insurance   ○ FICA tax

4. What is the total amount deducted for health insurance and union dues each pay period?
   ○ $6.00   ○ $40.00   ○ $92.00   ○ $46.00

5. How much money does Linda Wong's hometown receive directly from this paycheck?
   ○ $140.00   ○ $70.00   ○ $56.00   ○ $28.00

6. What is the total amount deducted from this paycheck?
   ○ $487.00   ○ $882.00   ○ $46.00   ○ $476.00

7. How much money has been deducted from Linda Wong's paycheck for the year to date?
   ○ $882.00   ○ $92.00   ○ $974.00   ○ $913.00

8. Which of the following statements about Linda Wong's deductions is true?
   ○ The deduction for FICA tax is less than the deduction for state taxes.
   ○ The combined deductions for health insurance and union dues are less than the deduction for local taxes.
   ○ The federal tax deduction is greater than the other deductions combined.
   ○ The federal tax deducted is greater than the state and local taxes combined.

9. How long is the pay period for each of Linda Wong's paychecks?
   ○ 1 day   ○ 1 month   ○ 1 week   ○ 2 weeks

10. What do the numbers on the second line below the words "GROSS PAY," "TAXES," "DEDUCTIONS," and "NET PAY" stand for?
    ○ amount of money for the year to date
    ○ amount of money the employee will receive for the next paycheck
    ○ amount of money the employee has earned so far at current job
    ○ amount of money the employee will earn next year at current job

11. About how much of her salary does Linda Wong receive as take-home pay?
    ○ all of it   ○ about one-half   ○ about one-third   ○ about two-thirds

12. How was Linda's net pay determined?
    ○ gross pay minus taxes and other deductions   ○ deductions minus gross pay
    ○ gross pay plus all deductions   ○ gross pay plus Social Security

B. Complete each sentence using information from the paycheck stub.

1. The amount of money that Linda Wong took home from this paycheck was _____.

2. The date that Linda received this paycheck was _____.

3. Linda Wong's Social Security number is _____.

4. Linda Wong's employer is _____.

5. Half of the cost of the FICA tax is deducted from Linda Wong's paycheck, and the other half is paid by _____. Therefore, the total amount of the FICA tax paid for Linda Wong during this pay period was _____.

Lesson 9

Plot

Reading a Literature Selection

▶ Background Information

This story about the destruction of Troy combines elements of Greek mythology and ancient history.

▶ Skill Focus

The plan of action or series of events in a story is called the **plot**. In most stories, the plot follows a five-part pattern.

1. **Beginning:** The beginning of the story introduces the main character and the conflict. It also establishes the setting.
2. **Rising Action:** The conflict develops as the characters struggle to achieve a goal or to solve a problem.
3. **Climax:** The climax is the most exciting event or the most dramatic moment—the story's turning point. At the climax, the reader can often predict the story's ending.
4. **Falling Action:** The events after the climax focus on how the story's conflict is resolved.
5. **Conclusion:** A final event often ties together all loose ends. Here all questions about the story's outcome are answered.

If you drew the plot of a story, it would look like the diagram below.

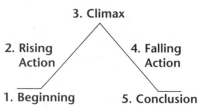

Use the diagram and these questions to help you follow the plot of a story.

1. What is the conflict that the characters face at the beginning of the story?
2. What do the characters do to resolve the conflict?
3. What is the climax?
4. How do the characters finally resolve the conflict?
5. Is the conclusion appropriate? Why or why not?

▶ Word Clues

When you read, you may come across a word that names a special person, place, or thing. If the paragraph has no context clues to explain the word, there may be a clue elsewhere. Read the sentence below.

> The siege of Troy[1] is not going well, thought Odysseus.

The raised number after the word *Troy* is a signal to look at the bottom of the page for a footnote with the same number. A footnote gives a brief definition or explanation of the word.

[1] **Troy** (TROY): an ancient city in what is now northwestern Turkey; scene of the Trojan War.

Use **footnote** clues to find the meaning of the six other numbered words in the selection.

▶ Strategy Tip

As you read, "The Gift of Betrayal," keep track of the plot. The questions and the diagram in the Skill Focus will help you follow the events. When you think the story has reached its climax, try to predict the conclusion.

The Gift of Betrayal

The siege of Troy[1] is not going well, thought Odysseus.[2] The kings and princes of Greece had been at war with the Trojans for ten long years. There had been a decade of bloody battles outside the walls of the strong city and of waiting for a stroke of luck to help conquer Troy.

Many valiant warriors on both sides had been slain. Odysseus wondered if the terrible death toll was too high for the rescue of one person. Yet, he told himself, the person in question was Helen,[3] the beautiful wife of Menelaus,[4] King of Sparta.[5] She had been kidnapped ten years before by Paris, son of the King of Troy. Her kidnapping had enraged the kings of the Greek cities. With a huge fleet, they had set sail across the Aegean Sea[6] to rescue Helen and destroy the Trojans. Yet the Trojans had held their own in their stout-walled city.

There must be a way to bring the wearying, terrible war to an end, thought Odysseus. Perhaps if they made a special offering to the gods, the gods might look kindly on their gift and reward them with the city of Troy. Odysseus pondered. Suddenly he was struck by an idea—a gift! A gift! They would win Troy with a gift!

Odysseus gathered the kings and princes of Greece together and presented his plan. They would build a glorious, huge, wonderful wooden horse. While the horse would seem magical and beautiful, its large belly would be hollow. Inside the horse, a hardy band of Greek warriors would conceal themselves. At the same time, the rest of the Greek warriors would appear to set sail for home in defeat. However, they would sail only to a small neighboring island, just out of sight of the

shore. There they would bide their time until the moment for attack.

The leaders of Greece accepted Odysseus' plan and set to work. They built their horse within sight of the walls of Troy. Its mane curved gracefully down a strong neck. The head was held high. The legs were the strong, sinewy legs of a charioteer's swift steed.

Finally, the horse was finished. Under cover of darkness, the small band of chosen warriors hid inside. The next day, the rest of the Greek warriors made a big show of leaving sadly, as if in defeat. They boarded their ships and quietly sailed out of the bay.

The Trojans were elated! With shouts of triumph, they swarmed out of their city onto the plain near the shore. They had been

[1] Troy (TROY): an ancient city in what is now northwestern Turkey; scene of the Trojan War.
[2] Odysseus (oh DIS yus): King of Ithaca; one of the Greek leaders in the Trojan War.
[3] Helen: wife of Menelaus, taken to Troy by Paris; known as the most beautiful woman in the world.
[4] Menelaus (men ə LAY əs): King of Sparta, after rescuing his wife Helen in the fall of Troy, returned to Sparta where he and Helen continued to reign.
[5] Sparta (SPAR tə): an ancient, powerful military city in southern Greece.
[6] Aegean (ee JEE ən) Sea: the arm of the Mediterranean Sea between Greece and Turkey.

imprisoned inside the city for years. Now the land was theirs again!

Yet what was this horse? Certainly, it was a thing of beauty, but why had the Greeks built it? Even more mysteriously, why had they left it behind? Was it a curse or a blessing? The horse did not answer, as it towered silently and woodenly over the Trojans. Its steady gaze was directed toward the sea, but the Trojans did not notice.

A Trojan priest, Laocoön,[7] approached the horse. He walked around the huge steed. He admired it, inspected it, struck it with his staff. A hollow sound rang out! The priest did not know why, but this sound bothered him. "I do not like this horse!" he cried. "We must burn it! It should be destroyed or else, I fear, it will destroy us! I fear the Greeks even when they bear gifts."

The people of Troy believed their priest. They began to move threateningly toward the horse, which could not move or defend itself. The men inside feared that their lives were at an end.

Then the gods interfered. They sent a huge sea serpent from out of the ocean onto the shore. The serpent twined its poisonous coils around the young sons of Laocoön. When the priest tried to save them, he too was trapped and slain. The serpent's appearance frightened the people of Troy. They took it as a sign that the gods were not pleased with the priest or his predictions.

Still the giant horse stood unmoving on the plains outside the city. The mystified Trojans wondered what it could be for.

Then some Trojan warriors rushed up to the people with a captured Greek slave. The slave told the Trojans that the Greeks had made the horse as a peace offering to the gods. The enemy had finally given up in defeat and sailed for home.

With songs of joy and triumph, the Trojans took the horse as their own, pulling it through the gates of their city. For them, the horse was a symbol of a hard-won victory.

For hours after they dragged the horse into the center of the city, the people of Troy celebrated their victory. They made offerings to the gods, feasted, sang, and danced. Finally, exhausted, they found their way home and went to bed.

As the city of Troy grew dark and silent, the horse appeared to gaze solemnly over it. A watching Trojan might have imagined the horse was standing guard. But it was not. Even as it stood in quiet majesty, the horse was betraying the city and its people.

The belly of the animal opened, and the Greek warriors silently crept out. They stole to the gates of the city and, just before dawn, opened the gates wide. Outside stood the Greek armies, who had sailed back to the shores of Troy in the dark of night.

The Greeks swept into the city, killing all who challenged them. As the Trojans rallied to defend their city, the fighting grew fierce. Warriors, priests, women, children, princes, and kings were all swept up in the jaws of battle.

Through it all, the horse stood motionlessly and quietly above the battle. Guard or betrayer, it had no further part to play in the fight for the proud city.

Although the Trojans fought bravely, in the end, the Greeks took the victory. The Trojans who survived were banished from their city. Helen was rescued and returned to her husband, Menelaus. Most of the Greeks immediately set sail for their native land.

Before the Greeks left, however, they set fire to Troy. As it burned, flames flickered and licked at the wooden feet of the horse. The scarlet, orange, and black colors of the fire cast an eerie glow on the steed. The treacherous horse of Troy caught fire, but still it did not move.

As the horse flared into full flame and burst into a shower of sparks and burning timber, Odysseus stood outside the walled city, pondering the sack of Troy. He was tired. The war had gone on too long, and too many friends had died in the fighting. Now he wanted to be in Ithaca, his home in Greece.

> *Still the giant horse stood unmoving on the plains outside the city. The mystified Trojans wondered what it could be for.*

---

[7] Laocoön (lay AHK ə wahn): a priest of Troy.

1. The captured Greek slave told the Trojans that the Greeks had made the horse as a peace offering to the gods. What effect did this information have on the Trojans?

_____

_____

_____

_____

2. What was there about the wooden horse that disturbed Laocoön?

_____

_____

_____

_____

3. Why did the wooden horse mystify the Trojans?

_____

_____

_____

4. Complete each statement with the correct word or phrase.

   Helen   Aegean Sea   Sparta   Odysseus

   a. The _____ lies between Greece on the west and Turkey on the east.

   b. _____, a city in ancient Greece, was home to Menelaus and Helen.

   c. The abduction of _____ by Paris started the Trojan War.

1. Why were the Greek warriors in the horse able to get to the gates of Troy unseen?

_____

_____

_____

_____

_____

2. How was the wooden horse a "gift of betrayal?"

_____

_____

_____

_____

_____

_____

3. a. The Trojans wondered whether the horse was a blessing or a curse. For whom was it a blessing? Explain.

_____

_____

_____

_____

_____

_____

   b. For whom was the wooden horse a curse? Explain.

_____

_____

_____

_____

Below are some events in the story of the wooden horse. On the lines provided in the plot diagram, write the letters of the appropriate events. First decide which event is the climax.

   a. Odysseus watches and ponders the fall of Troy.

   b. The Greek kings and princes accept Odysseus' plan to conquer Troy.

   c. Laocoön's warning to the Trojans to destroy the wooden horse is ignored.

   d. The Greeks build a wooden horse large enough to contain a band of armed warriors.

   e. The Greek warriors creep out of the belly of the wooden horse and open the gates of the city.

   f. The Trojans bring the wooden horse through the gates into their city.

   g. Before sailing out of the bay, the Greeks leave the wooden horse outside the gates of Troy.

   h. Under cover of darkness, the Greeks sail back to Troy.

   i. The Greeks storm the city of Troy and rescue Helen.

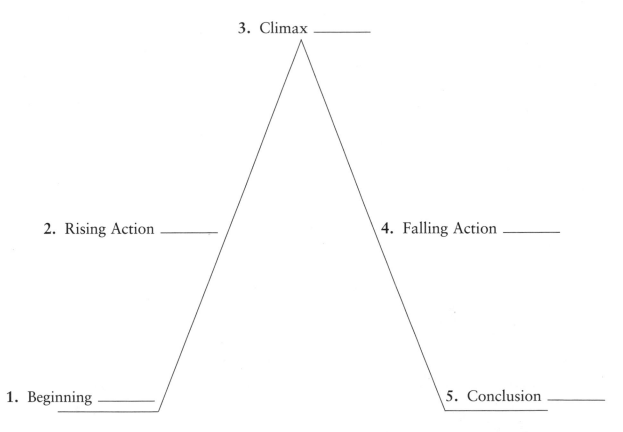

3. Climax _____

2. Rising Action _____

4. Falling Action _____

1. Beginning _____

5. Conclusion _____

▶ **Real Life Connections** From this age-old story comes the proverb, "Beware of Greeks bearing gifts." Why is this lesson still important today?

Cause and Effect

Reading a Social Studies Selection

▶ Background Information

In the following selection, you will read about the Bedouin and Masai.

The Bedouins live in the Middle East. Many still follow the traditional way of life that you will read about in the selection. However, since the mid-1990s, many Bedouins have left their nomadic lifestyle to live in modern cities. Many Middle Eastern nations have set up programs to encourage Bedouin settlement and a return to the traditional ways of life.

The Masai live in Kenya, a country on the east coast of Africa. Like the Bedouins, the Masai are nomads, wanderers, who rely on animals for food, clothing, and shelter.

Although these two groups live on different continents, they have much in common.

▶ Skill Focus

Many of the ideas that you read about in textbooks are connected by **cause and effect**. A cause is an underlying reason, condition, or situation that makes something happen. An effect is the result or outcome of a cause.

Often, several causes bring about a single effect, as shown in the following example.

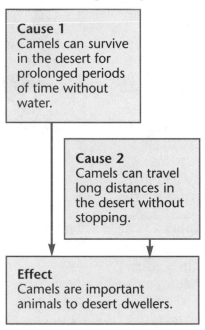

A single cause can also bring about several effects, as shown in this example.

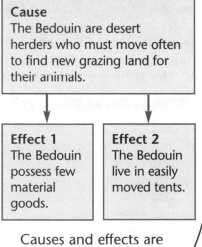

Causes and effects are often directly stated in a selection. However, you may have to infer, or figure out, a cause or an effect.

▶ Word Clues

Read the sentence below. Look for context clues that explain the underlined word.

Because these wells are shared in common and used equally by all, they are called underline communal wells.

If you do not know the meaning of the word *communal,* the first part of the sentence states what it means. A word meaning is often stated directly either before or after a new word. Definition clues may also be in the sentences before or after the sentence in which the unknown word appears.

Use **definition** context clues to find the meanings of the three underlined words in the selection.

▶ Strategy Tip

As you read about the Bedouin and the Masai, look for cause and effect connections. Ask yourself why these people live as they do. Try to understand the effects that their environments have on their lives.

The Bedouin and the Masai: Herders of Animals

In some remote areas of the world, there are groups of people whose lives are closely intertwined with the lives of their animals. These people, called herders, still live much as their ancestors did centuries ago.

Animals are important in every aspect of the herder's life. The wealth of a herder is measured by the size of the herd. Everyday life revolves around the care of the animals. Many customs and rituals have been influenced by the animals that enable the herder to survive. From their animals, herders get most of what they need to survive. The animals supply them not only with food, drink, and clothing, but also with shelter and fuel. In turn, the herders care for the animals. They take them to fresh pastures, care for the sick ones, and protect them from predators.

Unlike farmers, herders do not keep their animals in one place. Because the animals need more pasture than one small area can provide, the people and their herds move frequently from one grazing place to another.

Constant movement is a major feature of the lives of herders. They do not have permanent homes. As a result, their easily built dwellings can be carried with them or left behind. Herders possess few material belongings; they own only as much as they can transport with them.

Of all the herders still existing in various parts of the world, two groups are especially interesting. One group is the Bedouin of the Middle East, and the other is the Masai of eastern Africa.

The Bedouin

In the dry, vast deserts of the Middle East, herders of camels, sheep, and goats live an ancient, nomadic life. They are the Bedouin, the Arab inhabitants of the desert. With little grass in the harsh desert, the Bedouin move often to find new pastures for their animals.

A Bedouin camp is both beautiful and practical. Long, low, black tents, ingeniously adapted to the needs of Bedouin life, are pitched together on the white sand. Each tent is made from long strands of goat, camel, and

The camel has been essential to Bedouin life in the desert.

sheep hair. When wet, these fibers expand, making the tent waterproof. During the hot days, the sides of the tent are rolled up to provide shade and to let cool breezes through. At night, they are rolled down to keep out the cold wind. When the Bedouin decide to move their herds to new grazing land, they can lower their tents and pack their belongings within a few hours.

In the fall, winter, and spring, the Bedouin live and travel together in family groups of two to twenty tents. They move their herds across the desert, often following rain clouds. In the summer, the Bedouin gather together at wells, the only sources of water in the dry summer. Because these wells are shared in common and used equally by all, they are called communal wells. Hundreds of tents are pitched together in the vicinity of the communal well and remain there for three or four months.

✗✗ The Bedouin rely on their animals for most of their diet. Camel milk is the most important part of many meals. Sometimes it is drunk fresh, and other times it is made into <u>yogurt</u>. Yogurt is a semisolid food made from milk that is fermented by a bacterium.

Because the camels are so valuable, they are seldom killed to be eaten. On special occasions, however, the Bedouin enjoy camel meat as a festive treat. The Bedouin also make a kind of butter and a hard, white cheese from their sheep's milk.

✗ The Bedouin cherish and respect the camel. Various Bedouin groups prize a particular color camel—white, black, brown. The Arabic word for camel *(jamal)* comes from the same root as the Arabic word for beautiful *(jamil)*. Also, numerous Arabic words describe the various ages and kinds of camels.

In the past, the Bedouin herded only camels, the single-humped dromedary of the Arabian desert. The camel was not only the most important animal in the desert, but also the chief means of transportation for desert people. A camel can survive for prolonged periods of time without water and can also tolerate extreme heat. In addition, the camel has great endurance and courage.

Until modern times, the wealth of a Bedouin was measured only by the number of camels he owned. An average herd consisted of forty to fifty camels. Today sheep are becoming more and more important to the Bedouin economy. Because cars and trucks are now used as transportation in the desert, camels are no longer as valuable as they used to be. Consequently, raising sheep is becoming more profitable than herding camels.

Much of Bedouin life, however, remains unchanged. The people still travel the desert, following their herds and keeping up old traditions.

The Masai

The high, rolling, treeless plains in the countries of Kenya and Tanzania are unique to eastern Africa. They are called <u>savannas</u>. On these plains live the Masai. Although the Masai are herders of cattle, sheep, and goats, they value their cattle most. To them, no other possession is of equal worth. This attitude is the result of the important role cattle play in every aspect of Masai life.

A Masai village consists of a group of <u>bomas</u>. Built by the Masai women, bomas are dwellings made from a framework of twigs and covered by grass and leaves. To keep the structure warm and waterproof, it is plastered with a layer of cattle dung. Fences are put up

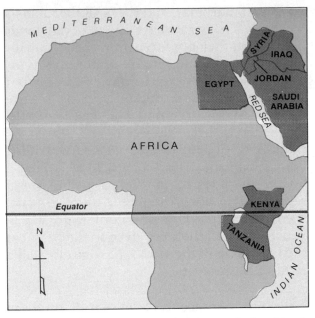

The Bedouin and Masai make their homes in the deserts of the Middle East and the savannas of eastern Africa.

around the boma village to protect the animals at night.

✗ Everyday life in the village revolves around the care of the cattle and other animals. Masai women and girls milk the cattle and prepare food using the milk. The men inspect the cattle for disease and treat any sick ones. During the day, the young boys take the cattle out to pasture and guard them from predators. When necessary, the boys help a pregnant animal give birth to a kid or calf.

When their cattle need new grazing land, the Masai move. If they come to a grazing place on the savanna where they have been before, the Masai patch up their old bomas. The women can do this task in half a day. If the grazing place is new, the women and young girls build new bomas. When staying in a place for a short while, the Masai live in dwellings made of mud and skin.

✔ From their cattle, the Masai get meat, milk, and blood for nourishment. After a cow is milked, the milk is divided into three parts. One part is drunk fresh. The second part is stored and becomes a kind of sour cheese. The third part is mixed with blood drawn from a cow to make a protein-rich drink. Cattle also provide the Masai with hides for clothing and bed covers.

Because cattle are so important to the Masai, a strong bond exists between them and their animals. They know each animal's voice and markings, and they call the animals by name. The Masai have few material goods because all they need to own is their animals. A Masai man cannot marry until he owns his own cattle. An average herd consists of about seventy-five head of cattle.

The Masai, a proud and noble people, have always been respected and feared by other African people. To become a warrior, a young man must prove himself by killing a lion with a spear. In the past, the Masai raided neighboring camps for cattle to make their own herds larger. According to Masai belief, all the cattle were given to the Masai at the beginning of the world. No one else had a right to possess any.

In recent years, the Masai have come to lead more peaceful lives. Still, modern civilization has not greatly affected them. The young people have the chance to go to the cities, but most Masai remain herders of cattle. They are close to their families and friends, and their love for their animals remains constant. They are proud to be Masai.

A Masai family in traditional dress stands in front of their boma. The fence in the background protects their animals at night.

Herders live a life that is unique in today's world. Living in close contact with nature, they have no need for luxury or conveniences. They remain in family groups, and they take pride in caring for the animals who ensure their survival.

RECALLING FACTS

1. How are the Bedouin dwellings different from those of the Masai?

_____

_____

_____

_____

_____

_____

2. Reread the paragraph that has XX next to it. Underline the sentence that states its main idea. Circle at least three sentences in the paragraph that give details in support of the main idea.

3. Reread the two paragraphs that have Xs next to them. Underline the sentence in each paragraph that states the paragraph's main idea.

4. Decide if each statement is true or false. Write *true* or *false* on the lines provided.

   a. The savannas of East Africa are suited to the raising of cattle, sheep, and goats.

   _____

   b. Along with milk and butter, yogurt is found in the dairy section of a supermarket.

   _____

   c. The Bedouin dwellings, found in the deserts of the Middle East, are called bomas.

   _____

   d. The Masai use sheep's milk to make a sour cheese and a protein-rich drink made from blood and milk.

   _____

1. List two ways in which the life of a farmer is different from the life of a herder.

   a. _____

   b. _____

2. What do the Bedouin and the Masai believe about land ownership? Explain.

   _____

   _____

3. Identify the following statements by writing *fact* or *opinion* on the lines provided.

   _____ a. Of all the groups of herders, the Bedouin and the Masai are the most interesting.

   _____ b. The Bedouin move often to find new pastures for their herds.

   _____ c. A Bedouin camp is both beautiful and practical.

   _____ d. The Masai have few material goods because their main goal is to own cattle.

   _____ e. The Masai are a proud and noble people who will never change their ways.

4. Reread the paragraph with a check mark next to it. Circle the letter next to the sentence that states the paragraph's main idea.
   a. The Masai get milk from their cattle.
   b. The Masai's cattle provide them with food, drink, and clothing.
   c. The Masai kill cattle for their blood.

5. How do you think the lives of the Bedouin and Masai herders may change in the coming years?

   _____

   _____

   _____

SKILL FOCUS

Answer the following questions based on the many cause and effect relationships described in the selection that you have just read.

1. Give two effects for each cause listed below.
   a. **Cause**   In the dry summer, a communal well is the Bedouin's only source of water.

   Effect _____

   _____

   Effect _____

   _____

b. Cause Trucks and cars have begun to replace the camel as a means of transportation in the desert.

Effect _____

_____

Effect _____

_____

2. Give two causes for each effect listed below.

   a. Cause _____

_____

   Cause _____

_____

   Effect In the past, the Masai raided neighboring camps for cattle.

   b. Cause _____

_____

   Cause _____

_____

   Effect Most Masai stay with their own people rather than move to cities.

3. Complete each of the following by giving one effect for the cause stated.
      a. Because animals influence how and where herders live, how they dress, and what they

   eat and drink, _____

      b. Because the camel can survive for long periods of time without water, _____

   _____

      c. When their cattle need new grazing land, the Masai _____

   _____

      d. When cars and trucks came into use in the desert, _____

   _____

4. Sometimes effects have to be inferred, or figured out, because they are not directly stated in a selection. Answer each of the following questions by inferring an effect.
      a. What will happen to the Bedouin way of life as sheep begin to replace camels?

   _____

   _____

      b. What will happen to the Masai way of life if more and more young people go to the

   cities? _____

   _____

▶ **Real Life Connections** Describe one aspect of the Bedouin or Masai way of life that appeals to you.

Classifying

Reading a Science Selection

▶ Background Information

What makes you different from a shark? You may answer this in many ways, but the fact that you have arms and legs and a shark has fins probably would come to your mind. Of course, this distinction is easy to make, but scientists use physical differences like these to classify animals.

About one million kinds of animals make up the animal kingdom. The following selection describes how scientists classify these animals according to their structures.

▶ Skill Focus

Sometimes information is organized by **classifying** similar objects or ideas into groups. Classifying makes it easier to see similarities and differences among these groups. It is therefore helpful for people who work with a great number of objects, as scientists do. When scientists classify plants and animals, they take large groups and break them up into smaller groups. The members of each smaller group are similar in some special way.

One way to group animals is according to habitat. For example, animals that live in water make up a large group. Sharks, shellfish, whales, certain frogs, and diving beetles belong to this large group of water dwellers. Water dwellers can be divided into two smaller groups: the saltwater group and the freshwater group. Whales belong to the saltwater group, while frogs belong to the fresh-water group.

A more common and useful way of grouping animals is according to their structure. For example, dogs, wolves, and coyotes are all built very much alike. They belong to a group called Canidae (KA nə dee). House cats, tigers, and cheetahs—all built alike—belong to a group called Felidae (FEE lə dee). By knowing an animal's body structure, you can put it into the right group, or classification.

When reading information about how animals are classified into groups, ask yourself such questions as the following:

1. What is similar about the animals classified in the same group?
2. How are the animals in one group different from animals in other groups?

▶ Word Clues

When you read a word that you do not know, look for context clues to help you. Context clues are nearby words and phrases that help make the meaning of the unknown word clearer. Read the sentences below.

Many lampreys are underlined{parasites}. Parasites are animals that obtain their food from other animals.

If you do not understand the word *parasites,* the next sentence defines the word for you.

Use **definition** context clues to find the meanings of the three underlined words in the selection.

▶ Strategy Tip

Preview the following selection before you read it. Look at the headings and boldfaced words. As you read "Classifying Animals," notice the similarities and differences among the classes of animals.

Classifying Animals

The animal kingdom can be divided into approximately twenty major groups, each of which is called a **phylum** (FY ləm). Members of each phylum have one or more body characteristics that are alike. For example, one phylum is called **Chordata** (kor DAT ə). The chordates are alike in that each animal in this group has a nerve cord along its back.

A phylum can be divided into even smaller groups, called **classes.** A class can be divided into **orders,** an order into **families,** and a family into **genera** (JEN ər ə). The word *genera* is plural; the singular form is *genus* (JEEN əs). A genus can be divided into **species** (SPEE sheez). The word *species* can be plural or singular. Look at Figure 1.

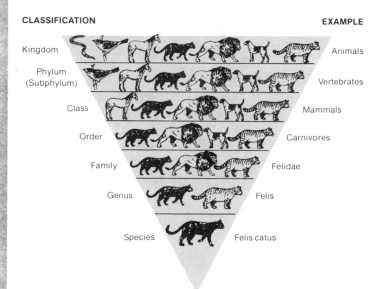

CLASSIFICATION   EXAMPLE

Kingdom — Animals
Phylum (Subphylum) — Vertebrates
Class — Mammals
Order — Carnivores
Family — Felidae
Genus — Felis
Species — Felis catus

Figure 1. These major classifications can also be subdivided.

A species is the smallest group into which an animal can be classified. Animals of the same species have the same basic body characteristics. They differ only in minor ways. Members of the same species can mate and reproduce. For example, all house cats belong to the species **Felis catus** (fee ləs KAT əs).

Two Groups of Chordates

House cats, bobcats, tigers, and fish all belong to the phylum Chordata because each has a nerve cord in its back. It is easy to see that a house cat is related to a bobcat and that both are related to tigers. However, it is not as easy to see that all cats are related to fish. A phylum is sometimes further broken down into groups called **subphyla** (SUB fy lə).

Cats, dogs, and fish all belong to an important subphylum called **Vertebrata** (ver tə BRAT ə). To understand how these animals are related, you have to understand their body structures. If you have ever eaten a whole fish, you know that it has a backbone and many other bones. X-ray photographs of a cat and a dog would show that their bodies have backbones too.

Any animal with a backbone is a **vertebrate** (VER tə brayt), which means having a backbone. Like all chordates, vertebrates have nerve cords. Unlike other chordates, vertebrates also have backbones to protect the nerve cords.

Seven Classes of Vertebrates

The subphylum Vertebrata is divided into seven classes, and the members of five of these classes are cold-blooded. *Cold-blooded* means "an animals' body temperature varies with the temperature of their surroundings." The members of the other two classes are warm-blooded. *Warm-blooded* means "an animals' body temperature stays about the same no matter what the temperature of their surroundings." Another similarity among vertebrates is that they breathe air by means of gills or lungs. Most vertebrates have two pairs of limbs, but some have wings or fins in place of legs.

Class 1. Agnatha (*Jawless Fish*)

Agnatha (AG nə thə) is a class of cold-blooded vertebrates that live in water and breathe by means of gills. However, unlike

Figure 2. A sea lamprey has no jaw. It clings to its prey with its mouth.

other classes of fish, they have no jaws, scales, or fins. Most members of this class live in oceans, but some live in fresh water. Lampreys and hagfishes belong to this class.

Many lampreys are parasites. Parasites are animals that obtain their food from other animals. The sea lamprey is such an animal. Having no jaws, it cannot bite or chew, but it can hold on to another animal by means of its round mouth. The lamprey then feeds on the blood of the other animal.

Class 2. Chondrichthyes (Cartilaginous Fish)

Sharks and their close relatives, the skates and rays, belong to a class of vertebrates called **Chondrichthyes** (kon DRIK thee eez). Like other classes of fish, members of this class are cold-blooded and breathe by means of gills. However, they do not have true scales or true backbones. Their backbones are made of cartilage, not bone. Cartilage is a tough, elastic material that is softer than bone. Scalelike plates protect the bodies of the animals in this class.

Sharks have streamlined bodies, two pairs of fins, and strong jaws. Some sharks are dangerous to people. Great white sharks are known to have attacked people and even boats. Other dangerous sharks are hammerheads and tiger sharks.

Rays and skates have broad, flat bodies. They move by flapping their large winglike fins. The stingray has a long tail.

Figure 3. A stingray is a close relative of the shark. It has a backbone made of cartilage.

Class 3. Osteichthyes (Bony Fish)

The class **Osteichthyes** (os tee IK thee eez) includes all bony fish. Bony fish are cold-blooded saltwater or freshwater vertebrates that breathe by means of gills. A few have lunglike air bladders that allow them to spend some time out of water. All bony fish have jaws and bony spinal columns. They have sets of paired fins that are supported by bony projections, called finrays. Many have unpaired fins as well. Their bodies are covered with flat scales. The fish uses its tail to push itself forward, and the streamlined shape of its body helps it move easily through the water.

There are more than 20,000 species of bony fish. The best known are those that people eat, such as sole, trout, perch, and bass.

Figure 4. Like most fish, the bass has a streamlined body. Instead of limbs, it has two pairs of fins.

Class 4. Amphibia (Amphibians)

Amphibia (am FIB ee ə) is a class of cold-blooded vertebrates that change from gill breathing to lung breathing as they mature. Frogs, toads, and salamanders belong to this class. All members of this class begin life as larvae. Larvae are the early forms of animals that change structurally when they mature. For example, a tadpole is the larva of a frog.

Figure 5. Salamanders have soft, moist skin. As adults, they breathe with lungs.

Most amphibians live in or near fresh water. Some live only on land but lay their eggs in water. Because most have soft, moist skin, land amphibians need damp surroundings. The salamander lives in wet, shady places.

Class 5. Reptilia (Reptiles)

The class **Reptilia** (rep TIL ee ə) includes turtles, lizards, snakes, and crocodiles. Except for snakes, all reptiles have two pairs of limbs. Snakes move by bending their bodies.

Figure 7. The Arctic tern uses its powerful wings to fly from pole to pole twice a year.

Class 7. Mammalia (Mammals)

The class **Mammalia** (mə MAY lee ə) includes hairy, intelligent, warm-blooded vertebrates. The females have mammary glands that produce milk for their young.

Mammals have two pairs of limbs and breathe by means of lungs. Although most live on land, the largest mammal, the whale, lives in water. There are 18 orders of mammals. Whales belong to the order **Cetacea** (see TAY shee ə). Dogs and cats belong to the order **Carnivora** (car NIV ə rə). Carnivores are animals that eat meat and have teeth designed for ripping and tearing.

Figure 6. Turtles are reptiles. They breathe air through their lungs.

Most reptiles are covered by hard scales or plates. Some live on land, and some live in water. All breathe by means of lungs. The ocean-going loggerhead turtle, for instance, can spend long periods under water before coming up for air. Some turtles have lived to be 150 years old.

Class 6. Aves (Birds)

Aves (AY veez) are warm-blooded vertebrates with one pair of wings and one pair of legs. Most birds use their wings to fly, but some, like the ostrich, use their wings only for balance. Birds breathe through lungs and have feathers. Their feathers keep them warm and help them to fly. Some birds <u>migrate</u> long distances. The word *migrate* means "to move from one region to another with the change of seasons." Arctic terns fly between the Arctic and the Antarctic twice a year.

Figure 8. Cats and dogs are mammals. The young of mammals receive milk from their mothers.

1. Arrange the following groups so that the largest is first and the smallest is last: class, family, order, species, kingdom, genus, subphylum, phylum.

   _____ _____

   _____ _____

   _____ _____

   _____ _____

2. What major characteristic distinguishes all vertebrates? _____

3. What two classes of vertebrates are warm-blooded? _____
   _____

4. How is a cold-blooded animal different from a warm-blooded animal?

   _____

   _____

   _____

5. List two examples of warm-blooded animals and two examples of cold-blooded animals.

   warm-blooded   cold-blooded

   _____ _____

   _____ _____

6. How do fish breathe?

   _____

7. How do reptiles, birds, mammals, and adult amphibians breathe?

   _____

8. Complete each sentence with the correct word below.

   cartilage   larvae   migrate

   a. Some animals _____ every fall.

   b. Human ears contain _____.

   c. The pond was full of mosquito

   _____.

1. Which includes a larger number of species, a phylum or a class? Why?

   _____

   _____

   _____

2. To what group do all animals belong?

   _____

3. Why are sharks vertebrates, even though they do not have hard bones?

   _____

   _____

4. What one characteristic do birds and mammals share that lampreys and mammals do not?

   _____

   _____

5. Based on the selection, to what class do you think goats belong?

   _____

6. The prefix in means "not" or "without." What do you think an invertebrate is?

   _____

   _____

A. Write the name for each of the classes of vertebrates mentioned in the selection. Under each class, write the names of some of the types of animals that belong to it.

Class 1	Class 2	Class 3	Class 4	Class 5	Class 6	Class 7
____	____	____	____	____	____	____
____	____	____	____	____	____	____
____	____	____	____	____	____	____
____	____	____	____	____	____	____
____	____	____	____	____	____	____

B. Go back to the selection, and reread the description of each class of vertebrates. Then complete the chart below by adding the characteristics of each group. The first one is done for you.

Class	Distinguishing Body Characteristics	Means of Breathing	Cold-blooded or Warm-blooded	Type of Skin Covering
Agnatha	no jaw no limbs	gills	cold-blooded	no scales
Chondrichthyes				
Osteichthyes				
Amphibia				
Reptilia				
Aves				
Mammalia				

▶ **Real Life Connections** Which classifications of animals described in this selection are common to your geographic area?

Lesson 12

Word Problems

Reading a Mathematics Selection

▶ **Background Information**

Problem solving is one of the most important skills in mathematics. "Reading Word Problems" gives you five steps that are useful in solving almost all problems in mathematics. Addition, subtraction, multiplication, or division of whole numbers and decimals are needed to solve these problems. Some of the problems in this selection require one operation, and some require two operations.

▶ **Skill Focus**

Most word problems can be solved using the same five-step process. When you try to solve any word problem, refer to the five steps below.

1. Read the problem. Be sure that you are familiar with all the words. If a picture is associated with the problem, be sure to read the labels. All problems ask you a question or require you to supply some information. Try to picture in your mind the information that is given in relation to the information that you are to supply. Read the problem again to be sure that you understand what you are to do.

2. Decide how to find the answer. It may be helpful to write a sentence about each fact that is given in the problem. After you determine the information needed to solve the problem, decide on the mathematical operations to use. Will the problem require one operation, or will it require two operations? If you need to use two operations, you need to write two mathematical sentences to find the answer. Be sure to look for key words to help you decide on the operations to use.

3. Estimate the answer. Use rounded numbers to make an estimate for each mathematical sentence that you use in solving the problem.

4. Carry out the plan. Solve each of the mathematical sentences that you have written.

5. Reread the problem. Is the answer logical? How close is the answer to your estimate? If it is not very close, rethink the problem. Have you made an error in writing the mathematical sentences or in carrying out the operations?

▶ **Word Clues**

As you read a word problem, look for key words that serve as clues to the operations needed in solving problems. For example, the word *difference* usually signals subtraction. The word *total* usually signals addition. Make sure that you know the meaning of the word *average.* The average is the sum of a group of numbers divided by the number of members in the group.

▶ **Strategy Tip**

As you read each word problem, consider whether you need to use one or two operations. Look for key words to help you determine whether to add, subtract, multiply, or divide. Be alert for numbers that are not needed.

Reading Word Problems

Research in the way in which animals live is important to saving the environment. Much of the research about animal life involves using numbers and solving problems.

Use the following five steps to solve word problems.

1. Read the problem.
2. Decide how to find the answer.
3. Estimate the answer.
4. Carry out the plan.
5. Reread the problem.

READ THE PROBLEM

In 1964, George Schaller studied the animals in Kanha National Park in India. One of the most common animals in the park was the axis deer. The largest herd Schaller saw in one month numbered 175 deer. The average herd that month numbered only 32.4 deer. What is the difference between the sizes of the largest herd and the average herd?

Read the problem again. Are there any words that you do not know? If so, look them up to find their meanings. Be aware that the proper nouns, or names, used in the problem usually cannot be found in a dictionary. The phrase *axis deer* is the name of a kind of deer.

Does this problem ask a question, or does it tell you to do something? Often questions are asked or instructions given in the last sentence of the problem.

DECIDE HOW TO FIND THE ANSWER

Of the three numbers mentioned in the problem, one is a date, and it is not used in solving the problem. The other two numbers are used in solving the problem. Write a short sentence about each number.

1. The largest herd had 175 deer.
2. The average herd had 32.4 deer.

Although the word *average* is used in the problem, you are not asked to find the average. It is given to you. The clue to what you are asked to find is in the phrase *what is the difference*. The largest herd is greater than the average herd. Write a mathematical sentence, or equation, that shows the difference between

the two herds. Let *n* be the unknown number that is the answer to the question.

$$175 - 32.4 = n$$

The solution to the equation will answer the question *What is the difference between the sizes of the largest herd and the average herd?* The letter *n* represents a number of deer. Because the average is a decimal, the number of deer in the answer will also be a decimal.

ESTIMATE THE ANSWER

In addition or subtraction, the most common way to estimate is to round each number to the highest place in the smaller number. In this problem, the highest place for the smaller number, 32.4, is the tens, so it is rounded to 30. The larger number, 175, is also rounded to the tens place, or 180. The following equation can be used for the estimate.

$$180 - 30 = n$$

Your estimate is 150.

CARRY OUT THE PLAN

$$
\begin{array}{r}
175.0 \\
-\ 32.4 \\
\hline
142.6
\end{array}
$$

Notice that it is helpful to rewrite 175 as 175.0 before subtracting.

REREAD THE PROBLEM

The difference between the sizes of the largest herd and the average herd is 142.6 deer. In this case, the answer is close to the estimate. If your answer is not close to your estimate, you should find out whether the error was in the equation or in carrying out the operation.

PRACTICE

Use the five steps to solve this problem.

Read: Tony Sinclair estimated that in the Serengeti National Park in Africa, about 52,000 wildebeest, a large antelope, die or are killed every year. About 11,400 are killed by lions, while hyenas kill about 7,500. The others are victims of disease or old age. Find out how many wildebeest die as a result of old age or disease.

The problem does not ask a question, but the last sentence tells you what to do. *Find out how many wildebeest die as a result of old age or disease.*

Decide: There are three numbers in the problem. Each stands for a fact about the wildebeest in the Serengeti Park. Write a sentence for each fact.

1. About 52,000 die or are killed each year.
2. Lions kill about 11,400.
3. Hyenas kill about 7,500.

The information you are to find is the *difference* between the total number that die or are killed and the *sum* of the wildebeest killed by lions and hyenas. Write equations that show how to solve the problem.

$$52,000 - s = d$$
$$11,400 + 7,500 = s$$

Which equation should you solve first? You must solve the equation that has one variable first. A variable is a letter that stands for a number.

Estimate: In addition and subtraction, you round to the highest place in the smaller number. In the equation $11,400 + 7,500 = s$, the smaller number is 7,500. The highest place in 7,500 is thousands, so round to thousands.

$$11,000 + 8,000 = s$$

A good estimate for s is 19,000.

Now round in the other equation. What is the smaller number? What is its highest place?

$$50,000 - 20,000 = d$$

A good estimate for the answer to the problem is 30,000 wildebeest.

Carry Out:

$$11,400 + 7,500 = 18,900$$
$$52,000 - 18,900 = 33,100$$

Reread: As a result of disease or old age, 33,100 wildebeest die each year. This is close to the estimate of 30,000 wildebeest.

RECALLING FACTS

1. Which step do you complete after you have decided on a plan?

2. When you estimate in addition or subtraction, which number do you use to determine to which place you should round?

3. In that number, to which place do you round?

4. In which sentence of a problem are you most likely to find the question or the directions for the information to be supplied?

5. When you are subtracting a decimal from a whole number, what should you do to the whole number?

6. Suppose that two equations are to be solved for a problem and that one equation contains one variable while the other equation contains two variables. Which equation do you solve first?

7. What is the last thing that you should do in solving a word problem?

INTERPRETING FACTS

1. In the problems in the selection, the letters *n, d,* and *s* are used as variables. What might these letters stand for?

_____

_____

_____

2. Only one of the five steps for problem solving can be done in a different order from the order given. Which step is it?

_____

_____

_____

SKILL FOCUS

Follow the steps to solve each problem.

1. **Read:** In 1968, George Schaller timed a tiger that was walking at normal speed. It traveled at 4 kilometers per hour. How many kilometers can a tiger cover in 12 hours if it continues at that speed?

   Decide: _____

   Estimate: _____

   Carry Out: _____

   Reread: _____

   _____

2. **Read:** Robert Yerkes tried to find how many tries different animals would need to learn that he had hidden their food in one of nine boxes. For each animal, he hid the food in the same box every try. Yerkes' results included the following:

   crow 50 tries   rat 170 tries

   pig 50 tries   monkey 132 tries

   Find the average for the animals listed.

   Decide: _____

   Estimate: _____

   Carry Out: _____

   Reread: _____

   _____

3. **Read:** One of the smallest animals at birth is the opossum, which averages only 2 grams in weight. If 13 opossums are born at one time, what is their total average weight?

Decide: _____

Estimate: _____

Carry Out: _____

Reread: _____

4. **Read:** A giraffe weighs about 38.5 kilograms at birth. How many newborn opossums (problem 3) would it take to weigh as much as one newborn giraffe?

Decide: _____

Estimate: _____

Carry Out: _____

Reread: _____

5. **Read:** A hibernating woodchuck breathes only once in 5 minutes. If a woodchuck hibernates for 2 months (60 days), how many breaths does it take?

Decide: _____

Estimate: _____

Carry Out: _____

Reread: _____

6. **Read:** George Schaller observed 129 fights in his study of male axis deer. In 114 of the fights, the deer with the larger antlers won. Of the 62 fights that he saw begin, the final winner started the fight 48 times. How many of the fights that Schaller saw were won by the deer with the shorter antlers?

Decide: _____

Estimate: _____

Carry Out: _____

Reread: _____

▶ **Real Life Connections** Make up a word problem about animals that live in your area.

Lesson 13

Syllables

Guide 4: Words with Two Consonants Between Two Sounded Vowels

A word that has two consonants between two sounded vowels is usually divided into syllables between the two consonants.

cactus   cac tus

Divide each word below into two syllables by writing each syllable separately on the line to the right of the word.

1. public _____
2. carbon _____
3. limber _____
4. walnut _____
5. contain _____
6. bargain _____
7. margin _____
8. engine _____
9. border _____
10. mixture _____
11. fertile _____
12. garden _____
13. chapter _____
14. oblong _____
15. discuss _____
16. surface _____
17. sentence _____
18. compare _____

Guide 5: Words with One Consonant Between Two Sounded Vowels

Guide 5a: A word that has one consonant between two sounded vowels, with the first vowel long, is usually divided into syllables before the consonant.

bacon   ba con

Guide 5b: A word that has one consonant between two sounded vowels, with the first vowel short, is usually divided into syllables after the consonant.

cabin   cab in

Say each of the words below to yourself. If the first vowel is long, use Guide 5a to divide the word into two syllables. If the first vowel is short, use Guide 5b. Write each syllable separately on the line to the right of the word.

1. tenant _____
2. hotel _____
3. camel _____
4. climate _____
5. modern _____
6. laser _____
7. topic _____
8. fever _____
9. minor _____
10. famine _____
11. limit _____
12. native _____
13. solid _____
14. canine _____
15. critic _____
16. moment _____
17. release _____
18. moment _____

Guide 6: Words with Blends

The word *between* has two consonants between two sounded vowels. Because *tw* is a consonant blend, you do not divide between the two consonants. The letters *tw* should be treated as a single consonant.

be tween

In a word that has three consonants between two vowels, two of the consonants may be a blend or a digraph. You treat the blend or digraph as one consonant. For example, *athlete* has a *th* digraph. You divide the word between the digraph and the consonant.

ath lete

Circle the blend or digraph in each of the words below. Then divide the word into two syllables by writing each syllable separately on the line to the right of the word.

1. secret _____
2. marshal _____
3. poultry _____
4. machine _____

5. concrete _____
6. complex _____
7. zebra _____
8. surprise _____

When a word ends in *-le*, the *-le* and the consonant before it make up a syllable, as in *gen tle.*

Divide the words below into two syllables by writing each syllable separately on the line to the right of the word.

1. bugle _____
2. ankle _____
3. tangle _____
4. staple _____

5. ladle _____
6. noble _____
7. uncle _____
8. candle _____

Divide each word below into syllables. Write the syllables separately on the line to the right of the word. On the line to the left of the word, write the number of the guide you used to divide each syllable. Some words have three syllables. The first one has been done for you.

__4, 5a__	consonant	__con so nant__	_____	phantom	_____
_____	danger	_____	_____	petal	_____
_____	carpenter	_____	_____	interest	_____
_____	member	_____	_____	patient	_____
_____	fragrance	_____	_____	particle	_____
_____	absolute	_____	_____	orthodox	_____
_____	holster	_____	_____	lemon	_____
_____	Atlantic	_____	_____	crumple	_____
_____	legal	_____	_____	embargo	_____

Lesson 14

Main Idea and Supporting Details

Many paragraphs that you read are packed with information. Knowing how to find the main idea and important details helps you understand the information in a paragraph. The **main idea** expresses the subject of a paragraph. A **major detail** is a supporting idea that is often an important example or a fact about the main idea. A paragraph usually contains more than one major detail.

The major details of a paragraph help develop or complete the thought expressed by the main idea. The main idea and major details work together as a unit to support one another. You could say that the main idea depends on major details.

Not all the details in a paragraph are major details. Paragraphs often contain details that are not important to the main idea. They are called **minor details.** They explain or tell more about the major details. The minor details add interest to the main idea, but the main idea does not depend on them.

The following paragraph is about the gaits of two different animals. Each animal uses a different type of leg movement. The main idea and two major details in the paragraph are diagrammed to show how the main idea depends on the major details.

Gaits, or the ways in which animals move their legs, differ in many ways. A moose with large antlers trots when it is in a hurry. When trotting, the moose moves a front leg and the opposite hind leg at the same time. In this way, two diagonal legs are in contact with the ground, giving the animal's body stable support. A camel, on the other hand, paces when it is in a hurry. In pacing, both legs on the same side of the body move together. This gait is useful only on flat land because it is not as stable as a trot.

In the diagram, the sentences that explain how the legs move when trotting and pacing are not listed as major details. They are minor details that explain the major details.

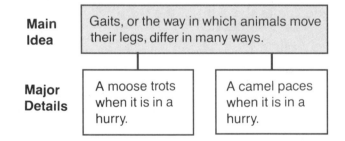

Main Idea: Gaits, or the way in which animals move their legs, differ in many ways.

Major Details: A moose trots when it is in a hurry. | A camel paces when it is in a hurry.

As you read the following paragraphs, look for main ideas and major details.

1. Four-legged animals have many different gaits. The slowest of the gaits, the walk, can be performed by all four-legged animals except kangaroos, wallabies, and some monkeys. Animals with short legs cannot gallop, because at some point in the stride all four feet must be off the ground. Only long-legged animals can push themselves

The springbok, a gazelle, pronks.

The springbok can also run quickly.

high enough to gallop. A much less common gait is the pronk, where all four of an animal's legs take off and land nearly together. Many deer and antelope use this gait.

2. How fast an animal is able to move depends on the length of its legs and its body size and weight. Animals with long legs can take greater strides and move faster than shorter legged animals. The deer, with its long legs and slimmer body, can move much faster than the pig. The pig, with its short legs and proportionally heavier body, cannot move as quickly. Massive animals with long legs, however, can often move very quickly despite their huge size. Such animals include buffalo and elephants.

3. The large front legs of the praying mantis enable it to catch prey, or living food. The mole uses its front legs to shovel through soil underground. It eats any earthworms it finds along the way. Many grasshoppers chirp by scraping together their third set of legs. The cassowary, a flightless bird, uses spurs on its legs to defend itself. Thus, animals use their legs for a variety of functions.

Complete the diagram for each paragraph. In the box labeled *Main Idea,* write the sentence that states the main idea as it appears in the paragraph. Use your own words for filling in the boxes labeled *Major Details.*

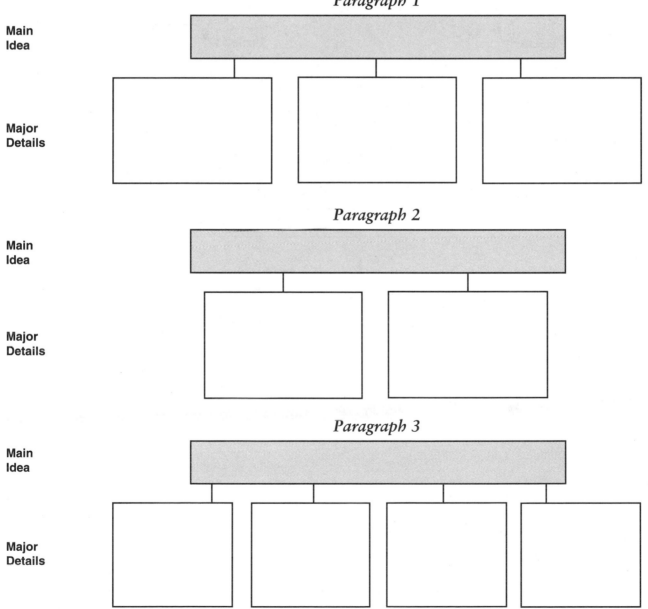

Paragraph 1

Main Idea

Major Details

Paragraph 2

Main Idea

Major Details

Paragraph 3

Main Idea

Major Details

Reading a Mail Order Catalog

Today it is not necessary to do all your shopping at a store. Many businesses permit people to shop through the mail. You can do so by using a **mail order catalog**—a book that lists things to buy.

Read the part of a mail order catalog for stereo equipment shown below. Then study the completed order form that follows it.

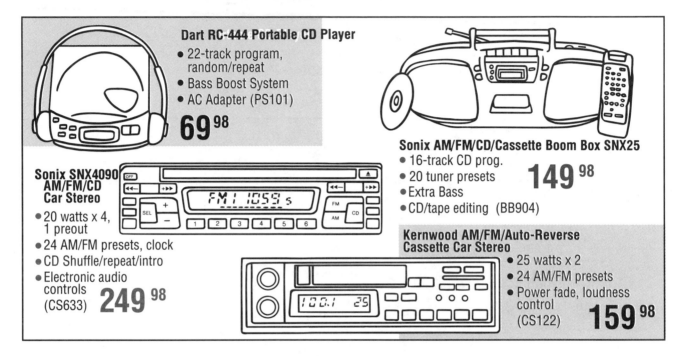

Dart RC-444 Portable CD Player
- 22-track program, random/repeat
- Bass Boost System
- AC Adapter (PS101)

69⁹⁸

Sonix AM/FM/CD/Cassette Boom Box SNX25
- 16-track CD prog.
- 20 tuner presets
- Extra Bass
- CD/tape editing (BB904)

149⁹⁸

Sonix SNX4090 AM/FM/CD Car Stereo
- 20 watts x 4, 1 preout
- 24 AM/FM presets, clock
- CD Shuffle/repeat/intro
- Electronic audio controls (CS633)

249⁹⁸

Kernwood AM/FM/Auto-Reverse Cassette Car Stereo
- 25 watts x 2
- 24 AM/FM presets
- Power fade, loudness control (CS122)

159⁹⁸

STEREO CITY 2200 Main Street, Midland, Texas 79701

Ordered by:

NAME   MR. LUIS HERNANDEZ

STREET ADDRESS   610 PINECREST ROAD   APT. 6A

CITY   WAYNE   STATE   NEW JERSEY   ZIP   07470

Just in case we have to phone you. . .

DAYTIME PHONE: AREA CODE (201)   337-9244

To send this order to a different address

NAME

STREET ADDRESS   APT.

CITY   STATE   ZIP

ORDER FORM
PLEASE COMPLETE ALL INFORMATION
AND MAIL TODAY

We offer four convenient methods of payment:

☐ CHECK OR MONEY ORDER ENCLOSED PAYABLE TO STEREO CITY

☐ ☑ ☐

CARD NUMBER: 5424-1601-6046-1382

SIGNATURE: DATE: 6/14/96

PAGE	ITEM	MODEL	CATALOG NUMBER					QUANTITY	PRICE EACH		TOTAL PRICE	
12	Portable CD Player	Dart RC-444	P	S	1	0	1	2	69	98	139	96
12	Car Stereo	SNX 4090	C	S	6	3	3	1	249	98	249	98

TOTAL ITEMS 3	Merchandise Total	389	94
	Handling Charge	2	00
	Subtotal	391	94
	TEXAS Residents ONLY: Sales Tax on Subtotal		
	Shipping charge: $4 per item	12	00
Thank you for your order	ORDER TOTAL	403	94

GUARANTEE OF SATISFACTION

You must be completely satisfied with every item purchased from Stereo City. If for any reason an item does not live up to your expectations, return it to us within two weeks for a refund or exchange, whichever you prefer.

Stereo City

A. Decide if the following information can be determined by using the mail order catalog and the order form. Write *yes* or *no* on the line.

—— 1. where to mail your completed form

—— 2. the length of time it takes to receive your merchandise

—— 3. whether you must pay sales tax

—— 4. the cost to ship each item

—— 5. the size of the CD car stereo

—— 6. if you can send a check for an order

—— 7. if you can return something you order and get your money back

—— 8. whether the Dart RC-444 portable CD player comes with a case

B. Use the information in the catalog and on the order form to answer each question.

1. How much does the Kernwood cassette car stereo cost? _____

2. If you order two items, what shipping charges do you have to pay? _____

3. If you order four items, what handling charges do you have to pay? _____

4. To whom is the merchandise being shipped? _____

5. How much time does the buyer have to return or exchange an item? _____

6. How is Mr. Hernandez paying for the merchandise he ordered? _____

7. Which piece of equipment in the catalog has CD/tape editing? _____

8. Which provides more presets, the Sonix boom box or the Sonix car stereo?

_____

9. Which product comes with an AC adapter? _____

10. Which car stereo includes a clock? _____

C. Complete the blank order form below. Show how you would order one Sonix boom box using a money order.

STEREO CITY 2200 Main Street, Midland, Texas 79701

Ordered by:

NAME_____

STREET ADDRESS_____ APT._____

CITY_____ STATE_____ ZIP_____

Just in case we have to phone you...

DAYTIME PHONE: AREA CODE ( )_____

To send this order to a different address

NAME_____

STREET ADDRESS_____ APT._____

CITY_____ STATE_____ ZIP_____

ORDER FORM
PLEASE COMPLETE ALL INFORMATION
AND MAIL TODAY

We offer four convenient methods of payment:

☑ CHECK OR MONEY ORDER ENCLOSED PAYABLE TO STEREO CITY

☐   ☐   ☐

CARD NUMBER:_____

SIGNATURE:_____ DATE:_____

PAGE	ITEM	MODEL	CATALOG NUMBER	QUANTITY	PRICE EACH	TOTAL PRICE

TOTAL ITEMS		
Merchandise Total		
Handling Charge		
Subtotal		
TEXAS Residents ONLY: Sales Tax on Subtotal		
Shipping charge: $4 per item		
Thank you for your order	ORDER TOTAL	

GUARANTEE OF SATISFACTION

You must be completely satisfied with every item purchased from Stereo City. If for any reason an item does not live up to your expectations, return it to us within two weeks for a refund or exchange, whichever you prefer.

Stereo City

Lesson 16 _____

Character

Reading a Literature Selection _____

▶ **Background Information**

In this true story of a modern-day hero, Roberto Clemente, you will read about a man who used the strength of his personality not only to join the ranks of baseball's greatest players, but also to help others.

▶ **Skill Focus**

The people in a story are called **characters**. Most stories have only one **main character**. The main character usually has a goal to achieve or a problem to solve. In a piece of fiction, the characters are made up by the author. In a biography or autobiography, the characters, of course, are real people. Look for clues to the main character's personality in what he or she says or does. When you read, keep in mind the following questions. They will help you understand the main character.

1. Who is the main character?
2. What is the goal or problem of the main character?

3. What does the main character do to achieve the goal or to solve the problem?
4. How do the actions reveal the personality of the main character?
5. How do the words reveal the personality of the main character?

▶ **Word Clues**

When you read a word that you do not know, look for context clues to help you understand it. Context clues are words near the unknown word that make its meaning clearer. Read the following sentences.

The plane was on a mission of mercy, carrying medical supplies to aid the people of Nicaragua, a Central American country that had been <u>devastated</u> by an earthquake. The tremors were violent enough to destroy buildings, reduce villages to ashes, and leave other property in ruin.

If you do not know the meaning of the word *devastated*, the phrases *to*

destroy buildings totally, *reduce villages to ashes*, and *leave other property in ruin* in the sentences that follow the word can help you. By reading these details, you can figure out that *devastated* means "totally destroyed or ruined."

Use **detail** context clues to find the meaning of the three underlined words in the selection.

▶ **Strategy Tip**

As you read "No Ordinary Baseball Player," think about questions that begin with *Who, What, How,* and *Why* to help you understand Roberto Clemente's personality. Think about his **actions** and **words**. Together, they will tell you much about who the character of Roberto Clemente was.

No Ordinary Baseball Player

The cargo plane rumbled down the runway at an airport near San Juan, Puerto Rico. In the humid evening air was a salty tang from the Atlantic Ocean, lying just beyond the city. It was New Year's Eve, 1972. The plane was on a mission of mercy, carrying medical supplies to aid the people of Nicaragua, a Central American country that had been devastated by an earthquake. The tremors were violent enough to destroy buildings totally, reduce villages to ashes, and leave other property in ruin. Many Nicaraguans who had survived were seriously injured; many were homeless.

As the plane took off, a bystander noticed flames licking at one of the engines. The plane began to wobble as it headed out to sea. The pilot radioed that the plane was turning back to the airport. Then, eyewitnesses said, that the plane suddenly dove into the ocean and disappeared.

News of the crash flashed across the island—and throughout the Americas. Roberto Clemente, a pro baseball star and hero of Puerto Rico, was among those killed in the accident.

It was Clemente who had organized the shipment of supplies to Nicaragua and who had decided to go along on the

Roberto Clemente won the batting championship four times.

flight. Part of the plane's cargo was a pair of artificial legs for a Nicaraguan boy who had lost his own. Clemente had wanted to make sure that the boy got his new ones—in person.

Why had this baseball superstar organized a mercy mission? Friends said it was typical of him. He was no ordinary person. From his childhood, they noted, Roberto Clemente was someone special.

Clemente was born in 1934 in Carolina, a lovely, old town on the island of Puerto Rico. He was the youngest of seven children in a family that did not have much money.

Clemente's father Melchor Clemente worked as a foreman at a sugar cane plantation, overseeing workers in the cane fields. From a distance, cane fields appear to be beautiful with their soft green leaves topped by snowy white tassels. Up close, the cane fields give a very different impression. The cane grows in tall, woody stems that are as thick and as tough as a young tree. The cane workers use large, heavy, swordlike knives with broad blades to chop the stalks. Even with the aid of these machetes, chopping sugar cane is an arduous task.

Experience quickly teaches cane cutters how to work hard, and Clemente's father taught all his children not to fear hard work. He told them that there was dignity in pushing themselves to do their best. Hard work would teach them honor and self-respect—values that would be of importance to them throughout their lives.

Like many of his friends, Clemente grew up playing baseball. Baseball may be the national pastime in most of the United States, but it is the national rage in Puerto Rico. After all, it can be played year 'round in the island's sunny, warm climate.

As a small boy, Clemente played so much ball, according to his mother, that he would forget to eat. His forgetfulness displeased his mother very much. Once time, his mother grew so exasperated that she tried to burn his bat—but to no avail.

Clemente didn't have much money for equipment. He often played with a cheap rubber ball, which he threw against a wall for hours on end. Sometimes, when he didn't have a ball, he would hit tin cans for batting practice.

By the time Clemente was eighteen, his long hours of practice and play were beginning to pay off. He was playing baseball for a professional team in Puerto Rico. He could throw a ball fast, he was a great fielder, and he could hit. Scouts from major league teams began to look him over.

In 1954, Clemente had a chance to prove himself to a major-league team. The Brooklyn Dodgers, the same team that had hired his idol Jackie Robinson, picked him up. The Dodgers sent him to play with their "farm team" based in Montreal, Canada.

The following season, the Pittsburgh Pirates hired Clemente, and he got to play in the major leagues for the first time. He spent the rest of his career with the Pirates.

> "If you have a chance and don't make the most of it, you are wasting your time on this earth."

A friend of Clemente's once said that he played every game as if it were the World Series. Once, early in his career, Roberto made a spectacular catch by jumping up against a stadium fence. His belt got caught in the fence, and he hung there until his teammates got him down! To Clemente, making the catch meant everything.

Clemente gave so much of himself to every play that he was often injured. Fans may cheer when an outfielder makes a spectacular catch against the stadium wall or dives into the turf to snag a grounder. Yet, few realize how hard the wall is or how fast the player is running when he hits it. After a few years, Clemente had so many breaks, tears, pulls, and aches in his body that he was sometimes unable to play.

Because his performance when he did play was so good, some fans and sportswriters became critical and accused him of being lazy. "He can't be that sick!" they would say. "He looked great on the field yesterday. If he could play so well yesterday, why is he on the sick list today?" They didn't realize how hard Clemente fought the pain of his injuries every time he played. He made playing look easy, but it wasn't.

The fans also didn't realize that even though he was often injured, Clemente played more games than any other Pittsburgh Pirate. In fifteen years, he never missed an opening game! The fans' attitude bothered Clemente's sense of dignity and self-respect. Hadn't his parents taught him always to work hard?

Clemente believed that he had a special responsibility. He was a Puerto Rican! He believed that he had to show the world how talented, hard-working, and caring the people of his island were. Clemente also wanted to throw farther, hit harder, and run faster than other players to prove himself.

He had little trouble proving himself. In eighteen years, he led the National League in batting four times, and he was elected Most Valuable Player once. He received the Golden Glove award for his fielding twelve times.

In the 1971 World Series, Clemente really showed his stuff. The Pirates were up against the Baltimore Orioles, a tough team to beat. The first two games went to the Orioles, and the losses scared some of the Pittsburgh players. Few teams that lose the first two games of a Series go on to win it.

Clemente didn't let this fact bother him. He played his best, getting at least one hit in each game. His fielding was great. He encouraged the other players.

The seventh and last game of the Series was very close. Three innings went by without a score on either side when Clemente suddenly hit a home run. Many of his teammates say that run helped them feel like winners. They played hard and kept the other team from scoring more than one run. In the eighth inning, the Pirates scored again. They won, two to one! Clemente was chosen the outstanding player of that Series.

Yet, the years of hard playing had taken their toll on Clemente. At one time he had thought of retiring after the 1971 Series. But when the Pirates won, he decided to stay on. He told a news reporter, "Money means nothing to me, but I love competition."

Besides, he had one more goal to achieve: to make three thousand hits in his career. He had only 118 hits to go. So Clemente went back to Pittsburgh for the 1972 baseball season. As he said, "If you have a chance and don't make the most of it, you are wasting your time on this earth." On the night of September 30, his dream came true. Roberto Clemente made his three thousandth hit!

When the season ended, Clemente went home to his wife and three sons in Puerto Rico. One of his many plans was to build a "Sports City," where the children of Puerto Rico could get free training in sports.

Before he could really get started, however, Nicaragua was struck by an earthquake. Thousands of people were without homes, medical help, food, and clothing. Clemente went right to work. He organized a relief operation with business friends. He found a plane to fly emergency supplies to Nicaragua. For a week, he was so wrapped up in getting emergency supplies to the earthquake victims that he hardly ate or slept. Finally, on December 31, 1972, the plane that was to take him to Nicaragua was ready. The cargo was aboard, and the plane was fueled up. Clemente kissed his wife goodbye and boarded the plane. Soon after they parted, the plane took off. Minutes later, Roberto Clemente was dead.

On August 6, 1973, Roberto Clemente became a member of the Baseball Hall of Fame. The first Hispanic player to be elected, Clemente was chosen for his outstanding baseball achievements and for his humanitarian concern for others.

RECALLING FACTS

1. Who is the main character of this story?

_____

2. What was the effect of Clemente's long hours of practice as a boy?

_____

_____

_____

3. How was Clemente like his father?

_____

_____

4. List two of Roberto Clemente's major baseball achievements.

_____

_____

_____

_____

5. Sequence the following events in the order in which they took place.

_____ Clemente makes his three thousandth hit.

_____ Pittsburgh drafts Roberto Clemente.

_____ Clemente is chosen the outstanding player of the 1971 World Series.

_____ Clemente becomes the first Hispanic player elected to the Baseball Hall of Fame.

6. List two details from the story that support this statement: Roberto Clemente cared about others.

_____

_____

_____

_____

7. Why was Clemente flying to Nicaragua?

_____

8. Circle the letter of the sentence that best expresses the main idea of this story.

    a. Many Puerto Ricans could be baseball stars.

    b. Hard work and talent helped Clemente achieve his goals.

    c. Talent is more important to success than hard work.

    d. All baseball players are humanitarians.

9. Complete each sentence with the correct word.

    machetes   exasperated   arduous

    a. Chopping sugar cane is a difficult and _____ task.

    b. Large steel _____ are used to cut heavy jungle vegetation.

    c. The young comedian's constant joking _____ his family.

INTERPRETING FACTS

1. Why might it have been important to Clemente to take artificial legs to the Nicaraguan boy himself?

_____

_____

_____

_____

2. Some fans thought Clemente was using his injuries as an excuse not to play. What fact proves them wrong?

_____

_____

3. Why was it so important for Clemente to work harder than anyone else?

_____

_____

_____

4. How do you think players would feel after losing the first two of seven games in a World Series?

_____

_____

_____

SKILL FOCUS

To answer questions 1 through 4, choose from among the following words:

    compassion   determination   pride

1. Which trait does Clemente show in achieving his goal to be an outstanding baseball player? _____

Which trait is evident in Clemente's feeling about being Puerto Rican? _____

Which trait is evident in Clemente's wanting to help victims? _____

2. a. Which trait is demonstrated in the following passage? _____

    Clemente also believed that he had a special responsibility. He was a Puerto Rican! He believed that he had to show the world how talented, hard-working, and caring the people of his island were.

    b. Go back to the selection and underline another passage that demonstrates this same trait.

3. **a.** Which trait is demonstrated in the following passage? _____

   Roberto wanted to throw farther, hit harder, and run faster than other players to prove himself.

   b. Go back to the selection and circle another passage that demonstrates this trait.

4. **a.** Which trait is demonstrated in the following passage? _____

   Part of the plane's cargo was a pair of artificial legs for a Nicaraguan boy who had lost his own. Roberto Clemente wanted to make sure that the boy got the new ones—in person.

   b. Go back to the selection and use parentheses to mark another passage that demonstrates this trait.

5. Roberto Clemente made the following statement. What quality does it reveal about him?

   "If you have a chance and don't make the most of it, you are wasting your time on this earth."

   _____

   _____

6. Which better demonstrates Clemente's caring, his aiding the Nicaraguan earthquake victims or his ambition to be a great baseball player? Explain.

   _____

   _____

7. How was Roberto Clemente more than just a baseball star?

   _____

   _____

   _____

   _____

8. In a paragraph of four sentences, tell why you would or would not have liked to have had Roberto Clemente for a friend.

   _____

   _____

   _____

   _____

   _____

   _____

   _____

   _____

   _____

▶ **Real Life Connections**   In your opinion, what was Roberto Clemente's best quality? How would having this quality help you do something positive for your community?

Statistics

Reading a Social Studies Selection

▶ Background Information

The 1990 United States Census found that 18.1 million Americans have their roots in Mexico, Cuba, or Puerto Rico. This selection gives statistics about these groups in several regions of the United States.

▶ Skill Focus

Statistics are numerical facts, frequently presented in a table, graph, or map. Statistical information can range from population figures to the prices of consumer goods. Because statistics can show important trends or patterns, people often use them to draw conclusions or make predictions.

Statistics, however, must be used with care. It is important to know whether the statistics that accompany a text are approximate or exact. When exact figures are not available, approximate numbers are often used. It is also important to know that statistics present only a partial picture. They cannot give reasons for a change in population or for the popularity of a certain product. Thus, other information is often necessary to interpret and use statistics effectively.

Use the following steps when reading and interpreting a table of statistics.

1. Identify the type of statistical information given in the table. The table title and the titles of the columns and rows tell what information is given.
2. Practice reading the statistics. Statistics often involve numbers in the millions. Be sure that you read the numbers correctly.
3. Study the table to find relationships among numbers. Compare in different columns and rows.
4. Use the statistics and accompanying text to draw conclusions about the events described in the table. You can use both statistics and information in the selection to draw your own conclusions and to evaluate the author's conclusions.
5. Use statistics to make projections or forecasts. Interpret both the statistics and the information in the selection to make predictions about future trends.
6. Compare your conclusions and interpretations with those of the author. Do you agree or disagree with the author? Why?

▶ Word Clues

Read the sentence below. Look for context clues that explain the underlined word.

> The United States is a nation of <u>immigrants</u>, or people who move to and settle in a new country.

If you don't know the meaning of the word *immigrants,* the word *or* can help you. *Immigrants* means "people who move to and settle in a new country." The word *immigrants* is explained in the appositive phrase set off by a comma.

Use **appositive phrases** set off by commas and/or the word *or* to find the meaning of the three underlined words in the selection.

▶ Strategy Tip

The information in "Latin Americans in the United States" will help you interpret the statistics in the table and on the map on page 69.

Latin Americans in the United States

The United States is a nation of immigrants, or people who move to and settle in a new country. Throughout this country's history, immigrants from every part of the world have poured into the United States. The 1990 U.S. Census showed that the largest group of immigrants came from Latin America.

Latin American immigrants have brought their language and cultures into the mainstream of U.S. life. While most Latin Americans who immigrate to the United States share a common language—Spanish—their cultural backgrounds vary.

Of the 22.8 million Latin Americans, almost 80 percent, or 18.1 million, are from three places: Mexico, Cuba, and Puerto Rico.

Population of Latin Americans in the United States

Spanish-Speaking Groups	1980	1990
Mexican	8,740,000	14,628,000
Puerto Rican	2,014,000	2,402,000
Cuban	803,000	1,071,000
Total:	11,557,000	18,101,000*

*includes other Latin Americans
Source: United States Bureau of the Census

Mexican Americans

Approximately 64 percent, or 14.6 million, of Latin Americans are Mexican Americans. Because Mexico shares a long border with the United States, the histories of the two countries are intertwined.

Mexicans have lived in what is now the United States for centuries. In 1609, a Mexican named Juan de Oñate founded a mission called Santa Fe, which is now Santa Fe, New Mexico. Between 1846 and 1848, the United States and Mexico fought each other in the Mexican War. As the victor, the United States gained possession of land that includes the present states of Texas, New Mexico, Arizona, Colorado, and California. In effect, Mexico had to give up half of its national territory. At that time, about 75,000 Mexicans lived in the area, which became the American Southwest.

Mexicans continued to immigrate to the Southwest, especially during the years of the Mexican Revolution, which took place between 1911 and 1920 and severely disrupted the Mexican economy. Before the revolution, in 1900, about one hundred thousand people of Mexican birth lived in the Southwest. After the revolution, by 1930, more than a million Mexicans had come into the United States.

Mexicans were attracted to the United States by the availability of jobs and the country's stable economy. Some immigrants found jobs in the vegetable fields and orchards of the Southwest, while others found factory jobs as the area became industrialized. By 1930, 180,000 Mexican Americans worked in agriculture, and another 150,000 were employed in industry.

✘ The Southwest remains the center of Mexican American culture in the United States. By 1960, approximately 3.5 million Mexican Americans lived in the Southwest. By 1980, California had the largest population of Mexican Americans. Chicanos are the fastest-growing minority group in Los Angeles, comprising almost 40 percent of the city's population. Texas, New Mexico, Arizona, and Colorado are other southwestern states with a large Mexican American population. There are also large communities of Mexican Americans in Illinois and Michigan.

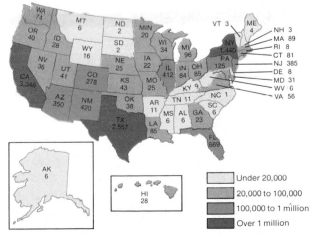

Latin Americans by State, 1990 (in thousands)

WA 74, OR 40, MT 6, ID 28, WY 16, ND 2, SD 2, MIN 20, WI 34, MI 96, VT 3, ME 4, NH 3, MA 89, RI 8, NY 1,440, PA 125, CT 81, NJ 385, DE 8, MD 31, WV 6, VA 56, NV 36, UT 41, CO 278, NE 25, IA 22, IL 412, IN 84, OH 85, KY 9, NC 1, CA 3,346, AZ 350, NM 420, KS 43, MO 25, OK 38, AR 11, TN 11, SC 6, MS 6, AL 6, GA 23, TX 2,557, LA 85, FL 668, AK 6, HI 28

- Under 20,000
- 20,000 to 100,000
- 100,000 to 1 million
- Over 1 million

César Cháves

Ruebén Blades

Antonia Novello

Tanya Leon

Jimmy Smits

Latin Americans have made tremendous contributions to many aspects of American life.

Puerto Ricans

Citizens of Puerto Rican <u>descent</u>, or origin, number 2.4 million and make up 10.5 percent of the Latin American population. The bond between the United States and Puerto Rico was forged in 1898 during the Spanish-American War. In that year, the United States annexed the former Spanish colony as part of its territory.

✔ In 1917, Congress granted U.S. citizenship to residents of Puerto Rico. In 1952, the U.S. Congress and the citizens of Puerto Rico agreed that the island would become a <u>commonwealth</u>, a republic with a constitutional government. Under this arrangement, the people of Puerto Rico drafted their own constitution, elected their own governor and legislature, and retained the rights of U.S. citizens. Included in these rights are the privileges of moving to the U.S. mainland without restriction and of traveling freely within its borders. In addition, the island of Puerto Rico enjoys the military protection of the United States.

Like Mexican Americans, many Puerto Ricans moved to the U.S. mainland in search of better job opportunities. Before World War II, only about 70,000 Puerto Ricans had moved to the mainland. After the war, the Puerto Rican population in the United States increased rapidly. By 1960, some 600,000 Puerto Ricans had come to the mainland. By 1980, nearly a million and a half Puerto Ricans lived in New York City alone. New York City remains the center of the Puerto Rican community in the U.S. mainland. Newark, Philadelphia, and Chicago also have large Puerto Rican communities.

Cuban Americans

Cuban Americans make up 4.7 percent of Latin Americans, over 1 million people. When a revolution brought Fidel Castro to power in Cuba in the early 1960s, thousands of Cubans fled the country. Between 1961 and 1970, over 200,000 Cubans immigrated to the United States. Many <u>resumed</u>, or restarted, the medical, legal, and teaching careers interrupted by their immigration.

Some Cubans fled their island homeland in small boats, heading toward the Florida coast only 100 miles (160 kilometers) away. Most settled in southern Florida. As a result, Miami, the city with the largest number of Cuban immigrants, took on a new appearance. Cuban restaurants, Cuban clothing stores, and Cuban newspapers sprang up to serve the new population. By the early 1980s, Miami, called Little Havana after

Cuba's capital city, had become the center of the Cuban community in the United States. Over half the city's population is Latin American, of which the overwhelming majority is Cuban. There are also many Cubans in New York City, Philadelphia, and New Orleans.

In the decade between 1980 and 1990, the Latin American population in the United States increased by more than 8 million. The Mexican American population nearly doubled, and there were significant increases in the Cuban and Puerto Rican populations. As the Latin American population grows, its influence on American culture grows stronger. Once again, America is changing to reflect its changing people.

RECALLING FACTS

1. Match the groups of Latin Americans with the cities of their greatest population.

—— New York City

—— Los Angeles

—— Miami

a. Mexican Americans

b. Cuban Americans

c. Puerto Ricans

2. Write the two causes for the single effect stated below.

Cause ———————————————

————————————————————

————————————————————

Cause ———————————————

————————————————————

————————————————————

Effect After the revolution, many Mexicans immigrated to the United States.

3. Reread the paragraph with an X next to it. Then underline the sentence that best states its main idea.

4. Complete each of the following statements.

   a. The number of Mexican immigrants to the United States increased greatly after ———————————.

   b. The number of Cuban immigrants to the United States increased greatly after ———————————.

   c. The number of Puerto Rican immigrants to the United States increased greatly after ———————.

5. Complete each sentence with the correct word.

   resumed   commonwealth   descent

   a. Canada is a ——————— of Great Britain.

   b. I am an American of Italian ———————.

   c. Pat ——————— a musical career after completing military service.

INTERPRETING FACTS

1. What unites most Latin Americans from Mexico, Cuba, and Puerto Rico? ————————————————

2. Why did most Cuban Americans immigrate to Florida?

————————————————————————————

3. How does the legal status of immigrants from Puerto Rico differ from that of Mexican and Cuban immigrants?

_____

_____

4. Over half the population of Miami, Florida, is Latin American. How has the growth of the Cuban community affected the culture of Miami?

_____

_____

5. On the line next to each of the following statements, write either *fact* or *opinion*.

_____ According to the 1990 Census, most Latin Americans are of Mexican descent.

_____ Schools in the United States should teach lessons in both Spanish and English.

_____ Cubans should be allowed free entry into the United States.

_____ According to the 1990 Census, New York City has the largest Puerto Rican population of any area in the United States.

6. Reread the paragraph with a check mark next to it. Write a sentence stating its main idea.

_____

_____

SKILL FOCUS

Use the selection and the table on page 69 to answer the following questions. To use the table, first read the title. Then read down the left column. There you will find the names of Spanish-speaking groups in the United States. Next, read across the rows to find out each group's population in 1980 and in 1990. The last row gives you total figures for the entire Latin American population in 1980 and in 1990.

1. Identify the type of statistical information given in the table.

   a. What is the title of the table? _____

   b. What years does the table cover? _____

   c. For what three groups of people are statistics given? _____

   _____

   _____

2. Practice reading the statistics.
   a. What was the Cuban American population in 1990? _____
   b. What was the total Latin American population in the United States in 1980?

   _____

3. Study the table to find relationships among numbers.

  a. What gain was there in the Latin American population between 1980 and 1990? _____

  b. Which Latin American group had the smallest population in both 1980 and 1990? _____

  c. Which Latin American group nearly doubled its population between 1980 and 1990? _____

4. Use the statistics and accompanying text to draw conclusions about the events described in the table. From these statistics, what conclusion can you draw about the Latin American population in the United States between 1980 and 1990?

_____

_____

5. Use statistics to make projections or forecasts.

  a. What trend or pattern do you see for the Latin American population in the United States?

_____

_____

  b. Based on the information given in the following table, predict the population growth for each group by the year 2000. Write your answers in the blank boxes under the heading *2000*. Be sure that you can explain your projections.

Latin Americans	1980	1990	2000
Mexican	8,740,000	14,628,000	
Puerto Rican	2,014,000	2,402,000	
Cuban	803,000	1,071,000	

6. Compare your conclusions and interpretations with those of the author.

_____

_____

_____

7. Use the statistics given on the population map on page 69 to answer the following questions. Write *T* for true or *F* for false on the line next to each of the following statements.

  _____ a. This population map indicates the number of Latin Americans living in the United States in 1990.

  _____ b. The population statistics are exact figures.

  _____ c. This map focuses on population figures rather than on ethnic groups.

  _____ d. Only four states have over 1 million Hispanics: California, Texas, New York, and Florida.

  _____ e. Only six states have a Hispanic population ranging from 100,000 to 1 million: Arizona, Colorado, New Mexico, Pennsylvania, New Jersey, and Illinois.

  _____ f. There are only 18 Latin Americans in Alaska.

▶ **Real Life Connections** In your opinion, what are the benefits from learning about and living with people from different cultures?

Cause and Effect

Reading a Science Selection

▶ Background Information

For centuries, people observed the regular thumping inside the chest—the heartbeat. They knew that a heartbeat was necessary for life, but real understanding of the heart and blood began less than 500 years ago.

▶ Skill Focus

A **cause** is a reason, condition, or situation that makes an event happen. The **effect** is the result of a cause. For example, you bleed when you get a cut. The cause is a cut. The effect is bleeding.

Sometimes one effect can have many causes. Read the following paragraph.

> Local blood banks have a shortage of blood. At this time of year, many donors are on vacation. Other donors are too busy to give blood. Several recent accidents have used up much of the stored blood.

The first sentence states the effect, which is a shortage of blood. The other three sentences give three causes of this effect.

Just as a single effect can have many causes, a single cause can have many effects.

Read this paragraph.

> Exercising regularly can be good for you. It can take inches off your waistline. It can build muscles. It can even help your heart and lungs work better.

As stated in the first sentence, the cause is exercising regularly. Three effects of this cause are found in the other three sentences.

Sometimes an effect can be the cause of another effect, forming a chain of causes and effects. Read the following paragraph.

> Many Americans are jogging. The exercise is helping to make them healthier. As a result, they have lower medical bills.

Better health, the effect of the first cause, is also the cause of lower medical bills. The following diagram shows this chain of causes and effects.

Cause
jogging

↓

Effect/Cause
better health

↓

Effect
lower medical bills

Recognizing patterns of cause and effect helps you understand how ideas are connected.

▶ Word Clues

Read the sentence below. Look for context clues that explain the underlined word.

> Arteries can stand up to this pressure without being damaged because they are <u>elastic</u>, or flexible.

If you do not know the meaning of the word *elastic*, the phrase *or flexible* can help you. This appositive phrase explains the word.

Use **appositive phrases** set off by commas or dashes to find the meanings of the three underlined words in the selection.

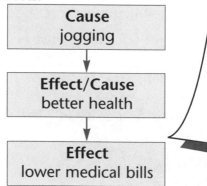

▶ Strategy Tip

As you read "The Human Circulatory System," notice the chain of causes and effects. The diagrams, labels, and captions will help you understand how the circulatory system functions.

The Human Circulatory System

The heart and the rest of the circulatory system function like a pump that is connected to many tubes. The tubes are filled with a fluid that the pump circulates, or moves in a cycle. The pump is the heart, the tubes are the blood vessels, and the fluid is blood.

Blood Vessels and Blood

There are three types of blood vessels in the human circulatory system: **arteries, veins,** and **capillaries.**

Arteries carry blood away from the heart. The heart forces blood into the arteries under great pressure. Arteries can stand up to this pressure without being damaged because they are elastic, or flexible. The walls of arteries are thick and have muscles that help move the blood. Look at Figure 1.

Veins carry blood back to the heart from all parts of the body. Their walls are much thinner than the walls of arteries. Veins have valves that prevent blood from backing up and keep it flowing toward the heart. Veins are located near the muscles of the body, such as those in the arms and legs. As the muscles contract and relax, they help push the blood that is in the veins toward the heart. Look at Figure 2.

Capillaries are the smallest blood vessels. They are so narrow that blood cells must travel through them in single file. Capillaries form a network throughout the body that connects small arteries to small veins.

Blood is made up primarily of a watery liquid called **plasma**. In addition to plasma, blood contains three kinds of cells: **red blood cells, white blood cells,** and **platelets** (PLAYT lits). Red blood cells carry oxygen to all parts of the body. White blood cells help the body fight disease. Platelets are necessary for blood clotting, so that bleeding stops after an injury.

The Heart

The heart is a muscle about the size of a person's clenched fist, and it is the hardest working muscle in the body. With each contraction, or beat, the heart moves blood throughout the body. Even when the body is at rest, the heart pumps 5 liters of blood per

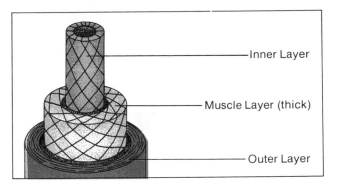

Figure 1. This diagram shows the three layers of an artery.

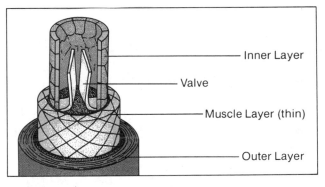

Figure 2. The walls of a vein are not as thick as the walls of an artery.

minute. During strenuous exercise, this rate is increased to 25 liters per minute. In a normal adult, the heart beats about 70 times a minute, 101,000 times a day, 36,800,000 times a year, and about 2.7 billion times in an average lifetime.

The heart is almost centered in the chest between the lungs. It is covered with a sac, called the **pericardium** (per ə KAHR dee əm). This sac is made up of two membrane layers that are separated by a fluid. The fluid acts as a cushion to prevent friction between the heart and the rib cage as the heart beats. The pericardium also attaches the heart to the surrounding tissues.

The heart has four chambers, or hollow cavities. The upper chambers are the right and left **atria** (AY tree ə; singular, *atrium*). The lower chambers are the right and left **ventricles** (VEN tri kəls). Valves between the atrium and ventricle on each side prevent blood from flowing backward. The body's biggest veins, the **venae cavae** (VEE nə KAY

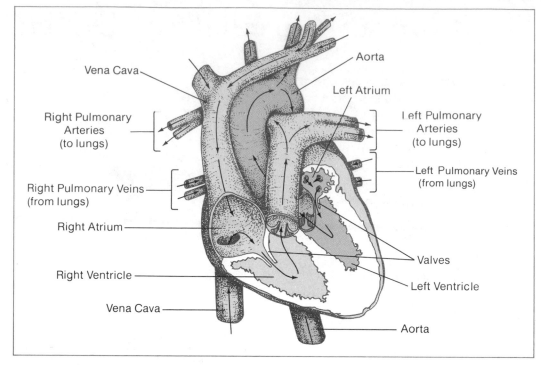

Figure 3. The human heart has four chambers.

vee; singular, *vena cava*), carry blood to the right atrium. This blood does not contain much oxygen because body cells have absorbed the oxygen that it was carrying. The right atrium contracts, which moves the oxygen-poor blood to the right ventricle. When the right ventricle contracts, it forces blood into the <u>pulmonary</u> arteries, which carry the blood to the lungs. In the lungs, the blood takes in oxygen and releases carbon dioxide. The oxygen-rich blood leaves the lungs through the pulmonary veins. The pulmonary veins carry blood to the left atrium, which moves the blood into the left ventricle by contracting. When the left ventricle contracts, it pushes blood into the **aorta** (ay OR tə), the body's main artery. From this artery, oxygen-rich blood travels to all parts of the body. Look at Figure 3.

The heart muscles contract and relax in a rhythmic manner that is called beating. When the ventricles contract, they force blood into the arteries. When the ventricles relax, the atria contract, pushing blood from each atrium into each ventricle. In this way, a constant supply of blood is moved through the heart, the lungs, and all parts of the body.

The rate at which the heart beats is not always constant. When resting, a person needs less oxygen than when active, and the heart beats more slowly. As a person becomes more active, the heart beats faster, and the body is provided with more oxygen.

Diseases of the Heart and Circulatory System

Changes in the circulatory system may cause health problems. One such change is atherosclerosis, in which fatty material accumulates on the inner walls of arteries and blocks blood flow. When this happens, the heart has to work harder to pump blood throughout the body. Sometimes, the arteries that supply the heart itself become clogged, eventually causing a heart attack. In a heart attack, part of the heart muscle dies because it doesn't receive blood.

Another condition that affects the circulatory system is hypertension, or high blood pressure. Blood pressure is the force exerted against the walls of blood vessels when the heart pumps blood through them. High blood pressure can damage not only the heart and blood vessels but other organs as well.

A stroke occurs when the blood flow to part of the brain is suddenly cut off by a blockage or rupture of a blood vessel. A stroke can cause the loss of the ability to speak or move, or it can even cause death. The effects of a stroke depend on what part of the brain is damaged.

People can reduce their risk of developing circulatory diseases by practicing good health habits. The most important habits to adopt are avoiding smoking and alcoholic drinks, exercising regularly, and eating a diet low in saturated fats and salt.

It Is important for people to have their blood pressure checked regularly.

RECALLING FACTS

1. What are the three main parts of the circulatory system?

_____

_____

2. In which direction from the heart do veins carry blood?

_____

3. In which direction do arteries carry blood?

_____

4. How does the structure of arteries help them do their job?

_____

_____

_____

5. What do red blood cells do?

_____

6. What do white blood cells do?

_____

7. What do platelets do?

_____

8. Complete each sentence by filling in the correct word.

   chambers   contractions   pulmonary

   a. _____ cause the heart muscle to beat.

   b. The human heart has four hollow cavities, or _____.

   c. The _____ arteries carry blood to the lungs.

1. How is the heart rate related to the body's need for oxygen?

   a. The heart rate controls the amount of blood going through the lungs to pick up oxygen for the rest of the body.

   b. The heart uses more oxygen when the body is resting than it does when the body is active.

   c. As the heart rate increases, the lungs and the rest of the body need less oxygen.

2. Blood doesn't flow upward from the ventricles to the atria because

   a. the atria are below the ventricles.

   b. the heart has valves between the atria and the ventricles.

   c. the ventricles do not hold blood.

3. Blood flowing from a cut contains

   a. plasma and red blood cells.

   b. arteries, veins, and capillaries.

   c. red blood cells, white blood cells, platelets, and plasma.

4. Blood entering the left atrium has

   a. more oxygen in it than blood entering the right atrium.

   b. less oxygen in it than blood entering the right atrium.

   c. the same amount of oxygen in it as blood entering the right atrium.

5. Why is exercise good for your heart?

   _____

   _____

   _____

Three chains of causes and effects can be made from the events listed below. Together, these chains describe how blood is circulated through the heart and body. To show the chains, draw an arrow from one event in the first column to an event in the second and third columns.

Cause	Effect/Cause	Effect
The venae cavae empty oxygen-poor blood into the right atrium, which contracts.	The blood is pushed into the right ventricle, which contracts.	Blood is forced into the pulmonary arteries, which carry it to the lungs to pick up oxygen.
The blood takes in oxygen and is carried to the left atrium by the pulmonary veins.	The blood moves through the capillaries and into veins.	Blood is forced into the aorta.
Oxygen-rich blood is carried throughout the body.	The blood is pumped into the left ventricle, which contracts.	Oxygen-poor blood returns to the heart through veins.

▶ Real Life Connections What kind of exercise do you do? How often do you exercise?

Word Problems

___ Reading a Mathematics Selection ___

▶ Background Information

Most word problems in mathematics give a question to be answered. You then use the steps necessary to answer the question. The following selection, however, poses problem situations. For those problems, use the information or facts given to determine the most logical question to ask and then solve the problem.

▶ Skill Focus

Use the following five steps to complete and solve most word problems.

First, read the problem. If it does not contain a question or directions, but gives a problem situation, or group of facts, you have to determine what the problem is yourself. To determine the problem, you need to understand all the information given. Try to picture the information in your mind. Then read the problem situation again to be sure that you know how the various facts are related.

Second, decide on a question to ask about the information provided in the problem situation, and decide how to answer the

question. First write a sentence about each fact. Then look for information that has *not* been provided that you can find using the information that *has* been provided. Write a question about the information that you want to find that logically connects the facts. Decide what operation or operations are necessary to answer the question you wrote. Write one or two mathematical sentences that describe the operation or operations.

Third, estimate the answer to the question that you wrote. This is one way to be sure that the question can be answered using the information given in the problem situation.

Fourth, carry out the plan. Solve the mathematical sentence or sentences that you wrote in the second step.

Fifth, reread the problem situation and your question. Is the answer to the question logical? Is it close to your estimate?

▶ Word Clues

Problem situations may involve two or more distances. If all the numbers in a problem situation are in

meters or *kilometers*, the problem probably involves addition or subtraction.

Sometimes the solution involves a *rate*, such as kilometers *per* hour or a *percent* of a whole. The word *per* always means that a rate is involved. Rates are found by division. Kilometers per hour is a rate that is found by dividing a number of kilometers by a number of hours. A percent is a rate found by dividing a number by 100. In actual problems, you need to divide sometimes and multiply at other times. The operation that you use depends on whether you want to find the rate or the total number.

▶ Strategy Tip

As you read "Completing and Solving Word Problems," you will see that the second problem-solving step is different from the one described here. Study the problem situations carefully before answering them.

Completing and Solving Word Problems

If you travel in the countries that border on or are located in the Caribbean Sea, you may need to know many facts. Although a map or other reference gives you important facts, it may not give the fact that you need. You have to determine first what fact you want to find from the information that you have and then decide how to find the answer. In other words, you make up a question, or complete the problem, whose answer will give you the fact that you need.

Use these five steps to complete a problem and to solve it.

1. Read the problem situation.

2. Decide on a question to ask about the facts in the situation and how to find the answer.

3. Estimate the answer.

4. Carry out the plan.

5. Reread the problem situation and your question.

READ THE PROBLEM SITUATION

You learn from a map that it is 402 kilometers from Nogales to Guaymas, 193 kilometers from Guaymas to Navojoa, 161 kilometers from Navojoa to Los Mochis, and 209 kilometers from Los Mochis to Culiacán.

Nogales, Guaymas, Navojoa, Los Mochis, and Culiacán are the names of cities in Mexico. After reading the information carefully, think about what problem you could solve using the information provided.

DECIDE ON A QUESTION TO ASK AND HOW TO FIND THE ANSWER

The problem situation gives you four facts. Write a short sentence about each.

1. It is 402 kilometers from Nogales to Guaymas.

2. It is 193 kilometers from Guaymas to Navojoa.

3. It is 161 kilometers from Navojoa to Los Mochis.

4. It is 209 kilometers from Los Mochis to Culiacán.

You want to make up a question that uses all four facts. Therefore, you need to find a mathematical operation that connects the four facts. When you want to connect more than two facts, the operation you use is often addition. If you add the four distances, you get the distance from Nogales to Culiacán. The question you want to answer, then, is *How far is it from Nogales to Culiacán?*

Write a mathematical sentence, or equation, connecting the four facts by addition.

$$402 + 193 + 161 + 209 = d$$

ESTIMATE THE ANSWER

Round each number to the nearest round number.

$$400 + 200 + 150 + 200 = 950$$

CARRY OUT THE PLAN

$$402 + 193 + 161 + 209 = 965$$

REREAD THE PROBLEM SITUATION AND YOUR QUESTION

After rereading the problem situation, write out a complete answer to the question that you wrote in the second step. *The distance from Nogales to Culiacán is 965 kilometers.* The answer is close to your estimate.

Complete and solve the following word problems.

Read: From 1493 until 1897, or for 404 years, Puerto Rico was a colony of Spain. From 1898 until 1951, Puerto Rico was a possession of the United States.

Make sure that you know what all the words mean. If you do not know the meaning of the word *colony*, for example, look it up in a dictionary.

Decide: From the information given, you know that Puerto Rico was a colony of Spain.

You also know that Puerto Rico was a possession of the United States for a number of years. What question does this information suggest? A logical question would be *How much longer was Puerto Rico a colony of Spain than it was a possession of the United States?*

This problem requires two operations. First you have to find how long Puerto Rico was a possession of the United States. Then you have to find how much longer Puerto Rico was a colony of Spain than it was a possession of the United States.

Choose variables, such as *U* and *t*, to stand for the answer to each step. Write equations that connect the information. Use a word clue. Problems that ask *how much*

longer or *how much more* can often be solved by subtraction.

$$1951 - 1898 = U$$
$$404 - U = t$$

Estimate: Since the smallest number in the problem has three places, you round all the numbers to the hundreds and estimate.

$$2000 - 1900 = 100$$
$$400 - 100 = 300$$

Carry Out: $1951 - 1898 = 53$
$$404 - 53 = 351$$

Reread: Puerto Rico was a colony of Spain for 351 years longer than it was a possession of the United States. The answer is close to your estimate.

RECALLING FACTS

1. To connect more than two numbers in a problem, which operation do you often use?

_____

2. If a problem contains the word clue *how much more*, which operation do you most often use to solve the problem?

_____

3. The Reread step involves two important parts. What are they?

   a. _____

   b. _____

4. What should you do if you do not understand a word in the problem?

_____

INTERPRETING FACTS

1. In the first problem situation in the selection, why would the question probably not be How much farther is it from Nogales to Guaymas than it is from Guaymas to Navojoa?

_____

_____

2. In the second problem situation in the selection, what can you infer about the status of Puerto Rico after 1951?

_____

_____

3. In the selection, the variables *d*, *U*, and *t* were used. What did they stand for?

_____

_____

4. What can you infer about the difference between the number of years Puerto Rico was a colony of Spain and the years since Puerto Rico ceased to be a U.S. possession?

_____

_____

Write the question that you think should be asked for each problem situation. Then write one or two equations as a plan, make an estimate, carry out your plan, and state the answer to the question in a complete sentence.

1. **Read:** On a road map of Cuba, José found that it was 96.5 kilometers from Havana to Matanzas and 35.5 kilometers from Matanzas to Varadero.

   Decide: _____

   _____

   Estimate: _____

   Carry Out: _____

   Reread: _____

   _____

2. **Read:** In Puerto Rico, the entrance to the Rio Abajo Commonwealth Forest is at kilometer 70.2 on Route 10. Dos Bacos Lake, in the forest, can be reached at kilometer 68 on Route 10.

   Decide: _____

   _____

   Estimate: _____

   Carry Out: _____

   Reread: _____

   _____

3. **Read:** From Tamazunchale in Mexico, the road climbs steadily into the mountains. You reach an elevation of 2,044.8 meters in 96.54 kilometers of driving.

   Decide: _____

   _____

   Estimate: _____

   Carry Out: _____

   Reread: _____

   _____

▶ **Real Life Connections** Think of your own problem situation based on your class, school, or community. Exchange problems with a partner and solve each other's problems.

Lesson 20

Accented Syllable and Schwa Sound

When words contain two syllables, one of the syllables is stressed, or accented, more than the other. In dictionaries, the **accent mark** (') is placed at the end of the syllable that is said with more stress. For example, the first syllable in the word *carrot* is said with more stress.

car' rot

In words with three syllables, the accent is usually on one of the first two syllables. When you are trying to pronounce a word with three syllables, such as *tradition*, stress the first syllable. If the word does not sound right, say it again, stressing the second syllable.

tra' di tion   tra di' tion

Say each of the following words to yourself. Write an accent mark after the syllable that should be stressed.

1. reg u lar   3. wal rus   5. con di tion   7. fi nal

2. ad di tion   4. pol i tics   6. dra mat ic   8. par ti tion

Words of four or more syllables usually have two accented syllables. In the word *composition*, the third syllable has the most stress. This syllable has the primary accent mark ('). The first syllable has more stress than the remaining two syllables but less than the third syllable. The secondary accent mark (') is placed after that syllable.

com' po si' tion

Say each of the following words to yourself. Write a primary accent mark after the syllable that has the most stress. Say the word again. Write a secondary accent mark after the syllable that has the second most stress.

1. in for ma tion   3. pan o ra ma   5. per son al i ty   7. a vi a tor

2. nav i ga tor   4. com pli ca tion 6. sal a man der   8. en thu si as tic

The vowels *a, e, i, o,* and *u* can all have the same sound. This is a soft sound like a short *u* pronounced lightly. This short, soft *u* sound is called the **schwa** sound. In dictionary respellings, the symbol ə stands for the schwa sound. If you look up the word *compete* in the dictionary, you will find it respelled this way.

kəm pēt'

Say each of the words below to yourself. Write an accent mark after the syllable that is stressed. Then circle the letter that stands for the schwa sound.

1. sec ond   3. haz ard   5. pi o neer   7. or i gin

2. ac count   4. ca det   6. dec o rate   8. fam i ly

Look at the words in the list above. Notice that the schwa sound always falls in an unaccented syllable of a word.

Lesson 21

Prefixes

A **prefix** is a word part that is added to the beginning of a word to change its meaning. Eight prefixes and their meanings are given below.

Prefix	Meaning	Prefix	Meaning
bi	having two, or happening every two	non	not
dis	away or opposite of	pre	before
mid	middle	semi	half or partly
mis	wrong or badly	trans	over, across, or beyond

Read each word below and the meaning that follows it. Write the correct prefix before each word.

1. _____ comfort   opposite of comfort
2. _____ monthly   happening every two months
3. _____ pay   pay before
4. _____ stop   no stops
5. _____ pacific   across the Pacific

6. _____ school   before regular school
7. _____ circle   half a circle
8. _____ week   middle of the week
9. _____ loyal   opposite of loyal
10. _____ spell   to spell wrong
11. _____ sweet   partly sweet

Use one of the words above to complete each sentence below.

1. This picture book is for _____ children.

2. _____ meetings will be held every Wednesday.

3. An aching tooth causes a lot of _____.

4. Proofread your composition to make sure that you did not _____ any words.

5. The team sat in a _____ around the coach.

6. A _____ magazine comes out six times a year.

7. The _____ ship left Los Angeles for Tokyo.

8. A traitor is _____ to his or her country.

9. The plane will fly _____ from New York to San Francisco.

10. We had to _____ our order from the Clarkstown Mail Order Company.

11. The recipe calls for honey and _____ chocolate.

Lesson 22

Suffixes

A **suffix** is a word part that is added to the end of a word to change its meaning. If the root word ends in *y* or *e*, its spelling may have to be changed.

When a word ends in *y* preceded by a consonant, change the *y* to *i* before adding suffixes that begin with a vowel.

defy + ance = defiance

When a word ends in *e*, drop the *e* before adding suffixes that begin with a vowel.

desire + able = desirable

Below are four suffixes and their meanings. Study them carefully.

Suffix	*Meaning*
able	that can be
al	the process of
ance	the act of
ant	that has or shows

Write the correct suffix after each word below. If the word ends in *y*, change the *y* to *i* before adding the suffix. If the word ends in *e*, drop the *e* before adding the suffix. The first one is done for you.

1. comply ___iance___ the act of complying

2. vary _____ that shows variety

3. compare _____ that can be compared

4. arrive _____ the process of arriving

5. defy _____ that shows defiance

6. envy _____ that can be envied

7. please _____ that shows pleasure

8. endure _____ the act of enduring

9. remedy _____ the process of remedying

10. rely _____ that can be relied on

Use one of the words above to complete each sentence below.

1. Rugby is a game _____ with football.

2. Mr. Matsumi and his children spent a _____ day in the park.

3. A runner must have great _____ to run twenty miles each day.

4. Lucia and Tomas are waiting for the _____ of their parent's plane.

5. This barometer gives a _____ weather forecast.

6. Carol appreciated the salesperson's _____ with her request for a refund.

7. The new community center started classes in _____ reading.

8. Mike has an _____ record of achievement in Spanish.

9. *Theatre* is a _____ spelling of *theater*.

10. LaTeena told us in a _____ manner that she was against our plans.

Lesson 23

Main Idea and Supporting Details

To understand a paragraph, it is important to know how the main idea of a paragraph is developed. The **main idea** is the most important idea in a paragraph. It states what the paragraph is about. Supporting details give more information about the main idea.

There are two kinds of supporting details. The most important details, called **major details**, tell about the main idea of a paragraph. Other details that are of less importance are called **minor details**. Minor details give more information about the major details.

As you read each of the following paragraphs, look for the main idea, major details, and minor details.

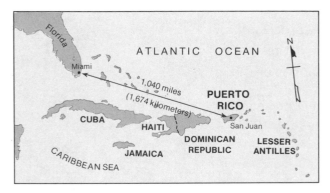

1. The island of Puerto Rico covers 3,435 square miles (8,897 square kilometers). The only two states that are smaller than Puerto Rico are Delaware and Rhode Island. Puerto Rico's 1990 population was about 3.5 million. Approximately one third of the people living in Puerto Rico live in San Juan. In fact, 58 percent of all Puerto Ricans live in the urban areas of San Juan, Ponce, Caguas, and Mayaguez, while 42 percent inhabit the rural areas. Indeed, Puerto Rico is a small but crowded island.

2. Only about one third of Puerto Rico's land is used for farming. Coffee, sugar cane, and tobacco are the island's leading crops. Most of the tobacco is used for cigars. Many fruits are also grown commercially for export. Such fruits include bananas, plantains, pineapples, avocados, coconuts, and oranges.

3. Puerto Rico's economy used to be based primarily on farm products, but today manufacturing is the main source of income.

86 Lesson 23 *Identifying the main idea and supporting details*

Agriculture accounts for only a small percentage of the value of goods produced in Puerto Rico annually. Manufactured products include petrochemicals, textiles, electronic equipment, and machinery. There are about 2,000 factories in Puerto Rico, with both American and Puerto Rican owners. The factories employ about 125,000 workers.

Complete the diagram for each paragraph. In the box labeled *Main Idea,* write the sentence that states the main idea as it appears in the paragraph. Use your own words when filling in the boxes labeled *Major Details* and *Minor Details.*

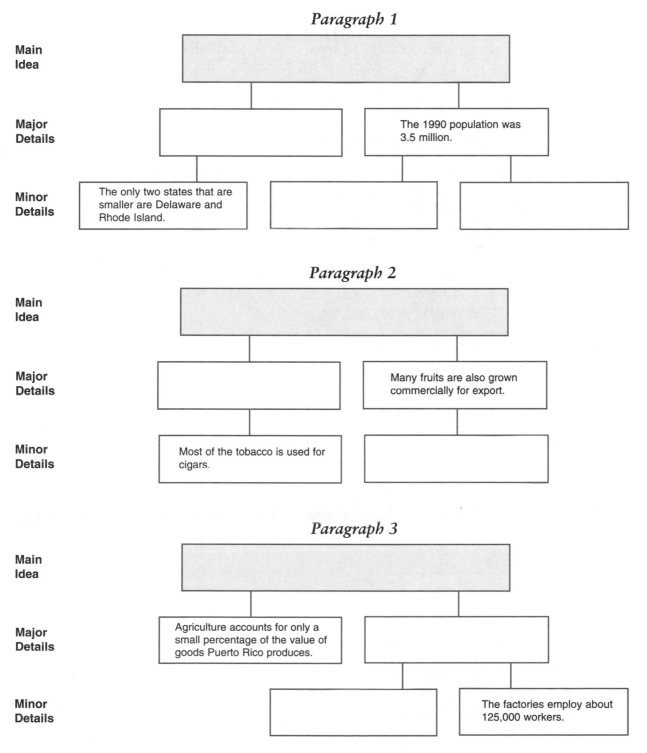

Paragraph 1

Main Idea

Major Details | The 1990 population was 3.5 million.

Minor Details | The only two states that are smaller are Delaware and Rhode Island.

Paragraph 2

Main Idea

Major Details | Many fruits are also grown commercially for export.

Minor Details | Most of the tobacco is used for cigars.

Paragraph 3

Main Idea

Major Details | Agriculture accounts for only a small percentage of the value of goods Puerto Rico produces.

Minor Details | The factories employ about 125,000 workers.

The Dictionary

Each word, abbreviation, prefix, suffix, or group of words that your dictionary explains is called an **entry word**. The entry word and all the information about it is called an **entry**. All entries are arranged in alphabetical order.

To help you find an entry quickly, **guide words** are printed in the upper left-hand and right-hand corners of each page. The upper left-hand guide word tells the first full entry on that page. The upper right-hand guide word tells the last entry that begins on the page.

In many dictionaries, dots divide entry words into **syllables**. Syllabification shows you where to divide a word when you cannot write it all on one line.

Respellings appear in parentheses after most entry words. The key to pronunciation is in the front or back of most dictionaries, and a shortened version appears at the bottom of every other page. A key word accompanying each symbol shows you how to pronounce the symbol correctly.

The definitions, or meanings, of entry words are grouped according to **parts of speech**. Some entry words appear as only one part of speech, as does *tractor*, which is a noun. Many words, however, can be used as several parts of speech. For example, *range* can be a verb, noun, or adjective.

If entry words can be used as more than one part of speech, abbreviated labels identify the group of meanings for each. For example, all the noun meanings of an entry word follow the abbreviation for noun, **n.**

An **idiom** is included at the end of the entry that is the key word of the idiom. An idiom is a group of words that has a different meaning from the meanings of the words by themselves.

On page 89 is part of a page from a dictionary. Use it to answer the following questions.

1. What are the guide words for this page? _____

2. What is the respelling of *plow*? _____

3. What is the fourth entry word on this page? _____

4. What is the second noun meaning of *plot*? _____

5. What sentence is given for the third transitive verb (**vt.**) meaning of *plow*?

_____

6. How big does a plover grow to be? _____

7. What two idioms are given for the word *plow*? _____

8. What are three types of pliers? _____

9. What key word is given in the pronunciation key for the long *e* sound? _____

10. What is the adjective form of the word *plow*? _____

11. Which entry word is a homograph, a word with the same spelling as another but with a

different meaning? _____

12. Which entry word means a pedestal _____

13. Which entry word can be used only as an adjective? _____

14. How do you spell the past tense of *plot*? _____

15. How would you divide the word *plumage* into syllables? _____

---

pliers   737   **plumate**

pli·ers (plī′ərz) *n.pl.* [< PLY¹] small pincers for gripping small objects, bending wire, etc.

plight¹ (plīt) *n.* [< Anglo-Fr. *plit*, for OFr. *pleit*, a fold] a condition or state of affairs; esp., an awkward, sad, or dangerous situation [the *plight* of the men trapped in the mine]

plight² (plīt) *vt.* [OE. *plihtan*, to pledge < *pliht*, danger] to pledge or promise, or bind by a pledge —**plight one's troth** to make a promise of marriage

Plim·soll mark (or **line**) (plim′sol, -säl, -sōl) [after S. *Plimsoll* (1824–98), Eng. statesman] a line or set of lines on the outside of merchant ships, showing the water level to which they may legally be loaded

☆**plink** (pliŋk) *n.* [echoic] a light, sharp, ringing or clinking sound —*vt., vi.* **1.** to make such sounds on (a piano, banjo, etc.) **2.** to shoot at (tin cans, etc.)

plinth (plinth) *n.* [< L. < Gr. *plinthos*, a brick, tile] **1.** the square block at the base of a column, pedestal, etc. **2.** the base on which a statue rests

Plin·y (plin′ē) **1.** (L. name *Gaius Plinius Secundus*) 23–79 A.D.; Rom. naturalist & writer: called *the Elder* **2.** (L. name *Gaius Plinius Caecilius Secundus*) 62?–113? A.D.; Rom. writer & statesman: called *the Younger*: nephew of *Pliny the Elder*

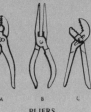

PLIERS
(A, slip joint; B, needle nose; C, arc joint)

plov·er (pluv′ər, plō′vər) *n., pl.* **plov′ers, plov′er**: see PLURAL, II, D, 1 [< OFr., ult. < L. *pluvia*, rain] a shore bird with a short tail, long, pointed wings, and a short beak

plow (plou) *n.* [ME. *ploh* < Late OE.] **1.** a farm implement used to cut and turn up the soil ☆**2.** anything like this; specif., a SNOWPLOW —*vt.* **1.** to cut and turn up (soil) with a plow **2.** to make furrows in with or as with a plow **3.** to make as if by plowing [he *plowed* his way through the crowd] **4.** to cut a way through (water) —*vi.* **1.** to use a plow in tilling the soil **2.** to cut a way (*through* water, etc.) **3.** to go forward with effort; plod **4.** to begin work vigorously (with *into*) **5.** to strike against forcefully (with *into*) —**plow back** to reinvest (profits) in the same business enterprise —**plow up 1.** to remove with a plow **2.** to till (soil) thoroughly —**plow′a·ble** *adj.* —**plow′er** *n.*

plow·boy (plou′boi′) *n.* **1.** formerly, a boy who led a team of horses drawing a plow **2.** a country boy

plow·man (plou′mən) *n., pl.* **-men 1.** a man who guides a plow **2.** a farm worker

plow·share (-sher′) *n.* the share, or cutting blade, of a moldboard plow

ploy (ploi) *n.* [? < (EM)PLOY] an action or maneuver intended to outwit or confuse another person in order to get the better of him

PLOVER
(to 11 in. high)

---

plot (plät) *n.* [OE., a piece of land] **1.** a small area of ground [a garden *plot*] **2.** a chart or diagram, as of a building or estate **3.** a secret, usually evil, scheme **4.** the plan of action of a play, novel, etc. —*vt.* **plot′ted, plot′ting 1.** *a*) to draw a plan of (a ship's course, etc.) *b*) to mark the position or course of on a map **2.** to make secret plans for [to *plot* a robbery] **3.** to plan the action of (a story, etc.) **4.** *a*) to determine the location of (a point) on a graph by means of coordinates *b*) to represent (an equation) by joining points on a graph to form a curve —*vi.* to plan together secretly; scheme [to *plot* against the king] — **plot′less** *adj.* —**plot′less·ness** *n.* —**plot′ter** *n.*

plum (plum) *n.* [OE. *plume*] **1.** *a*) any of various small trees bearing a smooth-skinned fruit with a flattened stone *b*) the fruit eaten as food **2.** a raisin, when used in pudding or cake [*plum* pudding] **3.** the dark bluish-red or reddish-purple color of some plums **4.** something excellent or desirable [the new contract is a rich *plum* for the company]

plum·age (plōo′mij) *n.* [MFr. < L. *pluma*, a feather] a bird's feathers

plu·mate (-māt, -mit) *adj.* [< L. *pluma*, a feather] *Zool.* resembling a feather, esp. in structure

fat, āpe, cär; ten, ēven; is, bīte; gō, hôrn, tōol, look; oil, out; up, fur; get; joy; yet; chin; she; thin, then; zh, leisure; ŋ, ring; ə for *a* in *ago*, *e* in *agent*, *i* in *sanity*, *o* in *comply*, *u* in *focus*; ' as in able (ā′b'l); Fr. bàl; ë, Fr. coeur; ö, Fr. feu; Fr. mon; ô, Fr. coq; ü, Fr. duc; r, Fr. cri; H, G. ich; kh, G. doch; ‡foreign; ☆ Americanism; < derived from. See inside front cover.

Lesson 25

Reading Forms

Everyone in the United States who is planning to work is required to have a **Social Security number.** Children who have bank accounts also must have a Social Security number. Assigned to you for life, the number belongs only to you. Because you must write your Social Security number on job applications, it is wise to get your number before applying for a job. Your Social Security number is needed for many other forms that you are required to complete, such as income tax forms. Memorizing the number may be helpful, because you are required to write it frequently.

The Social Security program is supported by money that is deducted, or taken out, from each of your paychecks. When you stop working because your health is poor or you reach retirement age, you receive money from the Social Security program each month. Also, if a working parent dies, the children in the family receive monthly Social Security checks for a set period.

To apply for a Social Security number, call, write, or visit the nearest Social Security office to get an application form like the one shown here. After you fill out the form and return it to the office, your Social Security card, with your number on it, will be mailed to you.

A. Fill in the space between the lines next to the phrase that correctly completes each sentence.

1. When filling out a Social Security application, you print the name that you now use in
   || item 1. || item 2. || item 3. || item 4.

2. You print the names of the city and state or foreign country where you were born in
   || item 2. || item 3. || item 7. || item 11.

3. Item 1 asks for your full name at birth, which according to this form means
   || your first name.
   || your first and last names.
   || your first, middle, and last names.
   || your first name, middle initial, and last name.

4. If the person applying for the card is a boy or a man, he would complete item 4 by
   || printing the word *male* in the box.
   || checking the box next to MALE.
   || checking the box next to FEMALE.
   || writing his age in the box.

5. If you give false information when applying for a Social Security number, you may have to
   || pay a fine.
   || go to prison.
   || pay a fine, go to prison, or both.
   || go without getting a Social Security number.

6. Which is the only voluntary item on the form?
   || item 3. || item 5. || item 11. || item 17.

7. If you answer *no* to the question in item 10, you are told to
   || enter the Social Security number previously assigned.
   || enter the name shown on the most recent Social Security card.
   || enter any different date of birth used on an earlier application.
   || go to item 14.

B. Write the answer to each question on the line provided. Use complete sentences.

1. Where is the only place on the application that you should not print or type?

2. What information does item 8 require? _____

_____

3. What two dates does *everyone* need to include on the application? _____

_____

4. If a father is filling out the form for his daughter, how would he respond to item 17?

_____

5. When would the information on the first line of item 1 differ from the information on the second line? _____

_____

SOCIAL SECURITY ADMINISTRATION
Application for a Social Security Card

Form Approved
OMB No. 0960-0066

INSTRUCTIONS
- Please read "How To Complete This Form" on page 2.
- Print or type using black or blue ink. DO NOT USE PENCIL.
- After you complete this form, take it or mail it along with the required documents to your nearest Social Security office.
- If you are completing this form for someone else, complete the items as they apply to that person. Then sign your name in question 16.

1 NAME
To Be Shown On Card

▶

FIRST	FULL MIDDLE NAME	LAST

FULL NAME AT BIRTH
IF OTHER THAN ABOVE

OTHER NAMES USED

FIRST	FULL MIDDLE NAME	LAST

2 MAILING ADDRESS
Do Not Abbreviate

▶

STREET ADDRESS, APT. NO., PO BOX, RURAL ROUTE NO.

CITY	STATE	ZIP CODE

3 CITIZENSHIP
(Check One)

☐ U.S. Citizen   ☐ Legal Alien Allowed To Work   ☐ Legal Alien Not Allowed To Work   ☐ Foreign Student Allowed Restricted Employment   ☐ Conditionally Legalized Alien Allowed To Work   ☐ Other (See Instructions On Page 2)

4 SEX   ☐ Male   ☐ Female

5 RACE/ETHNIC DESCRIPTION
(Check One Only–Voluntary)

☐ Asian, Asian-American or Pacific Islander   ☐ Hispanic   ☐ Black (Not Hispanic)   ☐ North American Indian or Alaskan Native   ☐ White (Not Hispanic) Indian or Alaskan Native

☐ Office Use Only

6 DATE OF BIRTH   Month/Day/Year

7 PLACE OF BIRTH
Do Not Abbreviate

CITY   STATE OR FOREIGN COUNTRY   FCI

8 MOTHER'S MAIDEN NAME

FIRST	FULL MIDDLE NAME	LAST

9 FATHER'S NAME

FIRST	FULL MIDDLE NAME	LAST

10 Has the person in item 1 ever received a Social Security number before?

☐ Yes (If "yes," answer items 11-13.)   ☐ No (If "no," go on to item 14.)   ☐ Don't Know (If "don't know," go on to item 14.)

11 Enter the Social Security number previously assigned to the person in item 1.

☐☐☐ – ☐☐ – ☐☐☐☐

12 Enter the name shown on the most recent Social Security card issued for the person in item 1.

FIRST	FULL MIDDLE NAME	LAST

13 Enter any different date of birth if used on an earlier application for a card. _____

MONTH   DAY   YEAR

14 TODAY'S DATE ▶ _____   **15 DAYTIME PHONE NUMBER** ▶ ( ) _____
MONTH   DAY   YEAR   AREA CODE

DELIBERATELY FURNISHING (OR CAUSING TO BE FURNISHED) FALSE INFORMATION ON THIS APPLICATION IS A CRIME PUNISHABLE BY FINE OR IMPRISONMENT, OR BOTH.

16 YOUR SIGNATURE

▶

17 YOUR RELATIONSHIP TO THE PERSON IN ITEM 1 IS:

☐ Self   ☐ Natural or Adoptive Parent   ☐ Legal Guardian   ☐ Other (Specify) _____

Form SS-5 (9/89) 5/88 edition may be used until supply is exhausted

Lesson 26 _____

Imagery

Reading a Literature Selection _____

▶ Background Information

"Hymn to the Nile" is an ancient song of praise to the river that nourished one of the world's great cultures.

▶ Skill Focus

A poem alerts the senses, arouses the emotions, and stirs the imagination. The poet does these things by using words to create **images,** or mental pictures.

Several images together in one poem are called **imagery.** Imagery often appeals to the senses, allowing the reader to see, hear, feel, taste, and smell what the poet describes.

Here is a simple factual statement:

> I ran along the beach through wet grass and mud and dove into the water.

A poet might express the same idea very differently. As you read the following poem, notice how the poet's use of imagery makes you sense familiar things in a new way.

> Slick grass clung to my bare feet,
> Tang of mud-earth prickled my nostrils;
> A honey warmth of new sun dissolved in my throat.
> Sunlight spackled the waves before me.
> I screeched as I hit the cold water!

By using such words and phrases as *sunlight spackled the waves, screeched, slick grass, tang of mud-earth,* and *prickled my nostrils,* the poet appeals to the five senses. These words and phrases create images that involve the reader. As you read a poem, look for the images that the poet has created.

▶ Word Clues

When you read, you may come across a word that names a special person, place, or thing. If no nearby context clues explain the word, there may be a clue elsewhere.

Read the following sentence.

> We adore you, O Nile![1]

The raised number after the word Nile is a signal to look at the bottom of the page for a footnote with the same number. A footnote gives a brief definition or explanation of the word.

[1]Nile: a river in Africa that runs north from Uganda through Egypt to the Mediterranean Sea; one of the world's longest rivers.

Use **footnote** context clues to find the meaning of the six other numbered words in the selection.

▶ Strategy Tip

You will find a poem easier to read if you are familiar with its special form. This poem has six stanzas, or sections. Each part of a stanza is called a line. The lines are numbered. As you read this poem, notice how the imagery puts the senses to work.

Hymn to the Nile

We adore you, O Nile![1]
We adore you, O Nile!
You spread yourself over this land, embracing the earth.
You come to give life to Egypt!
You spring from a dark, mysterious source.[2]   (5)
This day we celebrate the flood which overtakes our land, nourishing the
    orchards created by Ra.[3]
Your waters give life to the cattle and slake the thirst of the earth.
There is no end to your gifts, O inexhaustible one!
Your waters caress all growing things; even the gods depend on your
    bounty.

    You are the mighty Lord of the Fish—   (10)
    Your waters whisper along their course. . . .
    The birds fear your anger,
    and dare not disturb the growing seedlings and crops.
You create the golden kernels of corn.
You bring forth the pearls of barley.   (15)
On your banks the temples stand strong to welcome your worshippers.
If your waters do not rise and ebb each season,
If you cease your toil and work,
    then all that exists cries in anguish,
    the gods in heaven will suffer,   (20)
    and the faces of your worshippers will waste away.

    If the Nile smiles, the Earth is joyous;
    Every stomach is full of rejoicing,
    Every spine is happy,
    Every jawbone crushes its food.   (25)
Nimble fingers strum songs to you on the harp.
Women clap their hands and chant.
The feet of young men beat the earth in a gleeful dance of praise.
As the sunlight glints on your waters, the people rejoice . . . with great
    feasts they celebrate.

    You are the greatest jewel of Seb[4]—   (30)
You are a ship with great sails, advancing with the wind . . .
    when men and women see you rise before them, their hearts beat
    with joy.

[1]Nile: a river in Africa that runs north from Uganda through Egypt
to the Mediterranean Sea; one of the world's longest rivers.
[2]source: a river's point of origin.
[3]Ra: the Egyptian god of the sun.
[4]Seb: according to the ancient Egyptians, another name for Earth.

As you flow in a molten silver stream through the royal city,[5]
    the rich grow content with their good life;
    the poor are satisfied with their lot.   (35)
You make everything grow to full measure,
    and all that grows is for us, your children.
    If you did not nourish us, the country would fall exhausted;
    the bitter taste of gall[6] would fill our mouths,
    our dwellings would fall silent,   (40)
    and the dank smell of death would fill the land.

    O flood time of the Nile!
    O giver of Life!
We shall make offerings to you.
We shall give up great oxen.   (45)
We shall sacrifice birds to you.
For you our warriors will hunt down swift-footed gazelles.[7]
We shall prepare a pure bright flame to praise you.
    O, Nile, come and prosper!
We cannot live without our flocks.   (50)
Our flocks must feed in the orchards.
Only you can nourish them all.
    Come and prosper, come,
    O Nile, come and prosper!

[5]royal city: Cairo
[6]gall: bile, a bitter fluid secreted by the liver.
[7]gazelles (gə ZELZ): small antelopes

RECALLING FACTS

1. Is this hymn being sung during or before the Nile flood? Support your answer by referring to lines in the poem.

_____

2. How do people celebrate the flooding of the Nile?

_____

_____

3. Name the animals sacrificed to the Nile.

_____

_____

4. In line 30, to what is the Nile compared?
_____ In line 31? _____

5. What happens when the Nile smiles?

_____

_____

6. Decide if each statement is true or false. Write *true* or *false* on the line provided.

_____ a. Ra was an ancient Egyptian river god.

_____ b. The source of the Nile is the Mediterranean Sea.

_____ c. Seb was the ancient Egyptian name for Earth.

_____ d. Gazelles were swift Nile riverboats.

1. Why does the Nile merit such a song of praise?

_____

_____

2. The statements below are either facts or opinions. Fill in the space between the lines next to each statement that expresses a fact.
   ‖ **a.** The Nile is a river in Africa.
   ‖ **b.** The Nile is the source of happiness and joy for all Egyptians.
   ‖ **c.** The ancient Egyptians depended on the Nile's flood waters for survival.

3. Does the poet identify the source of the Nile? Support your answer by identifying the line in the poem.

_____

_____

4. What would happen if the Nile did not overflow its banks as expected?

_____

_____

5. How was the Nile the "Giver of Life" to Egypt?

_____

_____

SKILL FOCUS

1. The lines below are from the poem that you just read. In the space provided, identify the sense to which the image in each line appeals.

sight   sound   touch   taste   smell

_____ Your waters whisper along their course . . .

_____ Your waters give life to the cattle and slake the thirst of the earth.

_____ . . . sunlight glints on your waters . . .

_____ The feet of young men beat the earth . . .

_____ Nimble fingers strum songs to you on the harp.

_____ . . . the dank smell of death would fill the land.

_____ Your waters caress all growing things . . .

2. In each of the following lines, circle the word or phrase that creates a sense image. Then describe in one sentence what each image means or suggests to you.

a. As you flow in a molten silver stream through the royal city . . . (line 33)

_____

_____

b. For you our warriors will hunt down swift-footed gazelles. (line 47)

_____

_____

c. the bitter taste of gall would fill our mouths . . . (line 39)

_____

_____

_____

3. The imagery in this poem helps the reader see the Nile as the poet saw it. Of all the images in the poem, which one gives you the clearest picture of some aspect of the Nile River? Explain.

_____

_____

_____

4. a. In five or six sentences, write a factual description of the Nile, based on the information in the poem. Do not use any sense images.

_____

_____

_____

b. Reread the poem and your paragraph. Which evokes stronger feelings or emotions, the poem or the paragraph? Explain.

_____

_____

_____

5. What emotional effect did the Nile have on the poet?

_____

_____

_____

▶ **Real Life Connections** Without naming the actual place, write a descriptive sentence about an area in your community. Use words that appeal to the senses. Read your description to other students. Let them name or draw what you have described.

Comparing and Contrasting

Reading a Social Studies Selection

► Background Information

The advances of technology have changed many aspects of life. For instance, today we don't rely as heavily on natural water sources. Using such techniques as irrigation, we can bring water to places that don't naturally have it. This allows farmers to grow crops in areas where they couldn't otherwise.

However, this has not always been the case. Many ancient civilizations were built on the banks of rivers. These communities thrived because they never had to worry about droughts. Among these civilizations were the Egyptians, who built their civilization on the Nile.

The Nile River, bringing water and life to dry, desert lands, has always been Egypt's chief natural resource. The following selection discusses the Nile River and its importance to both ancient and modern Egypt.

► Skill Focus

When reading, you will often need to compare or contrast people, places, or events. To **compare**, look for similarities. To **contrast**, look for differences. By comparing and contrasting, you can learn about important relationships between people, places, or events.

A writer sometimes presents material about two related topics separately. The writer may discuss each topic in its own paragraph. Information about one topic is given first, followed by information about the second topic.

When organizing material in this way, the writer usually does not make direct comparisons and contrasts between the topics. Instead, the reader must first read the information given about the two topics and then look for similarities and differences. When reading material that requires you to make comparisons and contrasts, use the following steps.

1. Preview the selection to see how it is organized.
2. Read the selection carefully to identify ideas being compared and contrasted.
3. Go back over the selection. This time, locate specific information about the ideas being compared and contrasted.

► Word Clues

Read the sentences below. Look for context clues that explain the underlined word.

> In both ancient and modern times, the Nile River has been the source of Egypt's prosperity. The Nile has brought Egypt good fortune, wealth, and power.

If you do not know the meaning of the word *prosperity*, the phrase *good fortune, wealth, and power* can help you. *Prosperity* means "good fortune, wealth, success."

Use **detail** context clues to find the meaning of the three underlined words in the selection.

► Strategy Tip

Before you read "Egypt: Gift of the Nile," preview the selection. Read the headings and examine the map. As you read the selection, compare and contrast the ideas about the Nile River in ancient and modern Egypt.

Egypt: Gift of the Nile

Ancient Egypt was a great civilization that arose more than 5,000 years ago. Modern Egypt is one of the most powerful and most influential countries of the Arab world. In both ancient and modern times, the Nile River has been the source of Egypt's prosperity. The Nile has brought Egypt good fortune, wealth, and power.

The Nile River: Giver of Life

The Nile is the longest river in the world. From its source in the mountains of central Africa to its mouth at the Mediterranean Sea, the river flows northward for almost 4,150 miles (6,640 kilometers). Lake Victoria in Tanzania feeds one branch of the river. This branch is called the White Nile because of the color of the limestone particles that it carries. Another branch of the Nile begins in the highlands of Ethiopia. It is called the Blue Nile because its pure water reflects the color of the sky. These two branches meet at Khartoum (kar TOOM) in Sudan.

As the river flows north, it crosses 950 miles (1,520 kilometers) of Egypt's barren desert land. In the far south of Egypt, the Aswan (ahz WAHN) High Dam, built across the river, has been a major factor in controlling the waters of the Nile. Behind the dam lies Lake Nasser (NAS ə r), a huge lake created by engineers.

From the Aswan High Dam north to Cairo, the river winds through the desert, supporting life along its banks and farming in the Nile Valley. Fertile strips of land lie on both sides of the Nile. These strips of land, sometimes as wide as 14 miles (22.4 kilometers) or as narrow as 3 miles (4.8 kilometers), support nearly half of Egypt's population.

At Cairo, Egypt's capital and Africa's largest city, the Nile fans out into a fertile triangle of small tributaries and streams. This area is called the delta of the Nile. Stretching 90 miles (144 kilometers) from Cairo to the Mediterranean Sea, the delta is 150 miles (240 kilometers) wide at the coast. Yet, this small area of rich land supports the other half of the nation's population. In fact, the valley

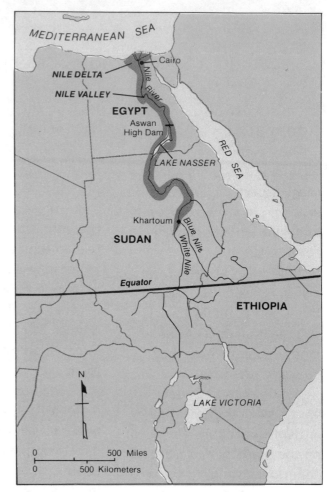

The Nile River irrigates long, narrow strips of land along its banks.

and the delta of the Nile together support almost the entire Egyptian population. Of Egypt's 386,000 square miles (1,003,600 square kilometers), only one-thirtieth is inhabited.

Ancient Egypt and the Nile

The Nile River enabled the ancient Egyptians not only to survive but also to develop an advanced civilization. Because the Nile brought water into the parched desert, the people there could grow crops and raise livestock. The river was also an essential artery for travel, communication, and trade.

Early Agriculture During a visit to Egypt, the Greek historian Herodotus declared that the land was "wholly the gift of the Nile." Every year, the ancient Egyptian farmer worked the land according to seasons that were based on the flow of the Nile. From June to September was the Flood. During this time, the Nile reached its highest level, flooding the irrigation systems that the farmers built. As the flood waters subsided, they deposited a rich, black silt. This layer of fertile earth left behind by the flood waters was planted and the crops harvested during the second season. Known as the Emergence, this season lasted from October to February. The last season from March to May was called the Drought. During this hot, dry season, nothing grew.

Wheat, the most important crop for the ancient Egyptian farmer, was used to make bread and to fatten cattle. Small plots of land were also planted with vegetables, such as beans, onions, garlic, and lentils. In addition to food, flax and papyrus reed grew along the banks of the Nile. Flax was used to make clothing and papyrus reed to make paper.

✔ Farmers developed systems of ditches and basins to trap the river's water. They invented water wheels to carry water from the river to the land. They learned to estimate the time and height of the Nile's floods. Yet, the river was still beyond their control. Some years it rose to enormous heights, washing away homes and killing livestock. Other years it did not flood at all, bringing famine to the land. This acute and general shortage of food often resulted in starvation and misery.

Transportation and Trade   For the early Egyptians, the Nile was a natural highway that linked the villages along its banks. The Nile was so important that even the language of ancient Egypt reflected the river's influence. The word for *travel* was either *khed,* to go downstream, or *khent,* to go upstream.

To travel on the Nile, the Egyptians built sailboats, called feluccas (fə LUK əs). Because the river flowed from south to north, these small, narrow boats could follow the river's current northward. Because the winds of the Mediterranean Sea blew north to south, the feluccas were propelled southward by their triangular sails. Routinely, merchants sailed from village to village with their wares, while grain barges floated north to the delta. During the construction of the great pyramids, river barges carried heavy stones to building sites.

The river also provided Egypt with a major route for trade with other countries. Egyptian traders sailed the Nile to do business with merchants from Syria and Mesopotamia (mes ə pə TAY mee ə). The Nile was a lifeline of commerce.

Modern Egypt and the Nile

The Nile is still the country's primary resource. Egypt's rapidly growing population remains concentrated along the Nile River valley and delta. However, the Aswan High Dam, completed in 1970, has changed the relationship between the Nile River and the Egyptian people. Not only has it affected farming in the Nile River valley, but it has also revolutionized the country's economy.

Modern Agriculture   Built across the Nile River in southern Egypt, the Aswan High Dam now controls the mighty river. Lake Nasser, extending 300 miles (480 kilometers) behind the dam into Sudan, collects the river water that the dam holds back.

The dam has affected Egypt's agriculture in several ways. The dam holds back the river during the high-water season, releasing the water in a constant flow to the north. Thus the dam has eliminated the annual flood and drought cycle along the Nile Valley. During several dry years in the 1970s, the dam provided Nile water to irrigate farmland and thereby prevented widespread famine.

Farmers can now rely on a steady, year-round supply of water to their land. To make use of the Nile's changed flow, new irrigation systems have been built. Modern diesel pumps bring the river water to the land, and large, heavy-duty tractors till and plant the earth. However, in some places, Egypt's farming traditions remain unchanged. Some farmers still turn the soil with ancient plows and irrigate the land with water wheels.

In modern times, cotton has become Egypt's most important crop. In fact, Egypt leads the world in cotton production. Cotton plants, which cannot survive floods, require a steady supply of water. The Aswan High Dam has, therefore, made cotton growing possible. In recent years, the Egyptian government has encouraged farmers to grow other crops, as well as cotton. Today Egypt also produces beans, corn, rice, sugar cane, and wheat.

In Egypt today, the feluccas have been replaced by more modern boats and steamers. However, these ancient vessels carry goods and people along the Nile today much as their ancestors did 4,000 years ago.

nutrients, it acted as a natural fertilizer for crops. Now, farmers have to enrich the soil with costly chemical fertilizers. The absence of silt is also seriously damaging the environment by causing the erosion of land along the Mediterranean coast near the Nile. In addition, the year-round plantings deplete the land, further reducing the soil's fertility.

Transportation, Commerce, and Industry
The Nile is still Egypt's most convenient means of transportation. Feluccas like those of ancient times still sail up and down the river. In addition, the barges and steamers that carry much of Egypt's commercial freight clog the great waterway. Construction materials, iron ore, agricultural products, and industrial equipment are all transported along the Nile. A network of highways and railroads also crisscrosses the Nile Valley.

In recent years, the power of the Nile has been harnessed for uses other than agriculture. Generators at the Aswan High Dam have tripled Egypt's output of electricity. This increased output has revolutionized Egypt's manufacturing capability. Electric power is vital to industrial production and has helped the country develop as a modern nation.

From ancient times to modern, Egypt has prospered. The Nile River has given the Egyptian people the gift of water and thereby the gift of life.

✘ The Aswan High Dam has also caused some problems for the Egyptian farmer. Besides water, the dam now holds back the rich silt that the Nile floods used to carry into the river valley. Because this silt was rich in

---

RECALLING FACTS

1. Sequence the following items in the order of the ancient Egyptian seasons.

    _____ Drought—time of dryness

    _____ Flood—time of high water

    _____ Emergence—time of planting

2. How did the Aswan High Dam prevent famine in Egypt during the dry years of the 1970s?

    _____

    _____

3. Write two causes for the following effect.

    Cause _____

    _____

    _____

    Cause _____

    _____

    _____

    Effect Egyptian farmers now need to fertilize their soil.

4. Use the map on page 98 to answer the following questions.
   a. In which direction from the Aswan High Dam is Lake Nasser? _____
   b. What major Egyptian city lies near the Mediterranean Sea?

   _____

5. Reread the paragraph that has an X next to it. Then underline the sentence that states the main idea of the paragraph.

6. Write the letter of the correct meaning on the line next to each word.

   _____ feluccas   a. fine-grained sediment carried by moving water

   _____ silt   b. scant supply of food, often resulting in starvation

   _____ famine   c. small, narrow boats propelled by triangular sails

INTERPRETING FACTS

1. Why is the Nile an easily navigable river?

   _____

   _____

2. What sort of land lies beyond the strips of fertile soil along both sides of the Nile Valley?

   _____

3. Identify each of the following statements as fact or opinion. Fill in the space between the lines next to each statement that expresses a fact.
   a. The Nile River crosses 950 miles (1,520 kilometers) of Egypt.
   b. Egypt should not have built the Aswan High Dam.
   c. The Aswan High Dam tripled Egypt's output of electricity.

4. Write the cause for the following effect.

   Cause _____

   Effect Egypt has become a leading world producer of textiles.

5. Explain the major drawback of the Aswan High Dam for Egypt's agriculture.

   _____

6. Reread the paragraph with a check mark next to it. Write a sentence describing its main idea.

   _____

SKILL FOCUS

1. The two charts at the top of the next page outline similarities and differences between ancient and modern Egypt. Look at the general topics listed in the middle column of these charts. Then reread the selection, looking for information about how ancient Egypt and

modern Egypt compare and contrast on these topics. When you have collected this information, write one sentence for each topic under each heading. The first sentence on each chart is done for you.

COMPARISONS		
Ancient Egypt	**Topic**	**Modern Egypt**
The Nile was Egypt's main source of water.	Source of Water	The Nile is still Egypt's main source of water.
_____ _____	Location of Population	_____ _____
_____ _____	Means of Transportation	_____ _____

CONTRASTS		
Ancient Egypt	**Topic**	**Modern Egypt**
Wheat was the main crop.	Major Crop	Cotton is the main crop.
_____ _____	Growing Season	_____ _____
_____ _____	Industry	_____ _____

ASWAN HIGH DAM	
Before 1970	**After 1970**
a. The Nile flooded the river valley every year.	**a.** _____ _____ _____
b. _____ _____	**b.** Droughts have been eliminated because surplus water is stored behind the dam.
c. The Nile carried rich silt into the river valley.	**c.** _____ _____

▶ **Real Life Connections** Which aspect of Egyptian culture would you be most interested in learning more about? Why?

Main Idea and Supporting Details

__ Reading a Science Selection __

▶ **Background Information**

This selection explains how plants and animals survive the harsh conditions of the desert.

▶ **Skill Focus**

Many paragraphs that you read are packed with information. To understand how ideas in a paragraph are related and which ideas are more important, look for the **main idea** and **supporting details**.

The sentence with the main idea expresses the subject of the paragraph. The **major details** give more information about the main idea. A paragraph may also include **minor details**, which provide information of less importance.

Read the following paragraph and the diagram.

(1) Desertlike areas occur in both the hot and cold regions of North America. (2) In the Arctic region, northern Canada and Alaska are tundra areas. (3) Hot desert regions cover parts of the southwestern United States. (4) Hot desert areas get very little rain during their short, mild winters.

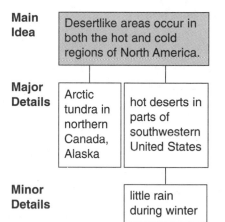

The first sentence states the main idea. The second and third sentences give important supporting information. The last sentence provides a minor detail about the supporting information in the third sentence. Not all major details have minor details.

When you read a selection that is packed with information, use the following steps.

1. Find the main idea in each paragraph.
2. Find the major details that develop and support each main idea.
3. Look for minor details that tell more about the major details.
4. After you have found all the major and minor details in a paragraph, arrange them to show how they are related. A

diagram is one way to organize information.

▶ **Word Clues**

Read the sentences below. Look for context clues that explain the underlined word.

The Empty Quarter, which is located in southeastern Saudi Arabia, is the largest expanse of sand in the world. Its spread covers almost a million square kilometers.

If you don't know the meaning of the word *expanse,* the word *spread* in the second sentence will help you. The words *expanse* and *spread* are synonyms.

Use **synonym** context clues to find the meaning of the three underlined words in the selection.

▶ **Strategy Tip**

As you read the selection, look for the main ideas and supporting details. Keep in mind how the major details support the main idea and how the minor details support the major details.

Hot Deserts

1. During summer days, temperatures in hot desert regions may soar to well over 38 degrees Celsius. However, as the sun sets, the temperature drops sharply. At night, temperatures may be more than 30 degrees lower than during the day. In the winter, deserts may even have freezing temperatures. In addition, the air is very dry. Over an average year, no more than 25 centimeters of rain falls. The desert's extreme environment is one of the most difficult areas on earth in which to live.

2. The Middle East has two desert regions. The Sahara, which stretches the full width of northern Africa, is the largest desert in the world. It covers more than 9 million square kilometers. A number of rivers flow into the Sahara, forming "islands" of living things throughout this barren region. The Empty Quarter, which is located in southeastern Saudi Arabia, is the largest expanse of sand in the world. Its spread covers almost a million square kilometers. Unlike the Sahara, the Empty Quarter has no rivers flowing into it. However, it does have <u>transient</u> streams. These temporary streams dry up and disappear during periods of drought.

3. Many kinds of organisms survive in deserts. At nightfall, birds, lizards, snakes, and small mammals scurry about in search of food. After a spring rain, the desert bursts into life as wildflowers quickly grow and blossom. How living things survive and reproduce in the desert has long fascinated scientists. By carefully studying and observing desert organisms, scientists can learn their secrets.

Desert Animals

4. Both warm-blooded and cold-blooded desert animals have ways to escape the desert heat. Warm-blooded desert animals, such as rats and mice, rest during the day, often staying in cool underground burrows. At night they search for food. Animals that are out during the day, such as cold-blooded lizards and snakes, are active only for short periods. As their body temperature rises, these reptiles move into the shade in order to cool down. In the early evening, when the sun

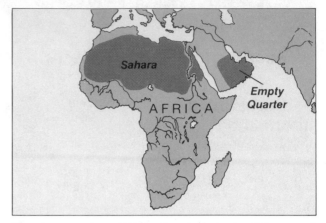

The deserts of the Middle East include the Sahara and the Empty Quarter.

grows weaker, the reptiles become more active and resume their search for food.

5. Getting enough water to survive is a major problem for all desert animals. Some desert animals, such as desert birds and bats, manage to find water holes. Other desert animals, such as the kangaroo rat and the related jerboa, get water only from the food that they eat. Because these animals eat mainly dry seeds, they must survive on a tiny amount of water.

Kangaroo rat

6. Most deserts have only a small number of frogs and toads because these animals must be near water to survive. Yet even these creatures have adapted to desert conditions. When small amounts of water collect in temporary streams, the desert-living frogs and

toads become active. After a rainfall, they lay their eggs. The eggs grow into tadpoles in a few days and into adults in just four weeks. When the puddles dry up, the adult frogs or toads dig into the ground. Their metabolism slows, and they stay beneath the ground until the next rain, which may be as much as a year away. Until then, their bodily activities continue at a reduced rate.

7. The camel—often called the ship of the desert—is one of the most successful desert animals. Camels can go for long periods without water, but eventually they must drink. When water becomes available to them after a long drought, they may drink 95 liters of water or more. When water is not available, what helps camels survive the desert heat is the fat stored in their humps. A camel's hump contains about 12 kilograms of fat. Fat is rich in hydrogen. As the fat is digested, hydrogen from the fat combines with oxygen in the air that the camel breathes. The result is H_2O, or water. Each kilogram of fat that a camel digests yields about a liter of water.

Camel

Desert Plants

8. Desert plants have different kinds of root systems that help them survive in an environment with little water. Some plants, such as **acacias** (ə KAY sh əz), have a thick **tap root** that grows deep into the ground until it reaches water. The tap roots of some plants go down more than 30 meters. While the tap root is growing toward water, plant growth above ground is not thick. However, after the tap root reaches water, the growth above

ground often becomes quite <u>dense</u>. Other desert plants have shallow roots that grow just below the surface of the ground and extend out from the plant for many meters.

Acacia

When rain comes, the root system acts like a large sponge, capturing most of the water that falls on it.

9. Other desert plants have different ways to survive despite the lack of water. The seeds of annuals, which grow, flower, and die in one season, are coated with a natural chemical that prevents them from <u>germinating</u>.

Cactus

However, water can wash away this chemical, allowing the seeds to sprout. The amount of water necessary to wash away the chemical is the same amount that the seed needs to sprout, grow, flower, and make new chemical-coated seeds for the next generation. **Succulents** (SUK you lənts), such as cactus, store water in their thick, fleshy stems for use during dry periods.

10. Plants need leaves to make food, but they lose much water through their leaves. Desert plants have different ways to reduce this loss. The leaves of many desert plants are small and covered with a waxy layer. Both the small leaf size and the waxy covering reduce water loss. Other desert plants grow leaves only after a rainfall. Then, when dry weather comes again, the leaves are quickly dropped, before much water is lost through them. Some plants, such as cactus, exhibit an extreme way to reduce water loss through leaves. They don't have leaves at all. Their stems carry out the food-producing function of leaves.

11. In spite of the harsh conditions of deserts, many organisms can survive in them, including human beings. In the future, more desert may be converted into farmland. Sophisticated irrigation techniques can increase the amount of land that can produce crops.

RECALLING FACTS

1. How much rainfall does a desert receive in an average year?

_____

_____

2. How many square kilometers does the Sahara Desert cover?

_____

_____

3. Where is the Empty Quarter?

_____

_____

4. Which desert has permanent rivers, the Sahara or the Empty Quarter?

_____

_____

5. How do mice and rats escape daytime desert heat?

_____

_____

6. Where do jerboas get the water that they need?

_____

7. What do frogs and toads do during a drought?

_____

8. How are frogs and toads able to reproduce in deserts?

_____

_____

9. How do camels get water without drinking?

_____

_____

_____

10. How does a tap root help an acacia survive in the desert?

_____

_____

_____

11. Where is most water lost from a plant?

_____

_____

12. Complete each statement with the correct word.

transient   dense   germinating

    a. Luckily, the unseasonable weather was ——————.

    b. The crops are —————————— in the field.

    c. The fog was so —————— that we couldn't see the road.

INTERPRETING FACTS

1. Because the Sahara covers about nine times more area than the Empty Quarter, but the Empty Quarter has a larger expanse of sand,

  || **a.** part of the Empty Quarter must be swamp.

  || **b.** part of the Sahara must be rocky or hilly.

  || **c.** part of the Sahara must be cold.

2. Desert animals are usually more active at night because

  || **a.** it is cooler at night.

  || **b.** they like the dark.

  || **c.** they are less likely to be attacked at night.

3. If you were stranded in a desert, your easiest water source would be plants that

  || **a.** have a tap root.

  || **b.** lose their leaves.

  || **c.** are succulents.

4. Desert mammals are more active

  || **a.** after dusk.

  || **b.** after dawn.

  || **c.** after a drought.

5. If a mammal's body temperature changes by several degrees,

  || **a.** then it may be hungry.

  || **b.** then it may be out at night.

  || **c.** then it may be sick.

SKILL FOCUS

When completed, the diagrams on the next page will show how the ideas in a paragraph are related. For each numbered paragraph, copy the sentence that states the main idea. Then write the major details that support or develop the main idea, using only key words or phrases. Finally, write the minor details, using only key words or phrases.

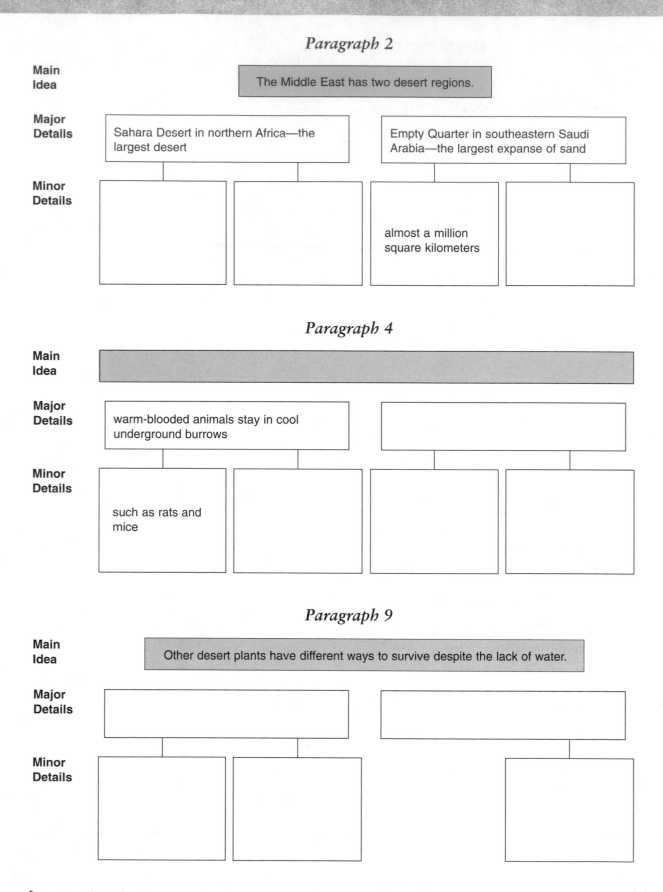

Paragraph 2

Main Idea

The Middle East has two desert regions.

Major Details

Sahara Desert in northern Africa—the largest desert

Empty Quarter in southeastern Saudi Arabia—the largest expanse of sand

Minor Details

almost a million square kilometers

Paragraph 4

Main Idea

Major Details

warm-blooded animals stay in cool underground burrows

Minor Details

such as rats and mice

Paragraph 9

Main Idea

Other desert plants have different ways to survive despite the lack of water.

Major Details

Minor Details

▶ **Real Life Connections** What is the largest desert area in the United States? Compile a list of facts about this region.

Geometric Terms

Reading a Mathematics Selection

▶ Background Information

Geometry dates back to the beginning of time. In ancient Egypt, architects used geometry to help them build great temples and pyramids. In ancient Babylonia, astronomers used geometry to help them observe the stars and planets. As a matter of fact, we still measure degrees and circles in the same way that the Babylonians did.

Both the Egyptians and the Babylonians could not have done many of the things that they did without the use of geometry. However, their knowledge of geometry was limited in comparison to what we now know about geometry. One reason for this is that in ancient times, they were only interested in practical geometry; they didn't worry about theory.

The Greeks were the first people to look at theory. They tried to prove things through mathematical statements. Today we have adopted a similar approach. This has led to a geometry that has both practical applications and theoretical proofs.

When you read about geometry, you must study the figures, as well as read the words. Whenever a geometric figure appears in the text, study it before reading further. The labels in some geometric figures indicate lengths.

▶ Skill Focus

Mathematics is concerned with more than just numbers. It also deals with shapes and sizes. This branch of mathematics is called **geometry.** In geometry you learn about different kinds of shapes and the terms used to name them. You also learn how to measure the shapes.

Before you can learn much about geometry, you need to know the names of different shapes. You probably already know some of them. When you have learned the meanings of the terms used in geometry, you can better use geometry to solve problems. Problems in geometry often involve finding the **perimeter** or the **area** of a figure.

It is also important to be able to recognize whether the two halves of a geometric figure match each other exactly. When they do, the figure is **symmetrical.** A symmetrical figure may have straight or curved sides. It may have two, three, four, or more sides. Some of the sides may be the same length, and some of the angles may be the same size.

▶ Word Clues

When reading the following selection, you will come across many words that contain prefixes. You will understand the names of geometric figures better if you know that *tri* means three, *quad* means four, *pent* means five, *hex* means six, and *rect* means right.

▶ Strategy Tip

When you read "Geometric Terms," be sure that you know the meanings of the labels, as well as the meanings of any special symbols, such as dotted lines. Remember to look for prefixes when you read the names of geometric figures.

Geometric Terms

If you fold a piece of paper in half and cut out a shape from the folded side, then unfold the paper, the two halves of the paper will be **symmetrical** (si MET ri kəl). In a symmetrical shape, the two halves match exactly. Here is a symmetrical geometric figure made by cutting folded paper.

Line of Symmetry

In the picture, the fold is shown as a dotted line, called the line of symmetry for the figure. The two halves on the sides of the line of symmetry match exactly. However, each half is a mirror image of the other half.

Some figures have more than one line of symmetry. Drawings of symmetrical figures usually show all the lines of symmetry. The circle is an exception to this rule because every line through the center of a circle is a line of symmetry.

Drawings give the properties, or characteristics, of some of the figures. One property of a figure is the distance around it, known as its **perimeter.** Another property is the amount of space it covers, or its **area.** For most geometric figures, a rule, or **formula,** tells how to find the area.

A figure with three straight sides is called a **triangle.** If two of the sides have the same length, the triangle is **isosceles** (eye SOS ə leez). An isosceles triangle has only one line of symmetry.

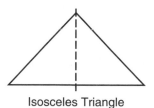

Isosceles Triangle

When all three sides of a triangle have the same length, it is **equilateral** (ee kwə LAT ər əl). An equilateral triangle has three lines of symmetry.

In this equilateral triangle, each side has a length of 3 meters. The label on each side is *3m,* which tells you the length of the side

(m is the abbreviation for meter). Because the perimeter is the distance around a figure, the perimeter of this triangle is 9 meters.

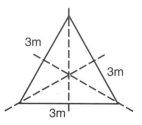

Fold a sheet of paper diagonally, or from corner to corner. Then fold it diagonally again, making sure that the two edges of the first fold meet. The result of the two folds is a right angle. In a **right triangle,** one of the three angles of the triangle is a right angle. A right triangle with two equal sides is also isosceles.

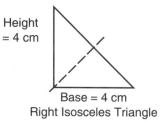

Right Isosceles Triangle

The sides of this right triangle are each 4 centimeters long *(cm* is the abbreviation for centimeter). If you know the length of the base of a triangle, as well as its height, you can figure out its area. Area is the space inside the lines of a figure.

Area is measured in square units. The formula for the area of a right triangle is $A = \frac{1}{2}bh$. The letter A stands for the number of square units in the area. The letter b stands for the length of the base, 4 centimeters. The letter h stands for the height, also 4 centimeters. To find the area of a right triangle, substitute numbers for the letters in the formula $A = \frac{1}{2}bh$. When two letters are written next to each other, or when a number is written next to a letter, they are multiplied. $A = \frac{1}{2}bh$ means

$$A = \frac{1}{2} \times b \times h$$

Therefore,

$$A = \frac{1}{2} \times 4 \times 4, \text{ or } 8$$

The area is 8 square centimeters, or 8 cm².

A figure with four straight sides and four right angles is a **rectangle.** The formula for the area of a rectangle is A = lw. Again, *A* stands for the number of square units in the area. The letter *l* stands for the number of units in the length. The letter *w* stands for the number of units in the width.

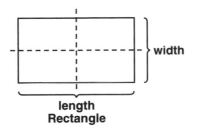

length
Rectangle

If the sides of a rectangle are the same length, the figure is a **square.**

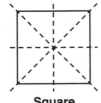

Square

A **rhombus** (ROM bəs) is like a square because it has four sides of the same length. It is different from a square because none of the angles is a right angle.

Rectangles, squares, and rhombuses are called **quadrilaterals** (kwod rə LAT ər əls). Any figure with four straight sides is a quadrilateral.

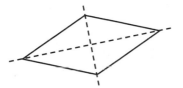

Rhombus

A **pentagon** (PEN tə gon) is any figure with five straight sides. This figure is a regular pentagon. A figure is **regular** if all the sides are the same length and all the angles are the same size.

Pentagon

A **hexagon** (HEK sə gon) is any figure with six straight sides.

Figures that have straight sides are called **polygons** (POL i gonz).

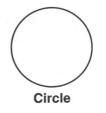

Circle

A **circle** does not have straight sides, and it is therefore not a polygon. All the points in a circle are the same distance from a single point, called the **center.** Every line through the center of the circle is a line of symmetry.

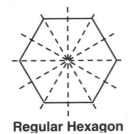

Regular Hexagon

Not every geometric figure has a line of symmetry. The following figures are three examples of polygons that are not symmetrical about any line.

A **scalene** (skay LEEN) triangle is a triangle in which no two sides are the same length.

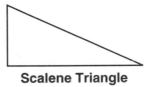

Scalene Triangle

A **trapezoid** (TRAP ə zoyd) is a quadrilateral in which two sides are **parallel.** Parallel sides do not meet no matter how far they are extended. The other two sides are not parallel.

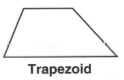

Trapezoid

A **parallelogram** (par ə LEL ə gram) is a quadrilateral in which both pairs of sides are parallel.

Parallelogram

1. Which figures in the selection are quadrilaterals?

_____

_____

2. Which figures in the selection have straight sides that are all the same length?

_____

_____

3. Name the figures that have exactly two lines of symmetry.

_____

_____

4. What is the distance around a geometric figure called?

_____

5. Which figures described in the selection have two or more sides that are parallel?

_____

_____

6. What is a circle?

_____

_____

INTERPRETING FACTS

1. What kind of triangle is this? _____

5 m   5 m
4 m

2. Suppose the two sides of a trapezoid that are not parallel have the same length. What would you call the figure? _____

3. A kite is a geometric figure with two equal short sides and two equal long sides, but it is not a rectangle. How would you classify a kite? _____

4. What is another name for a regular quadrilateral? _____

SKILL FOCUS

A. Draw a line of symmetry through each of the letters below. If a letter has no line of symmetry, circle it. The first one has been done for you. Then answer the following questions.

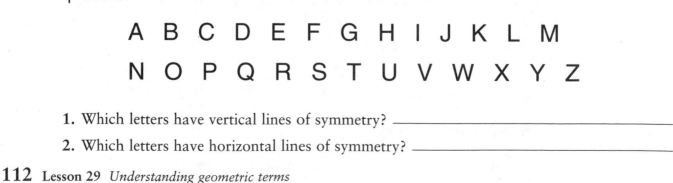

A B C D E F G H I J K L M
N O P Q R S T U V W X Y Z

1. Which letters have vertical lines of symmetry? _____

2. Which letters have horizontal lines of symmetry? _____

3. Which letters have two lines of symmetry? _____

4. Which letters have no lines of symmetry? _____

B. Answer the following questions about the perimeters of the geometric figures below. Remember to use units in your answers.

1. What is the perimeter of the rectangle shown below? _____

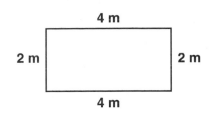

2. The polygon below is an equilateral triangle. What is its perimeter? _____

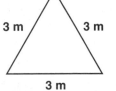

3. What is the perimeter of the rhombus below? _____

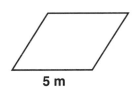

4. What is the perimeter of the parallelogram below? _____

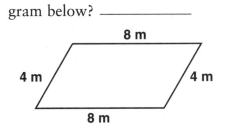

C. Answer the following questions about the areas of the geometric figures below.

1. A scalene triangle has sides that are 3m, 4m, and 5m, and it is also a right triangle. The 3m and 4m sides form the right angle. What is the area of the triangle?

   $A = \frac{1}{2}bh$ _____

2. What is the area of the rectangle below?

   $A = lw$ _____

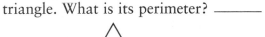

3. What is the area of the rectangle below?

   $A = lw$ _____

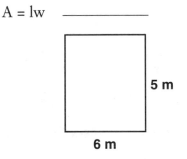

4. What is the area of the right triangle below?

   $A = \frac{1}{2}bh$ _____

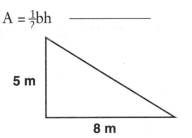

▶ **Real Life Connections** How would you go about finding the perimeter of your school building?

Synonyms and Antonyms

The word *synonym* comes from two Greek word parts, *syn* meaning together and *onyma* meaning a name. A **synonym** is a word having the same or nearly the same meaning as another word in the same language. For example, *constant* is a synonym for *unchanging*.

The word *antonym* comes from two Greek word parts, *anti* meaning opposite and *onyma* meaning a name. An **antonym** is a word that is opposite in meaning to another word. As an example, *polite* is an antonym of *rude*.

A. Underline the word that is the best synonym of the italicized word.

1. *apparent*
   a. amazing   c. alarming
   b. visible   d. impossible

2. *cautious*
   a. burning   c. careless
   b. clean   d. watchful

3. *challenge*
   a. dare   c. flavor
   b. change   d. plan

4. *detach*
   a. connect   c. warn
   b. poison   d. separate

5. *enthusiasm*
   a. dullness   c. tiredness
   b. eagerness   d. loveliness

6. *fascinate*
   a. charm   c. sweeten
   b. horrify   d. look

7. *mammoth*
   a. tiny   c. loud
   b. wicked   d. huge

8. *portion*
   a. ownership   c. section
   b. painting   d. covering

9. *rehearse*
   a. practice   c. command
   b. warn   d. relax

10. *triumph*
    a. defeat   c. reduction
    b. voyage   d. victory

B. Underline the word that is the best antonym of the italicized word.

1. *bright*
   a. dull   c. short
   b. shiny   d. forceful

2. *build*
   a. raise   c. add
   b. grow   d. destroy

3. *continue*
   a. maintain   c. begin
   b. end   d. remain

4. *disgrace*
   a. shame   c. honor
   b. disease   d. ugly

5. *filth*
   a. dirt   c. soap
   b. cleanliness d. refuge

6. *necessary*
   a. unimportant c. fancy
   b. needed   d. required

7. *pardon*
   a. forgive   c. fear
   b. overlook   d. punish

8. *quarrel*
   a. argue   c. agree
   b. grow   d. calm

9. *reduced*
   a. shrunk   c. correct
   b. increased   d. lowered

10. *temporary*
    a. raging   c. reasonable
    b. passing   d. permanent

Taking Notes: Summarizing

One way to take notes is to write a summary. A **summary** tells the most important ideas in as few words as possible. Summarizing helps you understand, remember, and review information.

Before writing a summary, carefully read the selection. Because a summary is much shorter than the whole selection, you need to decide which details are important. A good summary should include only the main ideas and major details in a selection.

Read the following selection. Underline the main ideas and major details that you think should be included in your summary. Then write a one-paragraph summary in your own words.

In recent years, Egyptian women have won new rights and have taken a greater role in public affairs. Some people credit this change to Jehan Sadat, wife of the late Egyptian president, Anwar Sadat. A well-known leader in the women's movement, Jehan Sadat encouraged her husband to take steps to improve the position of Egyptian women.

In 1979, President Sadat announced new laws giving women additional political and legal rights. He added 30 seats to the 360-seat Egyptian parliament. All the new seats were to be reserved for women representatives. At the same time, he decreed that one fifth of the members of local city councils should be women. When the newly elected women entered parliament, Jehan Sadat arranged a series of meetings for them. She encouraged the new members to ask a lot of questions and to raise issues that concerned them. "I'm very satisfied," Jehan Sadat said after the meetings, "because I fought for many, many years for this."

Jehan Sadat was not the only woman to influence public policy. Women gained important positions in several areas. Sadat

Jehan Sadat

appointed another woman, Aminah el-Said, chairperson of the board of the largest state-run Egyptian publishing house. Sadat had met el-Said in the early 1950s, when they were both on the staff of the publishing house.

Educated Egyptian women have moved into leading positions in a number of areas, including medicine, media, and education. For example, Dr. Haifaa Shanawany won international recognition for her family-oriented medical services throughout Asia, Africa, and Europe. The success of women leaders in Egypt has set an example for women in other Middle Eastern nations and helped them counter opposition to their new roles.

_____

_____

_____

_____

_____

_____

Taking Notes: Outlining

Another good way to understand and remember something you read is to make an **outline**. An outline can be written quickly and read easily. A good outline shows how the main idea and supporting details in a selection are organized.

Read the following paragraph. Then look at the outline next to it.

In 1922, archaeologist Howard Carter entered the four-room tomb of the Pharoah. Tutankhamun, who had been buried almost 3,300 years earlier. The largest room, the Antechamber, was 26 by 12 feet. Its contents included both everyday and religious objects. The Burial Chamber was 17 by 11 feet. It held objects for the last rites and the afterlife. Next to this room was the Treasury, which was 16 by $12\frac{1}{2}$ feet. This room contained mostly funerary equipment. The smallest room was the 14-by-$8\frac{1}{2}$-feet Annex. Provisions for the dead king were kept here.

The Tomb of Tutankhamun

I. Four rooms of the tomb
  A. Antechamber
    1. Largest room—26 by 12 feet
    2. Everyday and religious objects
  B. Burial Chamber
    1. 17 by 11 feet
    2. Objects for the last rites and afterlife
  C. Treasury
    1. 16 by $12\frac{1}{2}$ feet
    2. Funerary equipment
  D. Annex
    1. Smallest room—14 by $8\frac{1}{2}$ feet
    2. Provisions for the king

Notice that *Four rooms of the tomb,* the main idea of the paragraph, is written next to Roman numeral I. *Antechamber,* written next to capital letter A, is the first major detail about the rooms. Next to number 1 is the phrase *Largest room—26 by 12 feet,* a minor detail about the Antechamber. Notice the outline uses only words and phrases.

Several other things are important to know about outlining. Every outline should have a title. An outline should always include at least two main ideas; it can never have a Roman numeral I without a II. There should be at least two major details under each main idea and at least two minor details under each major detail.

Read the next four paragraphs about the rooms of Tutankhamun's tomb. Use the information in them to complete the outline.

As Carter entered the Antechamber, he thought it looked like a rummage sale. His procedure was to assign a number to each object for photographing and record keeping. It took seven weeks of careful work to record and remove the smaller objects, just to make room for dismantling the larger things. Three large animal-shaped couches, as well as royal thrones and ordinary stools, lined one wall. Four dismantled chariots were piled in a corner. Guarding a doorway were two life-size statues of the king.

Carter went to work next in the Burial Chamber. Taking apart the shrines, which almost filled the room, involved modern scaffolding and took four months. An elaborate pulley system was devised to open the coffins. Studying the king's mummy took eight months. In all, four shrines were nested inside one another protecting a stone sarcophagus. This held the outer coffin, which had two smaller coffins inside. Within the inner coffin lay the king. Covering his head was a great treasure, the Gold Mask.

Carter delayed work in the Treasury until the Burial Chamber had been emptied. It took a full winter to clear out the smaller objects to make room for dismantling the Canopic shrine. Removal of the shrine revealed a chest holding the king's internal organs. Of the many ritual images, 413 were shawabtys—workers to serve the king in the afterlife.

The Annex was discovered first but was cleared last. The clutter made clearing work space a complicated procedure. Using rope slings, archaeologists swung over the threshold to remove the objects. They found baskets and pottery jars filled with provisions for the dead king. Royal furniture and urns were among these common objects.

II. Antechamber

  A. Procedure

    1. Assigned each object a number

    2.

  B. Objects

    1. Three animal-shaped couches, royal thrones, and stools

    2.

    3.

III.

  A. Procedure

    1. Took apart shrines with scaffolding (4 months)

    2.

    3.

  B.

    1. Four shrines with sarcophagus inside

    2.

    3.

IV.

  A.

    1.

    2.

  B.

    1.

    2.

V.

  A.

    1.

    2.

  B.

    1.

    2.

Improving Reading Rate

A good reader is able to read at several speeds, depending on the material being read. When reading difficult or unfamiliar material, a good reader reads slower. For example, social studies, science, mathematics, and poetry may be more difficult to read than most literature. So these materials are read more slowly. Even literature can be difficult. Sometimes a reader needs to reread a paragraph to understand a complex idea. A good reader also slows down to read diagrams and maps with increased attention. You should be ready to adjust your reading rate to the difficulty of the reading.

The following selection can be used to check your reading rate. Use a watch or a clock with a second hand to time yourself. Start right on a minute, such as five minutes past ten o'clock. Write your starting time at the beginning of the selection. Then read the selection. Because it is a social studies selection, you should read it more slowly than you would read a story. Write your ending time at the end of the selection.

Starting time _____

The Temple of Dendur

The Temple of Dendur is one of the ancient monuments of the Nile River. It was built by the Emperor Augustus around 15 B.C.E., during the Roman occupation of Egypt. Between 1891 and 1902, a dam was built at Aswan, the ancient frontier between Egypt and Nubia. The dam regulated the water level of the Nile. By raising the water level, the dam caused some of the monuments at Dendur to be under water for nine months each year.

In the 1950s, the decision was made to build a new dam at Aswan. The Aswan High Dam would create a 3,000-square-mile lake. The advantages of the dam included providing more fertile land and hydroelectric power to Egypt's growing population. One disadvantage was that the lake would flood part of the Nubian desert, and the people living there would have to move elsewhere. Also, the ancient monuments at Dendur would be forever under the raised waters of the Nile.

To save the temples, shrines, and early Christian churches at Dendur, UNESCO began a worldwide campaign to move and reassemble as many of the buildings as possible. The United States contributed $16 million to help save the monuments. To show its appreciation, Egypt offered the United States the 2,000-year-old Temple of Dendur as a gift.

The Egyptian Department of Antiquities dismantled the Temple of Dendur in 1965. Due to the fragile nature of the stone, the masons carefully took the temple apart block by block, numbering each one. Detailed drawings of every part of the temple recorded the level, position, and number for each block, so that reassembling the temple would be simplified. The blocks were packed, loaded onto a barge, and floated to Elephantine Island. The temple that had stood on the banks of the Nile had been reduced to 640 crates that weighed over 800 tons.

In 1967, a committee appointed by President Johnson suggested that the temple should go to New York City's Metropolitan Museum. The temple would be a significant addition to the museum's already impressive Egyptian collection. In the summer of 1968, the crates containing the temple were put aboard the freighter *Concordia Star*, headed for the United States. Once the crates arrived at the Metropolitan Museum, they were stored in a large, inflated canvas and vinyl structure in a parking lot. They remained there for six years, until 1974, when they were transported by truck to their final home at the north end of the museum. Construction had begun that year on the Sackler Wing, an all-glass wing designed specifically to house the temple. By the end of the year, the first phase of construction—the platform for the temple with a garage and service area below it—was complete.

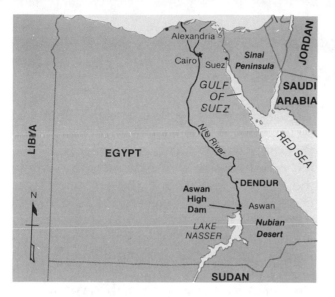

The temple was reassembled in the Sackler Wing to appear as it once did on the banks of the Nile. The platform it stands on looks much like an ancient wharf. A reflecting pool surrounds the platform, showing how the temple must have appeared in its original location on the Nile. Visitors to the museum have been admiring the Temple of Dendur since September 1978.

Words in selection: 658

	Hr.	Min.	Sec.
Ending time			
Starting time			
Total time			

$$\frac{\text{No. of words } 658}{\text{No. of seconds}} = \quad \times 60 = \quad \text{WPM}$$

To find the total time that it took you to read the selection, do the following: (1) Subtract your starting time from your ending time. (2) Divide the number of words in the selection by the remainder expressed in seconds.

For example, if it took you 3 minutes and 5 seconds ($3 \times 60 + 5 = 185$ seconds) to read the selection, you would have read 3.5 words per second ($658 \div 185 = 3.5$). (3) To find the number of words per minute (WPM), multiply your rate per second by 60. Your answer would be 210 WPM.

As each block was repaired, it was brought up to the platform to be assembled. The masons assembling the temple exhibited the same care as those who had dismantled it. They used padded pulleys to protect each stone while putting it into its proper place. When the temple had been set up, it was enclosed in a steel scaffold and covered as protection from the major construction going on around it.

Dendur is the only complete Egyptian temple in the Western Hemisphere. It is one of the latest examples of Egyptian architecture. Dendur has a gateway and a temple with floral columns on the front and three rooms beyond. The gateway and temple are made of pink sandstone.

To check your understanding of the selection, underline the answer to each question.

1. When was the Temple of Dendur built?
   a. around 15 B.C.E.
   b. between 1891 and 1902
   c. in 1974

2. Why was the temple moved?
   a. It was taking up too much space.
   b. It was falling apart.
   c. It would have been under water.

3. Why did Egypt give the Temple of Dendur to the United States?
   a. The United States started a campaign to move the temple.
   b. The United States helped dismantle Nubian monuments.
   c. The United States contributed money to save the Nubian monuments.

4. How were the monuments of the Nile to be saved?
   a. They would be taken apart and reassembled elsewhere.
   b. They would be packed in crates.
   c. They would be stored in warehouses.

5. Why were drawings made as the temple was dismantled?
   a. They would be sold to museums.
   b. They would make reassembly easier.
   c. They would stay in Egypt once the Temple was moved.

6. Where does the temple now stand?
   a. on the banks of the Nile
   b. at the Metropolitan Museum in New York City
   c. on Elephantine Island

Reading a Bank Statement

If you have a checking account, you receive a statement every month from your bank. The statement shows the two main types of activities that occurred during the month:

1. **deposits,** or how much money you put into your account
2. **withdrawals,** or the money that has been paid out of the account

The statement also shows the balance, or the amount of money remaining in your account, and charges, such as the service charge by the bank for processing checks. Canceled checks, or the checks that have been cashed, are returned with your statement.

Every time you write a check, you should record the following information in the checkbook register: the check number; the date; the person, business, or organization to whom the check is issued; and the amount of the check. You should also record the amount and date of any deposits made into your checking account. Accurate record keeping is essential for keeping track of your checking account. If your records are done correctly, the balance in your checkbook register should match the balance on the checking account statement exactly. This is called balancing a checking account. Study the checking account statement below and compare it to the checkbook register.

FROM: Big City Bank 111 E. Capital St., S.E. Washington, D.C. 20003	TELEPHONE ASSISTANCE NUMBER: 202-543-8002	ACCOUNT NUMBER: 2840264
		FOR THE PERIOD: 11/17/96-12/17/96

TO: Francine Harris 466 25th Street, N.W. Washington, D.C. 20020	ACTIVITY ON THIS STATEMENT: DEPOSITS 2 / CHECKS 6	

ENDING BALANCE ON PREVIOUS STATEMENT ⊕	DEPOSITS AND OTHER CREDITS ⊜	WITHDRAWALS AND FEES ⊖	BALANCE AS OF THIS STATEMENT DATE
$222.40	$1,308.35	$645.80	$884.95

DATE	DESCRIPTION	OTHER ACTIVITY	DEPOSITS	WITHDRAWALS	BALANCE
11/19	CHECK PAID-302			22.10	200.30
11/23	CHECK PAID-303			5.00	195.30
11/23	CHECK PAID-304			110.10	85.20
11/29	DEPOSIT		25.00		110.20
12/4	CHECK PAID-305			10.00	100.20
12/6	CHECK PAID-306			45.00	55.20
12/14	DEPOSIT		1283.35		1338.55
12/16	CHECK PAID-307			450.00	888.55
12/17	SERVICE CHARGE			3.60	884.95

		PLEASE BE SURE TO DEDUCT CHARGES THAT AFFECT YOUR ACCOUNT BALANCE FORWARD				BALANCE FORWARD	
NO.	DATE	ISSUED TO OR DESCRIPTION OF DEPOSIT	AMOUNT OF PAYMENT	OTHER DEDUCT	AMOUNT OF DEPOSIT	222	40
302	11/17	TO R & B GROCERIES	22 10			22	10
		FOR				200	30
303	11/17	TO SECOND ST. CINEMA	5 00			5	00
		FOR TICKET FOR MOVIE				195	30
304	11/20	TO MORGAN'S DEPT. STORE	110 10			110	10
		FOR				85	20
	11/29	TO DEPOSIT			25 00	25	00
		FOR BIRTHDAY GIFT				110	20
305	12/1	TO GIFTS & GAGS	10 00			10	00
		FOR GIFT-GRANDPA				100	20
306	12/2	TO DR. AUSTIN PHILLIPS	45 00			45	00
		FOR				55	20
	12/14	TO DEPOSIT			1283 35	1283	35
		FOR PAYCHECK				1338	55
307	12/14	TO BARNSTONE REALTY	450 00			450	00
		FOR RENT				888	55
		TO SERVICE CHARGE	3 60			3	60
		FOR				884	95

A. Circle the letter next to the answer to each question.

1. Which check number was written for the amount of $450.00?
   a. 1216   **b.** 307   **c.** 306   **d.** 183.46

2. On what date was there a balance of $110.20?
   a. November 17   **b.** November 23   **c.** November 29   **d.** December 4

3. What was the amount of check 305 to Gifts & Gags?
   a. $10.00   **b.** $46.05   **c.** $25.00   **d.** $110.10

4. On which date were two checks paid by the bank?
   a. November 19   **b.** November 23   **c.** November 29   **d.** December 16

5. What was the balance in the account after check 304 was paid?
   a. $85.20   **b.** $110.10   **c.** $110.20   **d.** $222.40

6. What was the period of time covered by this checking account statement?
   a. from November 19, 1996 to December 17, 1996
   b. from November through December 1996
   c. from November 17, 1996 to December 17, 1996
   d. from November 19, 1996 to December 19, 1996

7. Under which heading do you find out how much money is in the account on the day the statement was prepared?
   a. BALANCE
   b. ENDING BALANCE ON PREVIOUS STATEMENT
   c. BALANCE AS OF THIS STATEMENT DATE
   d. WITHDRAWALS AND FEES

8. Why was $25.00 added to the balance of $85.20 in the BALANCE column?
   a. A $25.00 check was paid.
   b. A $25.00 service charge was added.
   c. The bank made an error of $25.00.
   d. A $25.00 deposit was made.

9. What does the figure $55.20 represent?
   a. the ending balance on the previous statement
   b. the balance after check 306 was paid
   c. the balance before check 306 was paid
   d. the balance as of the date of this statement

10. What is the number 2840264?
    a. the account number for the person who received the statement
    b. the telephone number if help is needed with this account
    c. the ending balance on the previous month's statement
    d. the withdrawals and fees paid during this statement period

B. Read the sentences below, and write *true* or *false* on each line.

1. There was a balance of $85.20 on November 29. _____

2. The deposits that were made total $1,308.35. _____

3. The balance as of this statement date is $222.40. _____

4. The total of the checks paid and of other charges equals $645.80. _____

5. A check for the amount of $5.00 was paid on November 23. _____

6. After check 305 was paid, the balance in the account was $10.00. _____

7. Check 302 for $200.30 was paid on November 19. _____

8. Check 304 for $110.10 was paid on November 23. _____

9. Check 307 for $1,283.35 was paid on November 16. _____

Lesson 35 _____

Setting

Reading a Literature Selection _____

▶ **Background Information**

In "The Lifejacket," you will read about a girl's "near miss," or brush with death. People who have been through such an experience often have vivid memories of the event, even if it lasted only a few seconds.

▶ **Skill Focus**

Setting is the place and time of the events in a story. Events can happen in any place at any time. The setting of a story can be as ordinary as a school or as dramatic as a battlefield. The time can be now, the distant past, or many years from now.

Setting often contributes to a story's mood, or atmosphere. An author creates mood by using details, such as vivid phrases and images, to describe the setting. The mood of a story can be quiet, merry, or dangerous, and it can change as the plot develops.

Read the following paragraph. Look for details of setting that help build a mood of oncoming danger.

> No air moved under the swollen gray sky. The sounds on the prairie were unnaturally stilled. A bird darted on silent wings across the driveway and headed for cover in a bush by the side door. A woman, mopping the heat from her neck with a towel, came to the door. Her eyes searched the dark horizon. Would a twister come?

Phrases like _swollen gray sky, unnaturally stilled,_ and _dark horizon_ all contribute to the story's mood. The details help create a mood of anxious waiting for something dangerous.

The following questions will help you see how setting creates mood.

1. Where and when do the story's events take place?
2. What kind of mood does the author create?
3. What details of setting contribute to the mood?
4. Does the mood change?

▶ **Word Clues**

Read the sentences below. Look for context clues that explain the underlined word.

> Instead of shouting back, though, I looked down and decided to tighten the drawstring of my nylon slipover parka. I pulled it <u>taut</u> at the bottom and knotted it.

The word _taut_ is explained in the sentence that comes before it. The details help you understand that _taut_ means "pulled tight."

Use **detail** context clues to find the meaning of the three underlined words in the selection.

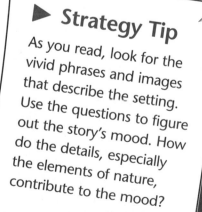

▶ **Strategy Tip**

As you read, look for the vivid phrases and images that describe the setting. Use the questions to figure out the story's mood. How do the details, especially the elements of nature, contribute to the mood?

The Lifejacket

Looming ahead of me was a small island, not much more than a rocky outcropping, several hundred yards offshore. It was an isolated island, difficult to get to, You couldn't land a boat on it. The only way to approach it was by crossing the causeway, a rocky path between it and the tip of Mosquito Head.

The wind whistled in gusts, plucking and shoving at me as I picked my way along the causeway's jagged rocks. If I had been alone, I probably would have felt great. I like that kind of weather. Thick clouds rumbled in from the ocean's horizon. The sharp wind and stinging spray were cold and raw. The coming storm made the ocean leap and churn. I love that kind of day.

Earlier, I had been bored. The sky had been a carnival blue, with cotton candy clouds floating in it. It had been almost too perfect. Then Sandy came by and tried to prod me into action. "Maisie—let's go down to the beach and look for shells." I wasn't interested.

"Then let's walk over to the island off Mosquito Head. Aren't you supposed to make a count of nesting sea birds for your science project?" she asked. Sandy had a point.

The island wasn't much to look at, I knew. It was just a mounded tumble of gray boulders and a few weeds. You'd never plan a picnic there. But it was a perfect spot for sea birds to build their nests. If I were looking for a variety of nesting sea birds to report on—and I was—that was the place to look.

So I laced on my thick-soled climbing boots, grabbed my slick parka, and started off with Sandy. I soon found myself relishing the salt spray on my face as I clambered over the rocks at a leisurely pace.

The wind caught my hair, and I felt it whip around my face. I turned into the wind, so that the jet-black strands blew off my face and streamed behind me. Just then, a voice broke into my daydream, calling, "Hey, hurry up, Maisie! Come on!"

It's Mei Ling, not Maisie, I thought. I hate my nickname. It makes me think of a ringleted, blonde porcelain doll, instead of me—Mei Ling, with my shiny, straight black hair and dark eyes that people said were beautiful. Sandy could really get on my nerves. Besides, right now my mind was set on a thoughtful walk to check the nesting birds, not on a cross-country dash!

Instead of shouting back, I looked down and decided to tighten the drawstring of my nylon slipover parka. I pulled it taut at the bottom and knotted it. It gave me a reason for staying where I was for a moment. As things turned out, it saved my life.

"What's the rush?" I said when I was close enough for Sandy to hear me over the moaning of the wind.

"I thought you had to check the island for your science project," Sandy said. "Let's keep together. In case you slip, I can help you."

"I can help myself."

Sandy was only two years older, but somehow she felt responsible for me.

"Look," she said, "the tide's starting in. A storm's blowing up, and pretty soon the waves will be rolling in over the causeway. It wouldn't be smart to get stuck on the island." She held up her fingers and counted off her points one by one, as if she were explaining something to a child. I'm fifteen, I thought. I'm not a child.

Sandy didn't notice my glare. She spun around and started towards the island. "Come on! Hurry!"

Between us and the mainland, the waves thundered against the causeway. Sandy was already way ahead of me. Now I'm supposed to run along and catch up, I thought angrily. Catching up was the last thing on my mind as I crossed the slippery rocks. Suddenly a tremendous wave spilled over me, knocking me off the causeway and dragging me down.

The icy wave shocked me like a jolt of electricity. I gasped, expecting to hit the rocks below. The next thing I knew, I was plunging down through murky, green water, with a distant, peaceful rumbling filling my ears.

The light over our dining room table has a special switch that my father wired up and that makes the light grow brighter or dimmer. As I moved through the icy water, the light faded. I thought of the way Mother darkens the dining room after supper, as if the room was a stage and the play had ended.

As the light faded, a huge fist seemed to be pressing on my chest. I wanted to breathe, and I couldn't. I kicked my feet and struggled toward the surface, the dim light above me. At last I bobbed up in the rolling surf about a hundred feet from the island—gagging, choking, and gasping for breath. A strong current was sweeping me out to sea, and my heavy, water-soaked climbing boots kept pulling me toward the bottom. I was terrified.

I tried to think, but my mind sputtered like a live wire. My heart thudded, and my whole body went into a <u>spasm,</u> like a bared nerve. The weight of my boots made it difficult to keep kicking, and I was too numb to untie them. "Help," I cried, "I don't want to die!" My eyes stung. I thought, how silly and wasteful to spill salty tears into the <u>briny</u> ocean.

A gull appeared above a storm-tossed wave. Its eyes swept over me and dismissed me from its search. It vanished beyond another foaming crest. I felt terribly alone.

Suddenly, I realized that I was floating on my back. An air bubble was trapped inside my nylon parka—a miracle was keeping me afloat.

The seconds passed, each one an eternity. When the churning swells lifted me skyward, I tried to catch sight of land. I did once, just long enough to see that I was being pulled farther out to sea. I didn't see Sandy. I hoped the wave hadn't knocked her into the water, too. I hoped she'd been too fast for it.

With each minute, the precious air bubble grew smaller. Was I still kicking my legs? I thought so, but my whole body was numb from the cold. I swallowed more and more of the salty, <u>frigid</u> water.

Another gull streaked across my sight, low on the water, like an arrow. I started to cry again. I wanted to finish my research paper, talk with Mother, kid Father—a million things. I wondered: If I drowned, would anyone ever find my body? I'd never felt so alone, so helpless, so abandoned. I think at that point I started to give up. I let my mind drift off to avoid thinking all those terrible thoughts. I guess I closed my eyes.

Something powerful clamped around my body. Sharks! I opened my eyes, started to scream, and looked straight up at the strangest of all birds, a helicopter. It hovered fifty feet above me, with a line dangling down to the rolling sea. The Coast Guard rescuer had an arm around my chest and bobbed next to me

> "I wondered: if I drowned, would anyone ever find my body? I'd never felt so alone, so helpless, so abandoned."

like a cork. In a minute or two, I was buckled into a harness. He signaled, and the rope pulled taut. Slowly, it lifted me from my watery grave—plucked me from the sea that had plucked me from the rocks.

Not until the next day did I learn that Sandy was also rescued by the Coast Guard. Fortunately, the Coast Guard, patrolling the coast for boaters in distress, had seen Sandy signaling for help. Sandy told them that I had been swept into the sea.

It was a while before I got out again to the island off Mosquito Head to count nesting sea birds. Before I went, I checked the weather bureau to be sure that there were no storms in the day's forecast. Also, I asked Sandy to go with me. I had learned my lesson well.

RECALLING FACTS

1. From what point of view—first person or third person—is this story written? Who is the narrator?

_____

_____

_____

2. Sequence the following events in the order in which they took place.

_____ Mei Ling, knocked over by a tremendous wave, plunges down through murky, green water.

_____ Mei Ling and Sandy go to the island off Mosquito Head.

_____ Mei Ling floats on her back.

_____ Mei Ling is rescued by a Coast Guard helicopter.

_____ Mei Ling's whole body grows numb from the cold.

3. a. With what does Mei Ling come into conflict?

_____

_____

b. How is Mei Ling's conflict resolved?

_____

_____

4. Answer each question by writing *yes* or *no* on the line provided.

a. Is a spasm a calm, regular movement?

_____

b. Is lake water usually briny? _____

c. Is frigid water cold enough to chill someone? _____

1. In what season of the year does the story take place? Give two or three details from the story to support your answer.

_____

_____

_____

2. **a.** Describe Mei Ling's personality.

_____

_____

_____

   b. Why do you think Mei Ling thinks about her family as she is pulled underwater?

_____

_____

_____

3. Why does Mei Ling resent Sandy's helping her?

_____

_____

_____

4. Why does Mei Ling gag and choke when she bobs to the surface?

_____

5. How does pulling a drawstring taut save Mei Ling's life?

_____

_____

_____

6. Mei Ling learns that it was foolish to go out to the island when a storm is approaching. What else does she learn?

_____

_____

_____

7. Think about the point of view from which this story is told. Why is it a good point of view for this story?

_____

_____

_____

_____

SKILL FOCUS

Details of setting help to create a story's mood. Answer the following questions on the lines provided.

1. When you first meet Mei Ling, the main character, she and a friend are on their way to a small island, several hundred yards offshore. As the girls clambered over the rocks at a leisurely pace, looking for nesting sea birds, "the wind whistled in gusts" and "thick clouds rumbled in from the ocean's horizon."

   a. What is the setting in this part of the story?

_____

   b. What is the mood, or atmosphere, in this part of the story?

_____

2. In the list below, circle the letter next to each detail of setting that contributes to the mood at the beginning of the story.
   a. The isolated island is a perfect spot to search for nesting sea birds.
   b. Mei Ling picks her way along the jagged rocks.
   c. Earlier in the day, Mei Ling had been bored.
   d. The stinging spray is cold and sharp.
   e. The wind whips around Mei Ling's face.

3. What suddenly happens to change the setting and the mood of the story?

   _____

   _____

   _____

   _____

4. Mei Ling suddenly finds herself "plunging down through murky, green water," feeling as if a huge fist pressed against her chest. Swept out to sea by a strong current, she feels her heart begin to thud, and her body goes into a spasm. She can't breathe. She bobs up and down—gagging, choking, and gasping for air.
   a. What is the setting in this part of the story?

   _____

   b. What kind of mood has the author created in describing this incident?

   _____

   _____

5. In the list below, circle the letter next to each detail of setting that contributes to the story's changed mood.
   a. Mei Ling is pulled under by her heavy, water-soaked climbing boots.
   b. The icy, churning swell lifts Mei Ling skyward.
   c. The gull vanishes beyond another foaming crest.
   d. The sky had been a carnival blue, with cotton candy clouds floating in it.
   e. With each minute, the precious air bubble grows smaller.

6. a. How does the storm influence the story's setting?

   _____

   _____

   _____

   b. What happens to the mood when the setting changes?

   _____

   _____

   _____

▶ Real Life Connections What lesson do you think Sandy learns?

Reading a Map

Reading a Social Studies Selection

▶ **Background Information**

Throughout the history of humankind, there have been many conquerors. Ghengis Khan spent his entire life conquering neighboring peoples and expanding the Mongolian Empire. Many Roman Emperors did the same for the Roman empire—so much so that at one time they ruled modern-day Great Britain.

Both the Mongolian and Roman Empires had their rise and fall in the distant past. If we want to examine conquerors, there is no need to go back that far.

In 1812, Napoleon Bonaparte invaded Russia in a war of conquest. More than a century later, Adolf Hitler launched a massive military campaign against the Soviet Union. The following selection describes the Russian campaigns of both Napoleon and Hitler.

▶ **Skill Focus**

A map provides a picture of a geographical area. In addition to showing the geography of an area, a map can give other important information. For example, a map can show the movement of troops in time of war. Studying troop movements on a map gives you a sense of an army's sweep from battle to battle. A map can indicate the path of an army's attack on a country or city and might also show the direction of its retreat.

A map often uses color and symbols to represent information. For example, a map of troop movements generally uses arrows to show the direction of the army's advance or retreat. Such a map often accompanies the description of a military campaign. Together, the map and the description give the reader a clear picture of an army's route.

The following questions will help you trace an army's route on a map. Be sure to read the captions and labels.

1. What geographical area does the map picture?
2. What event does the map depict?
3. Whose movements does the map trace?
4. What symbols indicate the direction of these movements?
5. What geographical features (rivers, regions) do the troop movements cross?
6. What does the map tell about the success or failure of the military campaign?

▶ **Word Clues**

Read the sentence below. Look for context clues that explain the underlined word.

But he was not prepared for the devastating enemy that would meet him in Moscow—the raw, bitter, bleak Russian winter.

If you do not know the meaning of the word *bleak,* the words *raw* and *bitter* can help you. The word *bleak* is grouped with other adjectives that also describe winter, so you can figure out that *bleak* means "piercing, cold, and cutting."

Use **grouping** clues to find the meaning of the three underlined words in the selection.

▶ **Strategy Tip**

The maps in the selection show the route of Napoleon's army in its advance to and retreat from Moscow and the movements of Hitler's army in the Soviet Union. As you read, trace these troop movements on the maps.

The Russian Winter

In 1812, Napoleon Bonaparte, Emperor of the French, led his Grand Army into Russia. He was prepared for the fierce resistance of the Russian people defending their homeland. He was prepared for the long march across Russian soil to Moscow, the capital city. But he was not prepared for the devastating enemy that met him in Moscow—the raw, bitter, bleak Russian winter.

In 1941, Adolf Hitler, leader of Nazi Germany, launched an attack against the Soviet Union, as Russia then was called. Hitler's military might was unequaled. His war machine had mowed down resistance in most of Europe. Hitler expected a short campaign but, like Napoleon before him, was taught a painful lesson. The Russian winter again came to the aid of the Soviet soldiers.

Napoleon's Grand Army

In 1804, Napoleon Bonaparte crowned himself Emperor of the French. The son of a minor noble family, Napoleon had gained power in France during the years of its bloody Revolution. From 1807 to 1812, he established an empire that stretched from the Atlantic Ocean to the borders of Russia.

Napoleon was a military genius who created his empire through wars of conquest. In 1812, however, Napoleon undertook a campaign that was to turn the tide of his fortunes.

For several years, Napoleon had kept an uneasy truce with Alexander I of Russia. Yet Alexander would not totally submit to the power-hungry Napoleon. In the spring of 1812, Napoleon decided to teach the Russians a lesson. He assembled an army of six hundred thousand men on the borders of Russia. The soldiers, recruited from twenty different nations in Napoleon's empire, were well trained, underline{efficient}, and well equipped. This military force was called the Grand Army. Napoleon, confident of a quick victory, predicted the conquest of Russia in five weeks.

The French Offensive

In the spring of 1812, Napoleon's army crossed the Neman River into Russia. The quick, decisive victory that Napoleon expected never happened. To his surprise, the Russians refused to stand and fight. Instead, they retreated eastward, burning their crops and homes as they went. The Grand Army followed, but its advance march soon became bogged down by slow-moving supply lines.

In August, the French and Russian armies engaged at Smolensk, in a battle that left over ten thousand dead on each side. Yet, the Russians were again able to retreat farther into Russian territory. Napoleon had won no decisive victory. He was now faced with a crucial decision. Should he continue to pursue

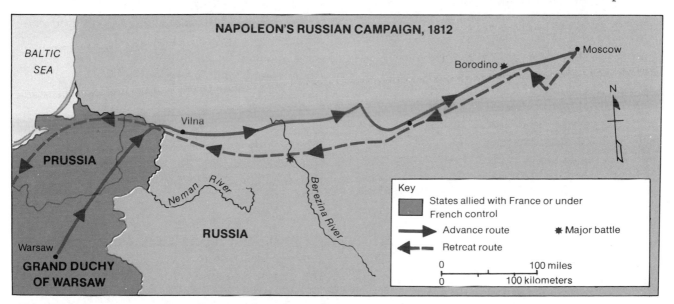

Napoleon's Russian campaign was doomed to failure because of the bitter Russian winter. In October 1812, Napoleon ordered the Grand Army to retreat from Moscow.

the Russian army? Or should he keep his army in Smolensk for the approaching winter?

Napoleon took the gamble of pressing on to Moscow, 280 miles (448 kilometers) away. On September 7, 1812, the French and Russian armies met in fierce battle at Borodino, 70 miles (112 kilometers) west of Moscow. By nightfall, thirty thousand French and forty-four thousand Russians lay dead, wounded, or maimed on the battlefield.

Again, the Russian army retreated to safety. Napoleon had a clear path to Moscow, but the occupation of the city became an empty victory. The Russians fled their capital. Soon after the French arrived, a raging fire destroyed two–thirds of the city. Napoleon offered a truce to Alexander I, but the Russian czar knew he could bide his time: "We shall let the Russian winter fight the war for us."

Napoleon soon realized he could not feed, clothe, and quarter his army in Moscow during the winter. In October 1812, he ordered his Grand Army to retreat from Moscow.

Winter Defeats Napoleon

✗ The French retreat turned into a nightmare. From fields and forests, the Russians launched hit–and–run attacks on the French. A short distance from Moscow, the temperature had already dropped to 25 degrees Fahrenheit (minus 4 degrees Celsius). On November 3, the winter's first snow came. Exhausted horses fell dead in their tracks. Cannons became stuck in the snow. Equipment had to be burned for fuel. Soldiers took ill and froze to death. The French soldiers dragged on, leaving the dead along every mile.

✔ At Smolensk, the French had hoped to establish winter quarters, but now Napoleon was in a race against time. The Russian army was gathering its strength. The French had to flee Russia to avoid certain defeat. At the Berezina (ber ə ZEE nə) River, the Russians nearly trapped the retreating French by burning the bridges over the swollen river. But Napoleon, by a stroke of luck, was able to build two new bridges. Thousands of French soldiers escaped, but at the cost of fifty thousand dead. Once across the Berezina, the tattered survivors limped toward Vilna.

On December 5, Napoleon left his soldiers to return to Paris. Of the six hundred thousand soldiers he had led into Russia, less than one hundred thousand came back.

The weakened French army continued its retreat westward across Europe. Soon, Britain, Austria, Russia, and Prussia formed a powerful alliance and attacked these stragglers. In March 1814, Paris was captured. Napoleon abdicated and went into exile. The Napoleonic empire was at an end.

Hitler's Operation Barbarossa

By early 1941, Adolf Hitler, leader of Nazi Germany, had seized control of most of Europe. To the east of Hitler's German empire was the Soviet Union. On June 22, 1941, without a declaration of war, Hitler began an invasion of the Soviet Union that was the largest military land campaign in history. The time had come, Hitler believed, to seize the rich farmlands and oil fields in the western part of the Soviet Union. Confident of a quick victory over the Soviet Union, Hitler expected the campaign to last no longer than three months. He planned to use the **blitzkreig** (blits KREEG), or "lightning war," tactics that had defeated the rest of Europe.

Hitler called the invasion Operation Barbarossa (bar bə RAHS ə). Frederick Barbarossa was the medieval German king who became Holy Roman Emperor and won great victories in the East. Over three million German soldiers massed on a 1,800-mile (2,880-kilometer) front to attack the Soviet Union and destroy the Red Army. The invasion had three broad thrusts: against Leningrad and Moscow and through the Ukraine.

Caught off guard by the invasion, Soviet leader Joseph Stalin instructed the Russian people to "scorch the earth" in front of the German invaders. Farms and factories were burned, destroyed, or rendered useless. During the first ten weeks of the invasion, the Germans pushed the front eastward, and the Russians suffered more than a million casualties.

The German Offensive

In the north, the Germans closed in on Leningrad. Despite great suffering, however, the people of Leningrad refused to surrender. As the battle of Leningrad dragged on into winter, the city's plight became desperate. The people of the city were trapped—surrounded on three sides by German soldiers. As food ran out, people died from malnutrition and disease. By the middle of the winter of 1941–1942, nearly four thousand people starved to death every day. Close to one million people died as a result of the siege.

In the center of Russia, Hitler's goal was the capture of Moscow. Because the Germans had anticipated a quick victory, they had made no plans for winter supplies. October arrived with heavy rains. "General Mud" slowed down the movement of the Germans' lightning attack. In charge of the defense of Moscow was Marshal Georgi Zhukov, who successfully used attack-and-retreat tactics against the Germans, just as the Russians had against Napoleon. Moscow would never be taken.

The Harshest Winter in Years

As Hitler's armies drew closer and closer to Moscow, an early, severe winter settled over the Soviet Union. In fact, the winter of 1941–42 was the harshest winter in years. Temperatures dropped to minus 65 degrees Fahrenheit (minus 48 degrees Celsius). Heavy snows fell. The German soldiers, completely unprepared for the Russian winter, froze in their light summer uniforms. The German tanks lay buried in the heavy snowbanks. The Russian winter brought the German offensive to a halt.

The Offensive Renewed

By the summer of 1942, Hitler had launched two new offensives. In the south, the Germans captured Sevastopol. With the fall of this city, the Germans had control of the Black Sea and were within striking distance of the Russian oil fields. Hitler then pushed east to Stalingrad, a great industrial city that stretched for 30 miles (48 kilometers) along the Volga River. Despite great suffering, Soviet defenders refused to give up Stalingrad.

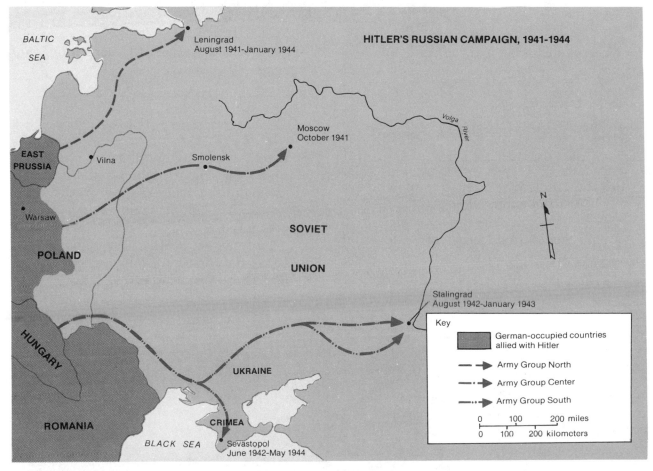

The five-month battle of Stalingrad, one of the most important battles of history, was a turning point in World War II. This German defeat ended Hitler's advance into the Soviet Union. After this victory, the Russian army advanced across eastern Europe. Berlin fell on May 2, 1945; five days later, Germany surrendered.

In November 1942, the Russians launched a counterattack. With little or no shelter from the winter cold in and around Stalingrad, German troops were further weakened by a lack of food and supplies. Not until January 1943 did the Germans give up their siege. Of the three hundred thousand Germans attacking Stalingrad, only ninety thousand starving soldiers were left. The loss of the battle for Stalingrad finally turned the tide against Hitler. The German victories were over, thanks in part to the Russian winter.

The German Retreat

During 1943 and 1944, the Soviet armies pushed the German front back toward the west. In the north, the Red Army broke the three-year siege of Leningrad with a surprise attack on January 15, 1944. Within two weeks, the heroic survivors of Leningrad saw their invaders depart. By March 1944, the Ukraine farming region was again in Soviet hands. On May 9, 1944, Sevastopol was liberated from the Germans. The Russians were now heading for Berlin.

For Hitler, the invasion of the Soviet Union had turned into a military disaster. For the Russian people, it brought unspeakable suffering. The total Soviet dead in World War II reached almost 23 million.

Russia's Icy Defender

The elements of nature must be reckoned with in any military campaign. Napoleon and Hitler both underestimated the severity of the Russian winter. Snow, ice, and freezing temperatures took their toll on both invading armies. For the Russian people, the winter was an icy defender.

RECALLING FACTS

1. Write two causes for the effect below.

   Cause ———————————————

   ——————————————————

   Cause ———————————————

   ——————————————————

   Effect Napoleon's occupation of Moscow was an empty victory.

2. What name did Hitler give to his invasion of the Soviet Union? Explain.

   ——————————————————

   ——————————————————

   ——————————————————

   ——————————————————

3. What tactics did the Russian army use when both Napoleon and Hitler first invaded Russian soil?

   ——————————————————

   ——————————————————

   ——————————————————

4. What was the name of Hitler's campaign against Russia?

   ——————————————————

   ——————————————————

5. Reread the paragraph that has an X next to it. Underline the sentence that states the main idea. Then circle at least three details that support the main idea of the paragraph.

6. Circle the correct meaning of the underlined word in each sentence.

   a. The driver of the car was <u>maimed</u> in the car accident.

      crippled   **responsible**

   b. The relay team had developed an <u>efficient</u> way of working together.

      effective   **wasteful**

   c. The commander has not yet decided where to <u>quarter</u> the new troops.

      punish   **house**

1. Write the cause for the following effect.

   Cause _____

   _____

   Effect Hitler and Napoleon both failed to consider the Russian winter as an important factor in their campaigns.

2. Why was the Russian winter harder on the invading armies than on the Russian army?

   _____

   _____

3. Who was probably responsible for setting the fire that destroyed two-thirds of Moscow soon after Napoleon occupied the city?

   _____

4. How did the geography of the Soviet Union make Hitler's blitzkreig attack less successful there than it had been in the rest of Europe?

   _____

5. What might have happened if there had been a late, mild winter in Russia in 1941?

   _____

   _____

6. How did the Russian campaigns of both Hitler and Napoleon contribute to the eventual defeat of their entire empires?

   _____

   _____

7. Reread the paragraph with a check mark next to it. Write a sentence stating its main idea.

   _____

SKILL FOCUS

Use the maps on pages 129 and 131 to answer the following questions.

1. What geographical area does the map picture?

   a. What area of the world is pictured on the first map? _____

   b. What area of the world is pictured on the second map? _____

2. What time period does the map depict?

   a. What is the time period of the first map? _____

   b. The second map? _____

3. Whose movements does the map trace?

a. What army's route is traced on the first map? _____

b. What army's route is traced on the second map? _____

4. What symbols indicate the direction of these movements?

a. Draw the symbol that shows Napoleon's advance to Moscow. _____

b. Draw the symbol that shows Napoleon's retreat from Moscow. _____

c. Draw the three symbols that show Hitler's offensives in the Soviet Union.

_____

5. What geographical features do the troop movements cross?

a. From where did Napoleon begin his invasion of Russia? _____

b. In what city did Napoleon on his advance engage in battle with the Russians?

_____

c. Approximately how far was Napoleon in his retreat out of Russia when he was almost

captured at the Berezina River? _____

d. Compare the route of Napoleon's advance and retreat. _____

_____

e. What city was the goal of Hitler's northern attack? _____

f. In which direction does Stalingrad lie from Moscow? _____

g. What region did the Germans have to cross to get to Stalingrad? _____

h. What is the most southern city that Hitler captured? _____

In what region is it located? _____

6. What does the map tell about the success or failure of the military campaign?

a. Which campaign was more ambitious in its attack? Explain.

_____

_____

b. Which campaign was fought for the longest time? Explain.

_____

_____

_____

c. Which campaign seems to have been more nearly victorious? Explain.

_____

_____

▶ **Real Life Connections** Find an updated map of Russia and the surrounding
countries. How have the countries' boundaries changed?

Cause and Effect

Reading a Science Selection

▶ Background Information

Almost everyone is interested in the weather. People rely heavily on daily weather forecasts. Weather forecasts depend on observations from weather stations throughout the world. The information is transmitted to forecast centers. Forecasters than analyze the information and predict what the weather will be like in their area.

Benjamin Franklin was one of the first people to realize that storms moved in a regular pattern. However, in the late 1700s, the storms moved faster than the mail could transmit the information. After the telegraph was perfected in the 1840s, information about weather systems could be sent at a faster rate. Today weather stations use high-tech equipment that not only records weather systems but also detects the intensity of the system.

In "Causes of Changing Weather," you will read about what causes several weather systems, as well as learn numerous important weather terms.

▶ Skill Focus

The **cause** of an event or condition is the reason it happens. The **effect** is the result of the cause. For example, cold weather results in higher heating bills. The cause is cold weather, and the effect is higher heating bills.

Causes and effects are usually stated directly. Sometimes, however, you have to infer, or figure out, a cause or an effect.

Read the following paragraph.

The weather report said that the hurricane would reach our beach community by 7:00 P.M., with winds up to 90 miles per hour before midnight. We made the necessary preparations. Given that it was the height of the tourist season, police warned that traffic would be heavier than usual on the small road leading to the highway.

If you think of the coming hurricane as a cause, you can infer the following effect: People will probably have to evacuate before the hurricane hits. To arrive at cause and effect inferences, you can use clues in the paragraph, along with what you know about the subject being discussed. In this example, you know that hurricanes can be dangerous and that people are often required to evacuate an area about to be hit.

▶ Word Clues

Read the sentence below. Look for context clues that explain the underlined word.

As light, warm air ascends, or rises, cooler air moves in to take its place, and air currents form.

If you do not know the meaning of the word *ascends,* the phrase *or rises* can help you. The phrase *or rises* is an appositive phrase. An appositive phrase explains a word coming before it and is set off from the word by commas or dashes.

Use **appositive phrases** to find the meaning of the three underlined words in the selection.

▶ Strategy Tip

The selection explains the causes and effects of weather systems. Every system, including fronts, cyclones, and anticyclones, has specific causes. Use the diagrams to help you understand the cause and effect patterns.

Causes of Changing Weather

To understand weather patterns, think of the blanket of air surrounding the earth as a liquid that can flow from place to place. Air does not have exactly the same characteristics everywhere on the globe. The air is cold in some places and hot in others. In some places, the air contains a lot of water vapor and is humid, while elsewhere it contains little water vapor and is dry.

A large body of air with certain characteristics, such as warmth and humidity, is known as an **air mass.** The amount of moisture in an air mass depends on where it develops, so air masses are classified according to where they are formed. Some air masses are formed above continents, and others are formed over oceans. Air masses usually cover thousands of square kilometers.

At any given time, there are several air masses over the United States, and their movement is a major contributor to our changing weather. The air masses over the United States also change their characteristics as they move from place to place. The four major air masses that affect the weather on the North American continent are shown in Figure 1.

Fronts

Where two air masses with different characteristics meet, a boundary, or **front,** forms, often causing unsettled weather. Where a mass of warm air meets and rides over a mass of cold air, a **warm front** is created, and showers usually occur. Where a mass of cold air meets and slides under warm air, a **cold front** forms, and violent storms may occur. In this case, the cold air pushes the warm air upward. If a cold front overtakes a warm front, the warm air is pushed up, forming a boundary called an **occluded** (ə KLOOD id) **front.** The occluded front occurs where the coldest air in the cold front meets cool air under the warm front. This type of front usually causes steady rain. Look at Figure 2.

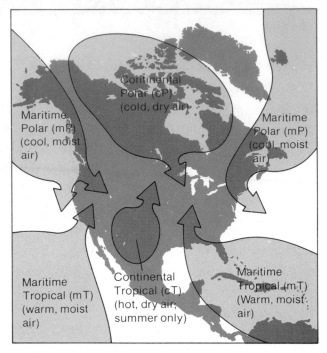

Figure 1. This diagram shows the air masses that affect weather in North America.

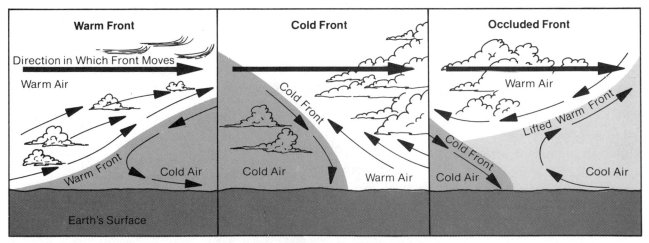

Figure 2. A front forms when two air masses with different characteristics meet.

If a warm air mass meets a cold air mass and neither of them moves, the resulting front is called a **stationary front.** This condition often results in rainfall throughout the area of the front.

Cyclones and Anticyclones

Another factor affecting weather is air pressure. Warm air is lighter than cold air and, as a result, has lower pressure than cold air. As light, warm air ascends, or rises, cooler air moves in to take its place, and air currents form. These wind currents spiral, or circle, around and into the centers of cyclones, where warm air is rising, forming what is called a **low** or a **cyclone.**

An area with cold, dry air has high pressure, and it is called a **high** or an **anticyclone.** Wind currents in a high pressure area descend, or fall, toward the earth and outward from the center of the anticyclone area. In North America, the wind currents in cyclones spiral in a counterclockwise direction, and those in anticyclones spiral in a clockwise direction.

Storms

Fronts and cyclones can result in severe weather called **storms.** The meeting of a warm and a cold front can result in a storm with heavy rain, lightning, and thunder. If a cold front meets a warm front in winter, there may be a heavy snowfall. If the temperature is less than minus 7 degress Celsius and the wind speed is above 56 kilometers per hour, a blizzard occurs.

When very strong cyclones develop over tropical oceans, they give rise to **hurricanes.** As the warm, moist air rises rapidly, cooler air moves in and the air begins to spin. Air pressure in the center drops, more cool air is drawn in, and the air spins even faster. This spinning system of rising air forms a cylinder of clouds, rain, and strong winds that may reach speeds of 120 to 130 kilometers per hour. At the center of a hurricane is an area of calm air called the eye. Look at Figure 3. As hurricanes move from the ocean onto land, they lose their source of warm, moist air, and their force diminishes, or decreases.

Tornadoes are among the most violent storms on earth. A tornado is a whirling, funnel-shaped cloud with wind speeds of over 350 kilometers per hour. These storms are most common during the summer in the states of the Great Plains. There, cool, dry air from the west meets warm, moist air from the Gulf of Mexico.

Tornadoes form high above the ground, and most of them stay in the sky. However, when a tornado touches down on the earth's surface, it leaves a path of destruction that

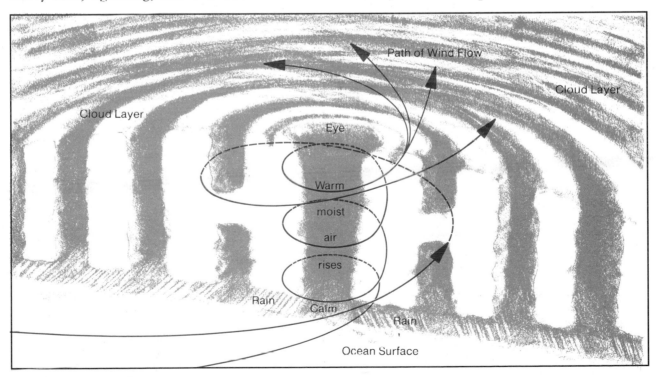

Figure 3. Hurricanes form over warm oceans.

averages about 6 kilometers long. The tornado wreaks this destruction in only a few minutes.

Weather Prediction

A major goal of weather science is to predict the weather, both for next week and for next year. Meteorologists, or scientists who study weather, collect data on temperature, humidity, wind speed, wind direction, and air pressure. Their sources of information are weather stations all over the world, weather balloons high in the atmosphere, and weather satellites in space. Today scientists use computers to analyze data and make predictions.

From their data, scientists construct weather maps, such as those that you see in newspapers and on television weather reports. The maps show highs (anticyclones), lows (cyclones), and fronts, as well as the direction in which the weather systems are moving. The maps are the basis for weather predictions. For example, fronts are associated with changing weather. Determining how fast a front is moving toward an area lets a weather forecaster predict when that area will be affected by the front.

Knowing future weather conditions is often very important. Farmers need to know about weather conditions in order to decide when to plant and harvest their crops. Many outdoor sports functions depend on clear weather. Airports use weather forecasts in scheduling takeoffs and landings, as well as in planning flight paths. Accurate weather forecasts also alert people to severe weather conditions that could endanger their lives or property.

RECALLING FACTS

1. What is a large body of air called?

2. What is a front?

3. What is an occluded front?

4. What is a cyclone?

5. What is an anticyclone?

6. In North America, does the air in an anticyclone move clockwise or counterclockwise?

7. Under what conditions does a blizzard occur?

8. What must happen for a hurricane to form?

9. Where are tornadoes most common in the United States?

_____

_____

10. Name four weather features that forecasters collect data on to make weather predictions.

_____

_____

_____

11. What are the sources of information for weather prediction?

_____

_____

12. Which air masses affect the weather on the west coast of the United States?

_____

_____

13. Complete each statement with one of the words below. Write the words on the lines provided.

    spiral   descend   diminishes

    a. An early frost _____ the orange crop.

    b. The elevator will _____ from the top floor.

    c. The snake can _____ around the tree.

INTERPRETING FACTS

1. Which of the three types of fronts would probably cause the longest period of rainy weather?
   a. cold
   b. warm
   c. stationary

2. If air pressure dropped steadily, you could expect the weather to
   a. become warmer.
   b. become cooler.
   c. remain the same.

SKILL FOCUS

A. Write the effect for each of the following causes.

1. **Cause** Two air masses with different characteristics meet.

   Effect _____

2. **Cause** A body of air is warmed.

   Effect _____

3. **Cause** A body of air is cooled.

   Effect _____

4. Cause A cold front meets a warm front in winter.

Effect _____

5. Cause A warm front meets a cold front in summer.

Effect _____

B. Write the cause for each of the following effects.

1. Cause _____

Effect A warm front forms, and showers usually occur.

2. Cause _____

Effect A cold front forms, and violent storms may occur.

3. Cause _____

Effect A stationary front forms, and rain may occur.

4. Cause _____

Effect A hurricane may occur.

C. Sometimes causes or effects are not stated in a selection. They have to be figured out, or inferred. For each cause given below, infer an effect and write it on the line provided. For each effect given, infer a cause and write it on the line provided.

1. Cause _____

Effect Weather forecasting is more accurate now than it was twenty years ago.

2. Cause _____

Effect A warm air mass contains a great deal of water vapor.

3. Cause _____

Effect Cold air pushes up warm air.

4. Cause As hurricanes move away from water, they lose their power.

Effect _____

▶ **Real Life Connections** Give an example of the best and the worst weather in your geographic area.

Graphs

Reading a Mathematics Selection

▶ Background Information

You come into contact with many different kinds of graphs in many different places almost every day. People of all walks of life and in all kinds of occupations use graphs because they convey information in a way that is easy to read and understand.

Conduct an experiment for one day. Open today's newspaper and count all the graphs that you find. Then do the same with a news magazine that you have at home or in your classroom. Finally, watch the news on television and count how many times you see a graph. When you have completed these three tasks, count the total number of graphs that you have seen. This number will probably be higher than you expected it to be.

Newspapers, news magazines, and the news on television often use graphs to present certain kinds of information. Without graphs, it would often take much longer to convey certain information. For this reason, graphs are an important mathematical tool.

Reading a graph is an important skill to learn. Read the title of the graph and the graph's labels and key first. They will help you understand what information is covered in the graph. When reading some graphs, it might be necessary for you to estimate the heights of bars or the steepness of lines. A straightedge ruler can be useful in reading bar or line graphs.

In the following selection, you will learn how to read bar graphs, circle graphs, and line graphs.

▶ Skill Focus

Graphs are used to show **data,** or information, that involve numbers in a form that is easy to read. The original numbers on which the graph is based may have been a detailed list, but a list does not show the relationships among the numbers. A graph makes these relationships more visible.

Different kinds of graphs are used for different purposes. **Bar graphs** are used to compare numbers that show information about the same thing at two or more different times, or about two or more different things at the same time. **Circle graphs** are used to compare the parts of a whole. Circle graphs often use percents. **Line graphs** are generally used to show how one or more kinds of information change over time.

To read a graph, you need to look at the words as well as the details. Important information is shown in the labels and title of the graph. Many graphs have **keys** that tell the meaning of different shadings, different colors, or different types of lines. Finally, to get the full meaning from a graph, you should read the text that comes before or after it.

▶ Word Clues

When reading this selection, be sure that you understand the special definitions of the following words: *data, axis, vertical, horizontal, sector.*

▶ Strategy Tip

When a numbered axis is not close to a bar or point on a graph, use a ruler to get an accurate reading. If a circle graph is labeled with percents, use them to find small differences that are not clear from just looking at the graph.

Reading Graphs

The information shown in a graph is called **data. Double bar graphs** compare two sets of data in the same graph. The double bar graph on this page compares the monthly precipitation in Rome, the capital of Italy, with the precipitation in Moscow, the capital of Russia. Precipitation is rain, snow, sleet, or hail.

First, read the title of the graph. The title tells you the kind of data that is in the graph. The title of this graph is *Average Monthly Precipitation in Rome and Moscow.*

Because this is a double bar graph, it has two sets of bars. One set represents the precipitation in Rome, and the other represents the precipitation in Moscow. You can learn what the bars stand for by looking at the **key.**

To find out the meaning of the data in the graph, read the labels on the **axes** (AK seez). The **vertical axis** is labeled *cm*. This label means that the precipitation is given in centimeters. The marks and numbers on the vertical axis show the number of centimeters. The **horizontal axis** has abbreviations for the names of the months.

By combining the information from the two axes with the information from the key, you can get information from the graph. For example, the amount of precipitation in Rome is about 7 centimeters in January. You can compare that with about 5 centimeters of precipitation in Moscow for the same month. (Most of the precipitation in Moscow in January is snow, and it is measured by melting it.)

Even without looking at the numbers on the vertical axis, you can learn a great deal from the shape of the graph. For example, you can see that most of the precipitation in Rome occurs in the autumn and winter, but most of the precipitation in Moscow occurs in the spring. You can also see that the average precipitation in either city is the same in April. The most precipitation in a single month occurs in Rome in October. In Moscow, the lowest average monthly precipitation occurs in September and December.

Sometimes it is helpful to look at the same information in more than one way. **Circle graphs** can be used to show the percentage of precipitation in the two cities during each of the four seasons.

Read the title of the circle graphs on the next page. Each circle graph is separated into four parts, called **sectors.** Each sector represents a season. Its size depends on how much of the precipitation for the whole year falls in that season. Each sector is labeled in two ways, with the name of a season and with a percent.

Presenting the data this way makes it easy to compare the precipitation on a seasonal basis. For example, 43 percent of the total precipitation in Rome falls during autumn. You can see that autumn brings the most precipitation to Rome, while spring brings the most to Moscow. A circle graph is therefore useful for showing how certain parts are related to the whole.

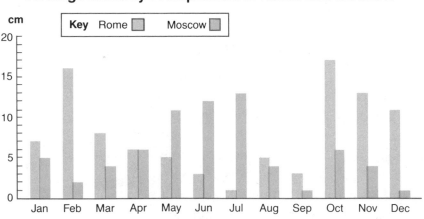

Average Monthly Precipitation in Rome and Moscow

Average Seasonal Precipitation in Rome and Moscow

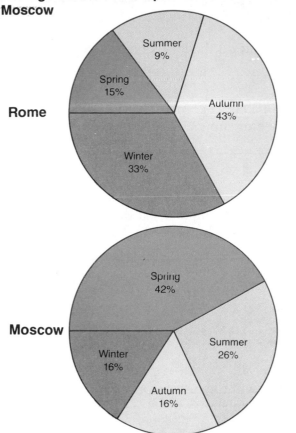

Notice that the circle graphs do not show the amount of precipitation. You can see that 16 percent of Moscow's precipitation occurs in autumn and 15 percent of Rome's precipitation occurs in spring, but without knowing the amounts in centimeters, you cannot tell that Moscow gets slightly more precipitation in autumn than Rome does in spring. In connection with the information in the double bar graph, however, you can find out that Rome actually gets more precipitation in spring than Moscow does in autumn.

A third type of graph is a **line graph**. Like the bar graph, a line graph can be used to show two related sets of data. To do so, two lines are used. The double line graph on this page compares another aspect of the climates of Rome and Moscow.

Read the title to find out the subject of the graph. The label on the vertical axis tells you that temperature is measured in Celsius units. The labels on the horizontal axis are the same as in the double bar graph on page 142. The key tells you which line shows temperature in Rome and which shows temperature in Moscow.

The graph shows that the average temperature in Moscow for a particular month is never as high as the average temperature in Rome for the same month. Summer in Moscow, however, is warmer than winter is in Rome.

The steepness of a line tells you how fast the data are changing. For example, in Moscow, the steep line shows that the temperature rises rapidly from February to May and falls rapidly from August to November. In Rome, the temperature changes more gradually during the whole year.

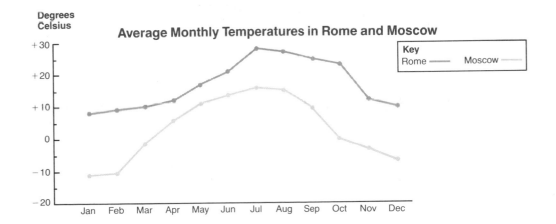

1. What is the information in a graph called? _____

2. For any kind of graph, what should you read first? _____

3. When a bar graph or line graph presents information about two different places, what information tells you which bar or line represents which place?

   _____

4. What do the labels on the axes tell you?

   _____

5. In a circle graph, what does the size of a sector show?

   _____

   _____

6. In a line graph, what does the steepness of a line show?

   _____

INTERPRETING FACTS

1. Combine the information from the double bar graph and the line graph in the selection. What can you say about the weather in Moscow in October?

   _____

   _____

2. The kind of bar graph used in the selection is sometimes called a vertical double bar graph. Why? _____

3. From the circle graphs, you can tell what percent of the precipitation in Rome occurs in autumn and what percent of the precipitation in Moscow occurs in spring. Suppose that the total annual precipitation in Rome is 95 centimeters and that the total in Moscow is 69 centimeters. Does more precipitation occur in Rome in autumn or in Moscow in spring?

   _____

4. If a line between two dots on a graph is horizontal, what does that tell you about the data?

   _____

SKILL FOCUS

A. Use the graphs in the selection to answer the following questions.

1. How many centimeters of precipitation does Rome get on the average in February? _____

2. How many more centimeters of precipitation occur in July in Moscow than in Rome? _____

3. In Rome, does more precipitation occur in summer and autumn combined or in spring and winter combined? _____

4. Which month shows the lowest amount of average precipitation in Rome? _____

5. In the hottest month, how much hotter is it in Rome than in Moscow? _____

6. In the coldest month, how much colder is it in Moscow than in Rome? _____

7. Which season has the lowest amount of precipitation in Rome? _____

B. People who study climate use a combination line and bar graph, as shown below. The line graph uses the vertical axis on the left, and it records temperatures. The bar graph uses the vertical axis on the right, and it records precipitation. Use the climate graph below to answer the following questions.

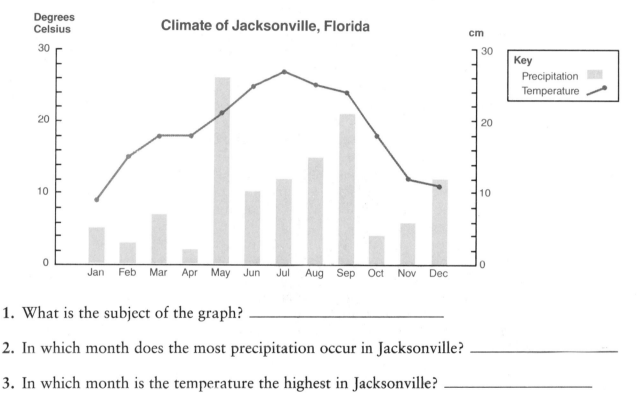

1. What is the subject of the graph? _____

2. In which month does the most precipitation occur in Jacksonville? _____

3. In which month is the temperature the highest in Jacksonville? _____

4. The average temperature in Jacksonville does not change much in which two-month period?

_____

5. Which month has the least amount of precipitation? _____

6. Which month has the lowest temperature? _____

7. How much precipitation occurs in September? _____

8. What is the average temperature in November? _____

▶ **Real Life Connections** Name an instance in your class in which a circle graph would make something easier to understand. Tell why you think so.

Fact and Opinion

As you read books, newspapers, or magazines, you should be able to distinguish facts from opinions. A statement of **fact** is information that can be proven to be true. A statement of **opinion** is a personal belief. There can be many different opinions on the same issue.

As you read the following paragraphs, think about which statements are facts and which are opinions.

The Stamp Act

The English government had great expenses as a result of the French and Indian War. Ruling the thirteen colonies and other areas, such as Canada, was a financial drain as well. The British needed new sources of revenue to pay the colonial governors and to support their soldiers. Parliament decided to raise money by taxing the colonists.

In 1764, British Prime Minister Grenville introduced to Parliament the Sugar Act, which placed a tax on sugar and other products imported by the colonists. A year later, Parliament passed the Stamp Act, which placed a tax on all legal documents, newspapers, playing cards, and dice. A stamp had to be placed on each of these items to show that the tax had been paid.

The colonists had every right to be infuriated. They were angered not so much over the cost of the tax as over the fact that they had no representatives in Parliament. The colonists believed that Parliament did not have the right to pass tax laws affecting them. Therefore, the Stamp Act was unfair. They argued that there could be "no taxation without representation." To the colonists, this was a valid argument. Because British subjects could not be taxed without the agreement of their representatives, why should the colonists be taxed without representation? As a result, the colonists did not accept these taxes.

In October 1765, representatives from nine colonies met at a Stamp Act Congress in New York. There they declared that only the colonists, not Parliament, had the right to tax the colonies, and they requested that the sugar and stamp acts be repealed.

Opposition to the Stamp Act, especially the refusal to buy British goods, helped to get the Stamp Act repealed in 1766. Even though Parliament passed more tax laws the next year, the colonists' reaction to the Stamp Act had important consequences. It helped to unite the colonists, who had formerly been unable to agree. Also, people who had voiced their opinions, such as Samuel Adams, John Adams, Patrick Henry, and George Washington, became America's greatest heroes.

Read the following statements, which are based on the selection. On the line next to each statement, write *F* if it is a statement of fact or *O* if it is an opinion.

_____ 1. Parliament decided to raise money by taxing the colonists.

_____ 2. In 1764, Prime Minister Grenville introduced the Sugar Act to Parliament.

_____ 3. The colonists had every right to be infuriated.

_____ 4. Parliament did not have the right to pass laws affecting the colonists.

_____ 5. The colonists had no representation in Parliament.

_____ 6. The Stamp Act was unfair.

_____ 7. The Stamp Act Congress met in October 1765.

_____ 8. Samuel Adams and Patrick Henry were two of America's greatest heroes.

Lesson 40

Inferences

Sometimes you can **infer**, or figure out, information that is not stated directly in a selection. If you go through the following steps, you will find it easier to infer information.

1. Read carefully.
2. Think about what you've read. Be sure you understand the information stated.
3. Read again and look for clues to information not stated.
4. Put together what is stated with information you already know. Use clues to help you make inferences.

As you read the following selection about weather forecasting, pay close attention to the facts. Use the facts to infer information that is not directly stated.

Weather Forecasting

1. Anyone can forecast weather conditions in his or her area for the next half hour or so just by looking at the sky. To make accurate predictions for the next day and beyond, however, meteorologists need information about a larger geographical area. For example, a good three-day forecast for the eastern United States requires information about today's weather for the entire Northern Hemisphere. Meteorologists get the information that they need from technological devices, such as radar and satellites.

2. One promising new technology for forecasting weather more accurately is Doppler radar. The old type of radar used in the past could show the location, movement, strength, and type of precipitation (rain, snow, or sleet) approaching an area. Doppler radar not only provides that information but also measures wind speed and direction and detects winds in clear air. It also can identify fronts—boundaries between masses of cool and warm air—even when they are not yet producing precipitation.

For each paragraph, put a check mark next to the statement that can be inferred. On the lines that follow, write the information given in the paragraph that has the clue that you found. Then explain how you inferred the information.

Paragraph 1 (check one)

_____ a. Three-day and five-day weather forecasts are not very accurate.

_____ b. Meteorologists use technological devices to study and forecast weather conditions.

_____ c. Weather satellites and radar provide information about large areas of the earth.

Clue _____

_____

Explanation _____

Paragraph 2 (check one)

_____ a. Identifying fronts helps meteorologists develop more accurate weather forecasts.

_____ b. Wind speed and direction could be measured with the old type of radar.

_____ c. Weather forecasters have stopped using the old type of radar.

Clue _____

_____

Explanation _____

Using an Index

The quickest way to find information in a text or reference book is to use the **index**. An index alphabetically lists the book's topics.

On the next page is part of an index from a science textbook. Find the topic *Vegetables*. Below it, two subtopics are listed alphabetically: *source of vitamin C* and *vitamins in*. Subtopics tell the specific kinds of information about the main topic.

The numbers after each topic or subtopic are the page numbers on which information is found. Numbers separated by commas indicate that the information appears only on the pages for which numbers are given.

Notice that some subtopics have words like *in* and *of* before them. These short words don't affect the alphabetical order of the subtopics.

Study the index on the next page. Then answer the following questions.

1. On which page(s) would you find information about weather balloons? ——————

2. How many subtopics are listed under the topic *Time*? ——————

3. On which page(s) would you find information about wood pulp? ——————

4. How many pages does the book have on time zones? ——————

5. On which page(s) would you find information about how water evaporates? ——————

6. Information about which two types of vitamins are found on page 65? ——————

7. On which page(s) would you find information about removing wax from cloth? ——————

8. Which five subtopics are listed under *Water Routes*? ——————————————

—————————————————————————————

9. On which page(s) would you find information about the effects of the moon on the tides?

——————

10. Which topic comes between *Vegetables* and *Venom, snake*? ——————

11. On which page(s) would you find information about Daylight Savings Time? ——————

12. If you wanted information about how moisture affects weather, which page would you

not look at between 248–253? ——————

13. On which page(s) would you find information about materials suspended in water? ——————

14. If the book had information about Telstar 1, after which major topic would it be listed?

——————————

15. If the book had information about the Triassic period, before which major topic would it

be listed? ——————————————

16. On which page(s) would you find information about the composition of sea water? ——————

17. On which page(s) would you find information about the U.S. Weather Bureau? ——————

18. On which page(s) would you find information about air pollution caused by volcanoes?

——————

Reading a Warranty

A **warranty** is a manufacturer's promise to the buyer that the product is well-made. According to this written guarantee, if the product does not continue to work properly for a given period, the company must repair or replace it at no cost to the buyer.

Many products that you purchase come with warranties. The terms of a warranty may influence your decision in buying a product. Therefore, you should read a warranty carefully before you purchase a product.

Most warranties include the following information.

Warranty period The amount of time from date of purchase during which the product is guaranteed by the manufacturer

Warranty coverage Exactly what the manufacturer is responsible for in the event that something goes wrong

Service agreement What to do after the warranty period runs out to get service from the company

Steps to take What the buyer must do to activate the warranty

Examine this warranty for a camcorder.

LIMITED NINETY DAY WARRANTY

SONIX warrants to the original consumer purchaser that your SONIX unit is free from any defects in material or workmanship for a period of ninety days from the date of purchase. If any such defect is discovered within the warranty period, SONIX will repair or replace the unit free of charge (except for a $4.00 charge for packing, return postage, and insurance), subject to verification of the defect or malfunction upon delivery or postage prepaid to

SONIX
Customer Service Division
1301 Third Avenue
New York, NY 10021

IMPORTANT

Please do not return your product to the store where it was purchased. SONIX accepts the responsibility of keeping you a satisfied customer. ALL RETURNS MUST HAVE WRITTEN AUTHORIZATION FROM
SONIX
1301 Third Avenue
New York, NY 10021

PLEASE WRITE FOR DETAILS.
This warranty does not apply to defects resulting from abuse, alteration or unreasonable use of the unit, resulting in cracked or broken cases or units damaged by excessive heat, and it does not apply to batteries. YOU MUST ENCLOSE PROOF OF DATE AND PLACE OF PURCHASE AND CHECK OR MONEY ORDER FOR $4.00 TO COVER HANDLING, OR WE CANNOT BE RESPONSIBLE FOR REPAIRS OR REPLACEMENT.

Any applicable implied warranties, including warranties of merchantability and fitness, are hereby limited to **ninety** days from date of purchase. Consequential or incidental damages resulting from a breach of any applicable express or implied warranties are hereby excluded. Some states do not allow limitations on how long implied warranties last and do not allow exclusion of incidental or consequential damages, so the above limitations and exclusions may not apply to you.

This warranty gives you specific legal rights, and you may also have other rights which may vary from state to state.

SERVICE AGREEMENT

If, after the ninety day limited warranty period, your SONIX unit requires service, SONIX will service the unit upon receipt, postage prepaid, with your check or money order in the sum of $10.00 to cover cost or repair, as well as return postage, insurance, and packing.

This service agreement does not apply to defects from abuse, alteration, or unreasonable use of the unit and does not apply to units that require service three years after the date of purchase.

IMPORTANT STEPS TO FOLLOW

Before returning the unit, you must write to

SONIX
1301 Third Avenue
New York, NY 10021
for a RETURN AUTHORIZATION LABEL, which must be applied to outside of return parcel.

Before returning this unit, replace the batteries (where applicable) with fresh ones, because exhausted or defective batteries are the most common cause of problems encountered. If service is still required,

1. Remove the batteries and pack unit with all its original accessories in a well-padded, heavy, corrugated box.
2. If the warranty period has not expired, enclose your sales receipt or photocopy of it to validate the date and place of purchase.
3. Enclose a check or money order payable to the order of SONIX for the sum of $4.00 (if the product is within the warranty period) or $10.00 (if the warranty period has expired.)

A. Decide if the following information can be determined from the warranty. Write *yes* or *no* on the lines.

1. where to send the product in the event of a defect _____

2. how long it will take to repair or replace a part in the event of a defect _____

3. what must accompany any products that are returned for repair or replacement _____

4. what steps to follow in the event of a problem after the warranty period is over _____

5. how long the product is under warranty _____

6. what to do with a product that becomes faulty three years after the purchase date _____

7. how to get a Return Authorization Label from the company _____

8. whether money must be enclosed with a returned product _____

9. where to telephone in case a product returned to the company is not sent back to the customer within ninety days _____

10. how frequently batteries need to be replaced in those products requiring batteries _____

B. Use the information provided on the warranty to complete each sentence.

1. The warranty period for this camcorder is _____.

2. To have a camcorder repaired or replaced, you are to send it to _____ rather than to the store where it was purchased.

3. If a one-day-old camcorder is found to be defective, repair or replacement is _____.

4. The company advises replacing the _____ with new ones before determining that the camcorder is defective.

5. If you get your brand-new camcorder home and find that it is defective, it will still cost you _____ to return it to the company. This charge covers _____ _____.

6. If you return a camcorder during the warranty period, you must include a sales receipt to prove _____.

7. If you return a camcorder at any time for repairs, you must enclose $4.00 for return postage, but you cannot send cash. You must send a _____ or _____.

8. To have a broken camcorder repaired when the warranty period is over, the company requires a check or money order for a total of _____ to fix it.

9. To return a defective camcorder to the company, a Return Authorization Label must be put on _____.

10. If a camcorder is given to you as a gift and it is defective, the company cannot be responsible for repairing it without _____.

Communications | # Conflict and Resolution

Reading a Literature Selection _____

▶ Background Information

In this story, the author's imagination takes the reader to a setting in the future. At the time that the story takes place, something very odd has happened to television viewing.

▶ Skill Focus

Often the characters in a story have a problem to solve. The struggle to solve the problem is called **conflict.** A character can face three main types of conflict.

Conflict with Self

A character may struggle with emotions or feelings within himself or herself. This struggle is an internal conflict. An example is a person trying to overcome jealousy of a friend's good fortune.

Conflict with Another Character

A character may struggle against another person. This struggle is an external conflict. An example is two athletes playing against each other in a tennis match.

Conflict with an Outside Force

A character may struggle against nature, society, technology, or a force over which he or she has no control. This struggle is also an external conflict. An example is a citizen fighting for the protection of an animal threatened with extinction.

By the end of a story, the character facing a conflict succeeds or fails in solving the problem. The way a conflict is settled is called the **resolution.** Conflict and resolution are part of a story's plot.

Stories sometimes have more than one conflict. When there is more than one conflict, the major, or more important, conflict involves the main character. The minor, or less important, conflict involves the other characters. As you read stories, look for the conflicts.

▶ Word Clues

Read the following sentences. Look for context clues that explain the underlined word.

> Once he fixed the computatime with a pushpin and a <u>smidgen</u> of tape. It was amazing what my brother could put together with a bit of this and a piece of that.

If you do not know the meaning of the word *smidgen,* the words *bit* and *piece* in the next sentence can help you. The words *smidgen, bit,* and *piece* are synonyms. They all mean small portions or parts of something larger.

Use **synonym** context clues to find the meaning of the three underlined words in the selection.

▶ Strategy Tip

As you read "Tuned-in Telenut," look for clues to the conflicts that the characters face. What is Jasmine's problem? How does she resolve it? What is Kamal's problem? How does he resolve it? Which conflict is the major conflict?

Tuned-in Telenut

Of course, I should have recognized the signs. But when it happens to someone close to you, you just refuse to believe the truth. I did notice that my brother was spending more and more time in his basement workshop. Once I even asked him, "What are you doing down there, Kamal?"

"Oh, I'm just experimenting," he said mysteriously. "Nothing to worry about, Jasmine."

I didn't worry about it then. Kamal was always doing experiments. He was a genius at constructing things. Once he fixed the computatime with a pushpin and a smidgen of tape. It was amazing what my brother could put together with a bit of this and a piece of that. He even built his own roboscanner and a merchanfone so that Mom could order groceries on the computer.

✔ On weekends, Kamal was always in his workshop before the rest of us woke up, and he was still there after we all went to bed. When he had to come up to eat, he had a faraway smile and a dazed look on his face. He seemed to have trouble answering the simplest of Dad's questions. At dinner, he often stared straight ahead, not seeing or hearing anything. He seemed <u>mesmerized</u>, hypnotized, almost in a trance. As soon as he could, he rushed back downstairs.

"What's Kamal experimenting with now?" Dad asked one day.

"I don't know," I said, but by then I had a terrible suspicion.

Later, I went downstairs and poked around. I hadn't searched very long when I found, hidden in the corner of the workshop, exactly what I had feared.

I trudged upstairs, not knowing how to get out of my predicament. The more I thought about my situation, the more difficult it became. I just couldn't decide what to do. I didn't want to tell on Kamal—I'd be getting him into a lot of hot water. On the other hand, I couldn't just stand by, knowing what

> *"Horrible!" I said with a shudder. "Thank goodness the age of television is over."*

he was doing, without trying to help him out of his trouble.

I decided to consult my logic synthesizer, which had been a lot of help with problem-solving homework. After you enter all the information about a problem, the synthesizer analyzes the data and helps you to select the best solution. I entered this statement: "I have a problem with my brother."

"Uh-oh," the synthesizer responded, "Kamal again. Name the problem."

I did. The synthesizer and I went back and forth for an hour. Finally, I slipped downstairs to the food center. Dad was busy microwaving dinner, while Mom was planning next week's dinners on the computamenu.

"Mom, Dad," I said, "Kamal is a telenut."

"Oh no!" Mom gasped.

I took a deep breath. "He has a television set and videotapes hidden downstairs."

Mom gasped again. "But that's illegal! Ever since the year two thousand twenty, only a few people have been allowed to watch television. And they're allowed to watch it only for research and experimental studies. How do you think Kamal got hold of a television set?"

"The same way that he got hold of the radar last year. He put it together himself. As for the videotapes, he must have found them in old, abandoned houses. The cleanup squads must have overlooked them."

"Doesn't Kamal realize what he's doing to himself?" Dad asked. "Back in two thousand ten, it was decided that television destroys the creative powers of the mind."

"I know," I said. "To think that in the nineteen nineties, over ninety-five percent of all Americans owned at least one television set."

"And the average person spent twenty-one hours a week in front of it," Mom added.

"Horrible!" I said with a shudder. "Thank goodness the age of television is over."

Just then Kamal wandered in. "Is it true, Kamal?" Dad asked. "Are you a telenut?"

Kamal's vacant expression and bloodshot eyes were answer enough.

"How could you?" Mom asked. "Don't you know you're letting your imagination wither and die?"

Kamal looked embarrassed. Sitting down at the kitchen table, he sighed and said, "Sometimes I'd like to stop being such a telenut. I know I'm breaking the law, but I can't help admiring the simplicity of the thing! You can learn a lot from watching television. No matter how complicated a problem is, it can be solved in one hour—actually in forty-six minutes, leaving out commercials. Amazing, isn't it? It makes life so simple."

Mom, Dad, and I looked at each other.

"You can learn a lot from commercials too," Kamal went on dreamily. "To get a date, all you need is the right mouthwash and deodorant. And to keep a marriage together, you should use certain brands of coffee and dishwashing detergent."

At this point, we knew Kamal was in real trouble. Nobody drank coffee any more, and no one needed detergents with the new ultrasonic dishwashers. Kamal was living in the ancient past.

"Kamal," Mom said, "You can learn things from books, too. Why not try scanning one for a change?"

"Scanning?" Kamal said blankly. "Oh, that. It's too much trouble watching the words move along the display. And there aren't enough pictures."

Mom turned to Dad. "Do you think it's too late for him?" she asked. "Is there any hope?"

"I don't know," Dad said, shaking his head. "They say that once you're a telenut, it's almost impossible to change."

"We've got to do something," Mom said.

"Is there no cure?"

"Some studies have shown that a telenut can be broken of the attraction slowly," I said. "We'll cut Kamal down one hour of television a day until he's down to an hour a week."

That's what we did. It wasn't easy for any of us. It was a huge struggle for Kamal, but he tried. He even made some decisions himself.

"This week, we cut out all quiz shows!" he would say bravely.

As we cut down his viewing time, Kamal grew shaky and <u>irritable</u>. He became so impatient that in the middle of a conversation, he would suddenly scream, "It's time for *Police Dog!*" or "I've got to know what's happening on *Rescue Squad!*" In his sleep, he muttered, "You, too, can get fast, fast, fast relief."

Kamal finally fought his way out of his telenuttery. Today he's a normal person, a typical teenager of the twenty-first century. His powers of thinking and logic were only temporarily damaged by his <u>harrowing</u> encounter with television. I know Kamal won't ever forget his terrifying experience of becoming a telenut.

Yet, he'll never be quite the person he once was. Every now and then, even today, he still gets that look in his eyes, and I know he's wondering what's happening on *My Mother, the Astronaut.*

1. Where and when does this story take place?

_____

_____

_____

2. Name three machines that give clues to the story's setting in time.

_____

_____

_____

3. From what point of view is the story told? Who is the narrator of the story?

_____

_____

_____

4. Why does Jasmine consult her logic synthesizer?

_____

_____

_____

5. Circle the correct meaning of the underlined word in each sentence below.

   a. Lost at sea for even one day can be a <u>harrowing</u> experience.

   frightening   wondering

   b. The audience was <u>mesmerized</u> by the effects of the lasers used in the light show.

   fascinated   startled

   c. When stuck in traffic jams, drivers often get <u>irritable</u>.

   concerned   annoyed

INTERPRETING FACTS

1. a. Describe Kamal's character.

_____

_____

   b. Describe Jasmine's attitude toward her brother.

_____

_____

2. Why is this a good point of view for this story?

_____

_____

3. Why does Kamal get hooked on television?

_____

_____

4. Will Kamal be able to stay away from television in the future? Explain.

_____

_____

5. Reread the paragraph with a check mark next to it. Write a sentence stating its main idea.

_____

6. Do you think watching television harms one's creativity? Explain.

_____

_____

SKILL FOCUS

Think about the major and minor conflicts in this story.

1. a. In the story, both Jasmine and Kamal face internal conflicts. Who faces the major, or more important, conflict? _____

b. How does this character come into conflict with himself or herself?

_____

_____

c. How is this major conflict gradually resolved?

_____

_____

2. a. There is also a minor conflict in the story. Who faces it? _____

b. Circle the statement that best describes the minor conflict. Then tell how the conflict is resolved.

Should Kamal give up television viewing?

Should Jasmine help Kamal give up television viewing?

Should Jasmine tell her parents about Kamal's attraction to television viewing?

_____

_____

3. In one or two sentences, explain how Kamal's and Jasmine's conflicts are alike or different.

_____

_____

_____

▶ **Real Life Connections** Imagine your neighborhood or community 100 years from today. Describe what you might see.

Lesson 44

Generalizations

Reading a Social Studies Selection

▶ **Background Information**

From early times to the present, people have found and invented ways to communicate. The history of communication contains many milestones that have changed the way that we live.

For example, in the eighteenth century, times were very different from what they are today. There were no televisions, radios, or telephones. These three inventions—all created within the last 120 years—are to communication what the automobile is to travel. They revolutionized the way that people travel.

In modern times, people invented even faster and farther reaching forms of communication. With the click of a mouse or the press of a button, we can quickly send information or messages almost anywhere in the world.

In "From Signal Fires to Lasers," you will read about key people who helped advance the science of communication to what we now have today.

▶ **Skill Focus**

Facts are an important part of history, but facts alone do not provide a complete understanding of historical developments. You must be able to make **generalizations**, or draw conclusions, from a sampling of facts or ideas. A generalization is a broad, main idea statement that includes or covers all the facts or ideas in a sampling. To be reasonable, a generalization must be based on more than one or two facts.

Examine the following facts.

> In 1868, the first type-writer came into use.
>
> In 1876, Alexander Graham Bell demonstrated his telephone, which could carry voice messages over electric wires.
>
> In 1877, Thomas Edison made the first working phonograph.

Based on these three facts, the following generalization can be made.

> During the late 1800s, a number of inventions resulted in improved communication.

All reasonable generalizations must be based on information that is true and can be proven.

▶ **Word Clues**

When you read a word that you don't know, look for context clues to help you understand it. Sometimes, however, there may be no context clues. Read the sentence below.

> During the 1800s, several inventors revolutionized the transmission of information.

You may not know the meaning of the word *transmission*. There are no context clues in the sentence to help you. You will have to look up the word in a dictionary.

When you come across a word that you don't know and there are no context clues, look up the word's meaning in a dictionary. You may find it more convenient to finish what you are reading before looking up the word.

Use a **dictionary** to find the meaning of the three underlined words in the selection.

▶ **Strategy Tip**

As you read "From Signal Fires to Lasers," look for patterns in the facts that are given. Make sure that the facts can be proven. Then make a reasonable generalization based on those facts.

From Signal Fires to Lasers

The history of communication is the story of people sharing ideas and information. The earliest means of long distance communication—such as messengers on foot and signal fires—were simple. Today we use more complex devices, such as lasers and satellites.

Ancient Times

The people of ancient civilizations shared ideas by talking. The first written language, called pictographic writing, was used about 3000 B.C.E by the Sumerians in the Middle East. From these symbolic pictures, a written language system eventually developed.

✗ Many ancient civilizations used various forms of written language. The Egyptians painted hieroglyphics on tomb walls and wrote them on papyrus scrolls. The Greeks wrote on wax tablets with a pointed tool called a stylus. The Romans spread important news in handwritten papers that were posted in public. These postings, called *Acta Diurna (Daily Events),* served as newspapers for Roman society.

During the Middle Ages, monks prepared illuminated manuscripts and so preserved the traditions of the ancient world for future generations.

The Middle Ages

✔ From 400 to 1400 C.E., Christian monks called scribes were among the few people in western Europe who could read and write. They slowly and painstakingly copied texts by hand. Most of the texts they copied were books on religious themes. Often they decorated the first letter of a paragraph with brilliant designs in gold, silver, and colored ink. These decorations are called illuminations.

The Renaissance

Between the 1300s and the 1600s, more and more people learned to read, and the demand for books greatly increased. With block printing, which replaced the slow copying of books by scribes, printers carved words into wood blocks. With these blocks, they stamped out many copies of a book.

The real revolution in printing in Europe came with the invention of movable type. Johannes Gutenberg, a German printer, made pieces of metal type for individual letters of the alphabet. The metal letters were set into frames that could be disassembled and the type used again. With the invention of movable type, the era of mass communication had begun.

Mass Communication

Printed information spread rapidly in the form of inexpensive newspapers, magazines, and books. Nations established postal services. Yet news could still travel only as fast as it could be carried.

In the 1800s, several inventors revolutionized the transmission of

As printed information spread, small newspaper and magazine stands began popping up in major cities.

information. Samuel Morse developed an electric telegraph that sent messages over long distances by wire. The messages were sent in a code of dots and dashes, called Morse code. By 1866, a telegraph cable across the floor of the Atlantic Ocean carried messages between Europe and America in a few minutes.

In 1876, Alexander Graham Bell demonstrated that his telephone could carry a voice message over electric wires. By the 1890s, Bell telephone systems were operating in most American cities. In 1877, Thomas Edison, another American inventor, recorded sound on a cylinder that was covered with foil to make the first working phonograph. In the 1890s, Edison and other inventors used a new celluloid film developed by George Eastman to produce the first motion pictures. By the end of the nineteenth century, the world was buzzing with sound and pictorial communication.

In the 1920s and 1930s, radio was a popular medium for entertainment and news.

Communication Through Space

By the end of the 1800s, scientists had discovered the existence of <u>electromagnetic</u> waves. In Italy, the wireless telegraph of Guglielmo Marconi could send electrical signals over a longer distance than had ever been done before. With the invention of Marconi's radio in 1895, the age of airwave communication was born. By the 1920s,

radio had become a popular form of entertainment.

Inventors were also working on the transmission of picture images by electromagnetic waves. Scotland's John Logie Baird developed a system of television transmission in 1926. By 1936, the British Broadcasting Corporation was sending out the first television broadcasts.

Communication satellites in space transmit telephone, radio, and other signals across the ocean.

Modern Communications

The advances in communications technology made in the second half of the twentieth century have been more far-reaching than those in the first half. Videocassettes and laser discs provide access to vast amounts of information. Facsimile, or fax, machines transmit printed information with the speed of a telephone call. Using telephone lines, computers in different locations can share information. Communication satellites orbit earth, relaying television, radio, and telephone signals in an instant, global communication network.

The use of <u>lasers</u> in communications technology has completely revolutionized communication systems. Fiber optics uses laser beams and thin, transparent glass fibers to transmit signals with great speed and accuracy. One laser disc can store an entire encyclopedia electronically. <u>Holography</u> uses lasers to produce three-dimensional photographic images. The advances of the last two decades are just the beginning of tomorrow's new communication systems.

1. Sequence the inventions below in correct historical order.

    _____ telegraph

    _____ lasers

    _____ movable type printing press

    _____ radio

    _____ communication satellite

2. Until very recently, what was the major difference between communication by telephone and communication by radio?

    _____

    _____

    _____

    _____

3. Reread the paragraph with an X next to it. Underline the sentence that states its main idea. Then circle three sentences containing details that support the main idea.

4. Complete each statement with the correct word below.

    lasers   holography   electromagnetic

    a. Radio broadcasts are transmitted through space by means of

        _____ waves.

    b. Using _____, the film maker was able to photograph a scary three-dimensional ghost.

    c. _____ produce a light beam so intense that it can melt steel.

INTERPRETING FACTS

1. What effect did the invention of movable type have on people's knowledge?

    _____

    _____

    _____

    _____

2. What had to be established before the telegraph and telephone could work?

    _____

    _____

3. Until the 1960s and 1970s, most information was stored and accessed in print form—in books, magazines, and newspapers. How has this changed in recent years?

    _____

    _____

    _____

    _____

    _____

    _____

SKILL FOCUS

Following the box on the next page are five groups of facts based on information in the selection. Read each group of facts carefully. Then, for each group, choose the most reasonable generalization. Write the letter of the statement on the line provided. You may go back to the selection if necessary.

Generalizations

a. Satellites have linked all parts of the world in a global communication network.

b. The use of electricity helped revolutionize long-distance communication.

c. Ancient civilizations used various forms of communication to spread news and pass on information.

d. Lasers have revolutionized communication systems.

e. Electromagnetic waves made it possible to send sounds and images through space.

---

1. Facts   Early Egyptians wrote in hieroglyphics on papyrus scrolls and tomb walls.

Early Greeks wrote on wax tablets with a stylus.

Early Romans spread important news in a written news sheet.

Generalization _____

2. Facts   In 1877, Thomas Edison recorded sound on the first working phonograph.

Samuel Morse's electric telegraph carried messages over wire in the early 1800s.

Alexander Graham Bell's telephone carried the human voice by electricity in 1876.

Generalization _____

3. Facts   Marconi's invention of the wireless telegraph showed that sound could be transmitted through space.

The invention of television made it possible to send picture images by electromagnetic waves.

The age of communication via airwaves began with the invention of the radio.

Generalization _____

4. Facts   Communication satellites orbit earth.

The satellites can send signals to any part of the world.

The satellites transmit radio, telephone, and television signals instantaneously.

Generalization _____

5. Facts   Lasers are used to produce three-dimensional photographic images.

Fiber optics uses lasers to transmit signals with great speed and accuracy.

An entire encyclopedia can be recorded on one laser disc.

Generalization _____

▶ **Real Life Connections** What kind of telephone will you use in the year 2050? What will computers be able to do? Make two predictions about the future.

Lesson 45

Diagrams

Reading a Science Selection

▶ **Background Information**

We often take the things that we have for granted. Our five senses (sight, sound, smell, taste, and touch) enable us to do so many things that we could not do without them. Although all five of the senses are important, for most people sight and sound are probably more important than the other senses. Take a minute to think about what your life would be like without sight or sound.

Although we cannot see sound, we depend on it every day. Sound is very important in communication, entertainment, and sometimes as a warning of danger.

Because sound is so important to us, scientists have studied diagrams of sound to see how sound is produced and how it travels. Scientists have figured out many of the principles of sound. In "Sound," you will be working with diagrams that scientists use to demonstrate the principles of sound.

▶ **Skill Focus**

Textbooks often contain **diagrams** to show what is being explained in the paragraphs. Diagrams can often be best understood if you read the paragraphs first, then look at the diagram. When you study diagrams, be sure to read the **caption** and the **labels**. They usually contain important information. As you study the diagram, think about the paragraphs that you just read. It may be helpful to go back to the paragraphs again and try to visualize the diagram.

Use the following steps for reading a selection with diagrams.

1. Read the paragraph or paragraphs before each diagram, and then study the diagram. Be sure to read the labels and caption with the diagram. The paragraph below the diagram may also explain what is pictured. Read that paragraph, too.

2. Read the rest of the paragraphs. Look back at the diagrams whenever you think they will help you.

3. After you have finished reading the paragraphs and studying the diagrams, look away from the selection. Try to picture what you have read and the details in the diagrams. If you are not able to do so, read the material again.

4. Follow this method until you understand all the ideas in the selection.

▶ **Word Clues**

Sometimes special words are explained in a paragraph and also shown in a diagram. When this happens, study both the text and the diagram until you understand the meaning of the words.

Use **diagram** clues as context clues to find the meaning of the three underlined words in the selection.

▶ **Strategy Tip**

While you read the selection, study the diagrams carefully. If necessary, go back and forth between the words in the selection and the information in the diagrams. Do so until you understand the information presented.

Sound

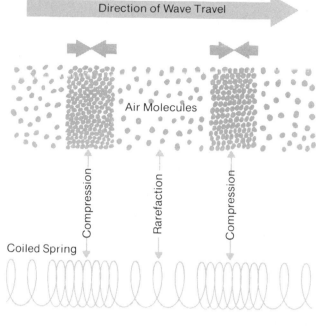

Figure 1. Sound waves are created by vibrations that produce areas of compression and rarefaction in the air.

What causes sound? Put your fingers on your throat as you talk, or watch the strings of a guitar as it is played. When you talk, you can feel movement in your throat. When a guitar is played, the strings move back and forth very quickly. These movements, called **vibrations**, produce sound.

Air is made up of tiny particles called **molecules** (MOL ə kyoolz) that can vibrate. A vibrating string starts sound waves in the air. When the string moves to the right, it pushes the air molecules that are next to it closer together. When the string moves back to the left, it leaves an area with fewer air molecules. An area of <u>compression</u> and an area of <u>rarefaction</u> (rair ə FAK shən) make up each sound wave.

Yet how does sound travel across a room? Air molecules pass their vibrations along to other air molecules. By means of this movement, sound gets from its vibrating source to the listener. As molecules become compressed, the compressions move outward through the medium, in this case the air. A medium is any substance—solid, liquid, or gas—that carries sound.

As the compressions move outward, each "layer" of molecules pushes the next layer. Rarefactions also move outward, layer by layer. This series of compressions and rarefactions makes up the waves that transmit sound energy through the medium.

A coiled spring is a useful image for visualizing wave motion. Picture yourself stretching such a spring across a smooth floor. Then suppose you pull several coils of the stretched spring together, causing a compression of the coils. When you release the coils, a disturbance, or pulse, moves along the spring. Although each coil does not move very far, the energy of the disturbance moves along the whole length of the spring. The disturbance in the spring causes coils farther along to be compressed. Each compression is then followed by a rarefaction, as shown in Figure 1.

Sound does not travel in a vacuum, which is a space that has nothing in it, not even air. Sound waves require a medium.

Pitch and Frequency

Sounds can be "high" or "low." **Pitch** is how high or how low a sound is. Pitch is determined by how fast the source of the sound vibrates. A guitar string that vibrates slowly produces fewer sound waves per second and a lower pitch than a string that vibrates rapidly.

Thus, pitch depends on **frequency**, which is the number of sound waves produced per second. Frequency is usually measured by calculating the number of waves that pass a point at a specific distance from the sound's source in one second. The number of waves that pass a specific point in one second is expressed in **hertz** (Hz). One hertz equals one complete wave per second. If a sound is low-pitched, fewer waves pass a specific point per second than if the sound is high-pitched.

Frequency is related to the length of a sound wave. In Figure 2, notice points X and Y on each set of waves. The distance between these two points is called a **wavelength**. As you can see, the low-pitched sound waves have a longer wavelength than the high-pitched sound waves. Figure 3 shows the frequency range of human hearing. It is much greater than the frequency range that can be produced by the human voice.

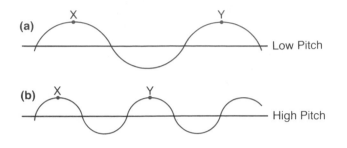

Figure 2. A sound with a short wavelength has a high pitch, and vice versa.

Musical Instruments

In stringed instruments, the vibration of the strings produces sound. In wind instruments, such as trumpets and trombones, a column of air inside the instrument vibrates to produce sound. The length of the column of air determines the pitch of the sound. The player varies pitch on the trumpet by opening and closing its valves and on the trombone by moving the slide. Making sounds in this way is similar to blowing across the tops of bottles filled with different amounts of water.

Clarinets and saxophones are wind instruments with a reed that vibrates and causes the column of air within the instrument to vibrate. Musicians produce different pitches on these instruments by opening and closing the keys and finger holes.

Drums, cymbals, and bells produce sound when parts of these instruments vibrate. The drum cover, or head, vibrates when struck, and the metal in cymbals and bells vibrates.

Amplitude

Increasing the frequency of sound waves increases the pitch, but it does not affect how loud or soft a sound is. Loudness is related to the amount of energy in a sound wave. You can do a simple test of the energy in a sound wave in the following way. Fold a small piece of paper into a V, and place it over a string on a piano or guitar. When you pluck the string gently, the paper vibrates only slightly. When you pluck the string with more force, however, the paper vibrates a great deal. Figure 4 shows sound waves of the same frequency, the first of which is soft and the second, loud. The difference between the two diagrams is the amplitude, or height, of the waves. Loud sounds have greater amplitudes than soft sounds.

The loudness of a sound is measured in **decibels**. A soft whisper registers at about 10 to 15 decibels. Very loud music registers at about 100 decibels. Loud noises can cause hearing loss over a period of time.

Speed

Have you ever estimated how far away a thunderstorm was by counting the seconds between the time you saw the lightning and the time you heard the thunder? The lightning and the thunder were produced at the same time. Light travels so quickly that you saw the lightning at almost the same instant it

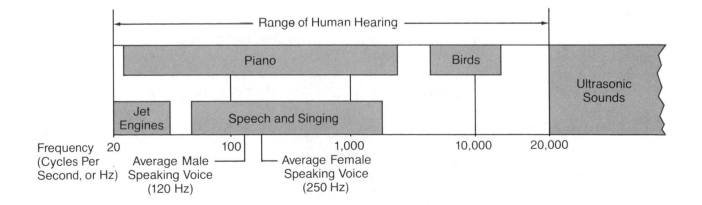

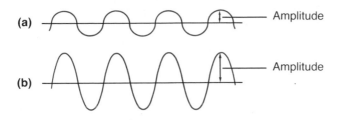

Figure 4. Loud sound waves have great amplitudes, and vice versa.

occurred. Sound, however, travels more slowly. The speed of sound is generally given as 340 meters per second at an air temperature of 10 degrees Celsius. However, the speed of sound depends on the medium that sound waves are traveling through and on the temperature of the medium.

Sound travels faster through earth or metal than through air, and it travels faster at warm temperatures than at cold temperatures. For example, sound travels 331 meters per second in air at 0 degrees Celsius. It travels 343 meters per second in air at 20 degrees Celsius. In seawater at 25 degrees Celsius, sound travels 1,531 meters per second. Sound travels through wood at about 3,850 meters per second.

Sound Reflection

Another characteristic of sound waves is that they bounce back from hard, smooth surfaces. On some surfaces, sound waves bounce back in such a way that the reflected sound is much like the original one. Yet, there is a distinct time lapse between the original and the reflected sounds. This effect is an **echo.** Bats use echoes to locate food. They send out high-frequency sound waves that bounce off insects, among other things, and are reflected back to their ears.

Scientists and engineers are interested in how sound waves are reflected because reflected sound affects the ability of people to hear in places like theaters and classrooms. The study of sound is called **acoustics** (ə KOOS tiks). A band shell has a shape that is designed to reflect sound out to the audience. In theaters and auditoriums, the walls and floors are often covered with thick drapes and carpets. The soft, irregular surfaces of these materials are filled with tiny holes that absorb sound waves so that they do not bounce. Thus, these soft surfaces eliminate echoes and other interference, making it easier to hear.

The study of sound wave reflection and travel has led to important uses of sound. **Sonar,** or sound navigation ranging, is based on sending out sound waves under water and listening to their echoes. Ships use sonar to detect unseen underwater obstacles, thus preventing collisions. It is also used by rescue missions to locate sunken ships.

Sound is also used in a medical process called **ultrasound.** One of the things that ultrasound can do is to give doctors and prospective parents a look at the developing baby within the mother's body. A small device that generates sound waves is placed over the mother's abdomen. This device bounces sound waves off the developing baby's body. These reflected sound waves are picked up and converted to signals on a television-type monitor. The image, called a sonogram, is fuzzy, but it gives a view of the developing baby that no one ever had before.

Sonograms are useful in a number of ways. With the sonogram, doctors can tell the size of the baby and, in some cases, whether it is healthy. Sonograms can confirm the presence of twins and the sex of the offspring. In the future, new medical uses for ultrasound may be perfected.

RECALLING FACTS

1. To produce sound, what must the sound source do?_____

2. Name the two parts of a sound wave.

_____

3. What is the frequency of a sound?

_____

_____

4. What is the range of sound frequencies that humans can hear? _____

5. What does one hertz equal?

_____

_____

6. In what way does a sound with a frequency of 10,000 Hz sound different from one with a frequency of 5,000 Hz?

_____

_____

7. If two sounds are different only in their degree of loudness, how are their sound waves different?

_____

8. How is the loudness of a sound measured? _____

9. Generally, what is the speed of sound in air? _____

10. What conditions affect how fast sound travels? _____

_____

11. How does an echo occur?

_____

_____

_____

12. What is acoustics? _____

13. How is the reflection of sound waves controlled in theaters and auditoriums?

_____

_____

_____

14. How does sonar work?

_____

_____

15. Name one way ultrasound is used in medicine. _____

_____

_____

16. Draw a line to match each word with its explanation.

compression	area where molecules are close together
rarefaction	height of a sound wave, or loudness
amplitude	area where molecules are far apart

INTERPRETING FACTS

1. A bell jar is a device from which all the air can be removed. If a ringing bell is placed in a bell jar and the air is withdrawn, what occurs?
   - ‖ a. The sound of the bell can be heard.
   - ‖ b. The sound of the bell cannot be heard.
   - ‖ c. The sound of the bell disappears and then reappears.

2. Western movies often show scouts putting an ear to the ground to hear if they are being followed. Based on what you know about sound, does this make sense?
   - ‖ a. No. Sound travels faster through air than through earth.
   - ‖ b. Yes. Sound travels faster through earth than through air.
   - ‖ c. No. Sound travels at the same speed through earth and air.

3. A sound with a frequency of 20,000 hertz
   || a. produces 20,000 waves per second.
   || b. moves very slowly in warm air.
   || c. has a very low pitch.

4. When are noises louder?
   || a. on a cold day
   || b. on a warm day
   || c. They are equally loud on warm and cold days.

5. Ultrasonic sounds are
   || a. above the range of human hearing.
   || b. louder than a sonic boom.
   || c. not produced by vibrations.

6. Dogs can hear some sounds that humans cannot. What can you tell about these sounds?
   || They have high amplitude.
   || They have a frequency above 20,000 Hz.
   || They have a frequency between 20-20,000 Hz.

SKILL FOCUS

1. Explain Figure 1 in your own words.
   _____
   _____
   _____
   _____
   _____
   _____
   _____
   _____

2. Explain Figure 2 in your own words.
   _____
   _____
   _____

3. Use Figure 3 to answer the following two questions.
   a. Could you hear a sound that registers 22,000 hertz? Explain. _____
   _____

   b. Could a person sing a note that registers 800 hertz? Explain. _____
   _____

4. Decide which of the three diagrams below can be used to answer the following questions. Write the letter of the correct diagram on the line.

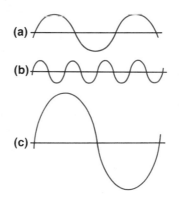

(a)

(b)

(c)

_____ Which sound wave has the highest pitch?

_____ Which sound wave has the softest sound?

_____ Which sound wave has the loudest sound?

_____ Which sound wave has a moderate pitch?

_____ Which sound wave has the shortest wavelength?

_____ Which sound wave has the lowest pitch?

▶ **Real Life Connections** Give two examples of how sound affects you at home or in school.

Equations

___ Reading a Mathematics Selection ___

▶ Background Information

You have probably been solving equations for years now—you have probably just never realized it. When you start reading the following selection, you will read about variables. You will see x's and y's in the problems. Don't worry about this term and these symbols. You already know how to solve equations.

For example, if you have 8 baseball cards and 4 people, how many cards should each person get? Each person should get 2 baseball cards. Now, you may not know it, but you just solved a variable equation, which would look like this: $4x = 8$. You will find that solving equations is something that you already understand, but never really thought that you did.

There is another important thing to know about solving equations. You will use your knowledge about solving equations throughout the rest of your life. While there may be other math concepts that only nuclear physicists or mathematicians use, solving equations is a concept that everyone uses. People in all fields frequently use algebra. Solving equations is one of the most basic of algebra skills.

▶ Skill Focus

When you solve a word problem, you state the plan for the solution in the form of a mathematical sentence. If the sentence has an equal sign, it is an **equation**. Most equations include a **variable**, or unknown number, represented by a symbol such as n, t, or x. To solve the equation, you must find a number to assign to the variable.

In general, to arrive at the unknown number, use the opposite operation of that shown in the equation. If an equation uses addition, you find the answer by subtracting. If an equation uses subtraction, you add. The same is true of multiplication and division.

Equations that have only one operation can be solved in a single step. Equations with more than a single operation require more steps.

▶ Word Clues

Solving equations is a large part of algebra. The word *algebra* comes from an Arabic word that means to *restore*. When you solve an equation, you restore the sentence to a simple form. In this simple form, a variable appears on one side of the equal sign, and a single number is on the other side.

Look at the following equation.

$$3x + 2 = 14$$

The solution is given as $x = 4$, which is the restored version of the equation. The solution assigns a meaning or a value to the variable.

▶ Strategy Tip

As you read equations, pay attention to the signs of operation. In algebra, you omit the multiplication sign when a product is formed from a number and a variable. Thus, $3y$ means the same as $3 \times y$, or 3 multiplied by y.

Reading Equations

Frequently, writing a mathematical sentence is the best way of stating the plan for a problem's solution. A mathematical sentence that has an equal sign is called an **equation**. Solving equations is one of the main parts of a branch of mathematics known as **algebra**.

Read the following problem.

A telephone call from White Plains, New York, to Atlanta, Georgia, during the day costs $0.62 for the first minute and more for each additional minute. If a two-minute call costs $1.05, how much does an additional minute cost?

The following equation describes the problem.

$$x + 62 = 105$$

This is one of the simplest kinds of equations for solving problems. The letter x represents the cost of an additional minute, and all costs are given in cents. To solve such an equation, you must isolate, or set apart, the x on one side of the equal sign. You can do so by subtracting 62 from each side of the equation.

$$x + 62 - 62 = 105 - 62$$
$$x = 43$$

It costs $0.43 for each additional minute.

Similarly, to solve the following equation, isolate the x by adding 37 to each side:

$$x - 37 = 98$$
$$x - 37 + 37 = 98 + 37$$
$$x = 135$$

If you look carefully at both equations, you can see that the operation used to solve each equation is the opposite of that shown in the equation.

Here is another problem.

Suppose that a phone call in your immediate area costs only $0.09, no matter how long you talk. If you spent $0.54 on local phone calls one evening, how many calls did you make?

A problem like this results in a different kind of equation.

$$9x = 54$$

In this case, the letter x represents the number of local phone calls. In algebra, $9x$ means 9 times x. To solve such an equation, isolate the x by dividing each side by the numerical factor, in this case 9. Again, perform the opposite operation to solve this equation. Since multiplication is shown in the equation, you solve it by division.

$$9x \div 9 = 54 \div 9$$
$$x = 6$$

You made 6 local phone calls.

Suppose that the night and weekend rate from White Plains to Atlanta is $0.24 for the first minute and $0.18 for each additional minute. If a call from White Plains to Atlanta on a Sunday cost $1.50, how long was the call?

If you let the letter x equal the number of additional minutes, you get the following equation.

$$18x + 24 = 150$$

This is a two-step equation. First you must isolate the expression with the x in it; then you must isolate the x. To isolate the expression with x in it, use the opposite operation from that shown in the equation: subtract 24 from each side of the equation.

$$18x + 24 - 24 = 150 - 24$$
$$18x = 126$$

Then isolate the x by dividing by 18.

$$18x \div 18 = 126 \div 18$$
$$x = 7$$

The number of additional minutes is 7, so the total time of the call is 8 minutes.

1. When a mathematical sentence contains an equal sign, what is the sentence called?
   _____

2. When you solve an equation, what must you do to the variable? _____

3. An equation consists of a number added to a variable, and that expression is equal to another number. How do you solve the equation.
   _____

   _____

4. A number and a variable are written together with no space or operation sign between them. What does this expression mean?
   _____

   _____

5. What do you call an equation that involves both a product and a sum?
   _____

6. An equation consists of a variable multiplied by a number, and that expression is equal to another number. How do you solve the equation?
   _____

   _____

   _____

7. What is the first step in solving the equation $18x + 24 = 150$?
   _____

8. What is the second step in solving the equation $18x + 24 = 150$?
   _____

1. What is the first step in solving the equation $x \div 4 = 3$? _____

2. In the equation $x = 6y$, x and y are whole numbers. How much larger is x than y?
   _____

3. In the equation $n + 16 = p$, which is larger, n or p? _____

4. In the equation $s - 42 = t$, which is larger, s or t? _____

Solve each equation. Use the space to the right of each equation to work it out.

1. $x + 4 = 13$

   $x =$ _____

2. $x + 18 = 47$

   $x =$ _____

3. $x + 5 = 18$

   $x =$ _____

4. $x + 16 = 38$

   $x =$ _____

5. $x - 3 = 14$

$x =$ _____

6. $x - 17 = 23$

$x =$ _____

7. $x - 19 = 7$

$x =$ _____

8. $34 = x - 12$

$x =$ _____

9. $3 = x - 47$

$x =$ _____

10. $x - 5 = 9$

$x =$ _____

11. $3x = 9$

$x =$ _____

12. $13x = 117$

$x =$ _____

13. $6x = 51$

$x =$ _____

14. $2x = 10$

$x =$ _____

15. $3x = 24$

$x =$ _____

16. $10x - 150$

$x =$ _____

17. $17x = 51$

$x =$ _____

18. $0.5x = 9$

$x =$ _____

19. $4x = 36$

$x =$ _____

20. $6x = 66$

$x =$ _____

21. $2x + 3 = 11$

$x =$ _____

22. $7x + 9 = 23$

$x =$ _____

23. $13x + 11 = 50$

$x =$ _____

24. $2x - 3 = 11$

$x =$ _____

25. $9 = 2x - 7$

$x =$ _____

26. $14x - 3 = 11$

$x =$ _____

27. $14x - 11 = 3$

$x =$ _____

28. $11x + 3 = 14$

$x =$ _____

29. $3x - 11 = 14$

$x =$ _____

30. $49 = 6x + 7$

$x =$ _____

▶ **Real Life Connections** Create the equations for three math problems based on buying items in a fast-food restaurant. Exchange problems with a partner and solve each other's equations.

Propaganda

A **fact** is information that can be proven to be true or checked to be sure it is accurate. This is a statement of fact: The artist Vincent van Gogh was born on March 30, 1853.

An **opinion** is a personal belief or feeling. It is what someone thinks is true. Here is a statement of opinion: Vincent van Gogh is the best painter the world has ever known.

If people believe that their opinions are very important, they may try to convince others to agree with them. When people want to convince others to believe something, do something, or buy something, they can use **propaganda**. Most advertisements use some kind of propaganda to talk consumers into buying a product or service. Political candidates often use propaganda to convince people to vote for them.

Following are six different types of propaganda devices. Read the description of how each type works and the example of it.

1. **Name Calling:** This device gives a bad name to someone or something in order to convince people to avoid the person or product.

   Example: The difference between our milk and the popular Alpha Milk is that Alpha Milk does not taste as fresh.

2. **Glad Names:** This device states positive things about the listeners or readers to convince them to agree with what they hear or see.

   Example: You're honest and hard working. Vote for the honest, hard-working candidate for senator— Ann Fong.

3. **Testimonial:** This device uses the sponsorship or support of a well-known personality. It is based on the idea that people will do something because the person they admire says that it is a good thing to do.

   Example: Raoul Hernandez, president of Hernandez Electronics, drinks A-O-K orange juice. Be a winner, too—with A-O-K!

4. **Transfer:** This device attempts to transfer to a product, person, or idea the good qualities belonging to something else or someone else. People then associate these qualities with the product, person, or idea.

   Example: Some of the world's most famous chefs eat at The Gold Kettle when they visit Chicago.

5. **Emotional Words:** This device uses words, particularly adjectives, that appeal to listeners' or readers' feelings or emotions.

   Example: A summer at Camp Echo makes campers active, happy, and healthy.

6. **Faulty Cause and Effect:** This device attempts to convince people that if they do something, such as buy a certain product, something good will happen. However, the cause and effect are not really related.

   Example: Play tennis with a Slammo tennis racket, and you'll never lose another game!

A. Fill in the circle next to the type of propaganda that each of the following statements uses.

1. Vote for Carol Luchenski for Congress. Governor Byron is voting for her, too.
   ○ transfer   ○ emotional words   ○ testimonial

2. Beautiful hair like yours deserves the best—Silk'n'Shine shampoo.
   ○ faulty cause and effect   ○ glad names   ○ name calling

3. *Monsters from the Moon* is a gory, violent, and downright frightening book.
   ○ emotional words   ○ name calling   ○ glad names

4. Snow Bunny ski jackets are made of the same material as the astronauts' suits.
   ○ testimonial   ○ transfer   ○ emotional words

5. The Culver may cost the same as the Liberty sedan, but repair costs will be twice as much.
   ○ name calling   ○ faulty cause and effect   ○ glad names

6. Use a Nelson camera, and you'll never take a bad snapshot again.
   ○ glad names   ○ testimonial   ○ faulty cause and effect

7. Many of the world's best skiers spend their winters skiing the Rocky Mountains.
   ○ transfer   ○ emotional words   ○ glad names

B. Read each of the following statements. On the line provided for each statement, first write the type of propaganda used. Then write the words that give you a clue about the device used.

1. Hockey star Greg Fleming uses Hi-Glo toothpaste every morning and evening. You, too, can be a star. Use Hi-Glo.

   _____

2. Your newborn baby is one of a kind. So use Dinkies—the one-of-a-kind diaper for your special little person.

   _____

3. Wear Miller jeans, and you'll be the most popular kid in your neighborhood.

   _____

4. The C. C. Cycle is fast, flashy, and fun to ride.

   _____

5. Haircuts by Shavers & Company make you look like you've been sheared.

   _____

6. You deserve luxury. Come live at Highgate, the city's newest condominium apartments.

   _____

7. The Marquis Quasi-Diamonds look as sparkling as the Crown Jewels.

   _____

8. Why do movie stars Heather Harris and Floyd Little look so good? They are members of the Northern Health and Athletic Club. You can meet Heather and Floyd by joining Northern!

   _____

9. Use Peterson's Plumbers the next time your kitchen sink has a leak, and it will never leak again.

   _____

10. Chez Hamburger home cooking is as good as the best French cuisine in Paris.

   _____

Reading Classified Ads

You do not always have to do your shopping at a store. Sometimes, what you are thinking of buying, such as a motorcycle, furniture, or camping equipment, could be less expensive if it has been previously owned. In such a case, read the **classified ad** section in the newspaper.

Study the following classified ads from the newspaper. Notice that the ads often use abbreviations to save space.

MERCHANDISE OFFERINGS (3200)

Telephones & Answering Machines 3204

One-Stop Shopping for all your telephone needs. Desk-style and Wall Phones, Cordless Phones, Answering Machines, LOW, LOW, PRICES. PHONE FACTORY, Route 6 in Middletown, Open 10-10.

Cordless telephone—make or receive calls up to 600' away from your installed phone. $45. Call 9-4 328-6365

Phone with built-in answerer. Digital recording, no tapes. 12-function remote. Asking $80. Call Ms. Ling at 298-4133.

RC-200 Telephone Ans Mac. Dual-cassette system. Auto date/time. Never been used. $65.
Call Mon or Tue 673-0443

THE TELEPHONE ANSWERING MACHINE
Source-RCs, SOUNDSO, RECORD-A PHONES, TELE-MATES, & MORE.
Best prices.
Call Jack Lewis 295-1880

ATTENTION DOCTORS. Forget your inefficient & costly answering services. I'll install Tele-Mate 1800 system in your office. For info. call Sharon Amis 673-2111.

Slimlite Desk-Style Phones. Touchtone dialing, attractive slim style. In white or assorted colors. ONLY $29. RAY'S COMMUNICATION CENTER 42 W. Borden St.

VCRs   3207

Sonix 2-head VCR. 1 month/8-event timer. Remote on-screen programming. 155-channel capacity. Auto scan memory. Paid $169, will sacrifice for $75. 595-6021 eves.

Soundo VCR—older model with no fancy features, but still works great. Perfect for kids' TV. $40 or best offer. 964-2120

WHY BUY NEW?
Rebuilt/reconditioned VCRs. Major brands, recent models. All with 60-day money-back guarantee. Work performed by trained technicians.
The VCR Barn
240 So. Main St. (Rte. 16), Hanover
Open Tues-Sat
9-6, Sun 12-5

General Electronics VCR. Never used, still in original box. Digital quartz tuning. Timer recording with bar-code scanner. TV/VCR unified remote. Fast search, slow-motion, frame advance, and more. Sells for $449 new. A bargain at $275. 898-7297. Ask for Rosa.

SAVE $ $ $! ! !
Every in-stock VCR now on sale. Today through Sat. RAY'S COMMUNICATION CENTER, 42 W. Borden St.

A. On the line next to each advertised item in the left-hand column, write the letter of the way you would purchase it in the right-hand column.

1. ____ older Soundo VCR

2. ____ RC-200 answering machine

3. ____ new General Electronics VCR

4. ____ Sonix 2-head VCR

5. ____ wall telephones

6. ____ Slimlite desk-style phones

7. ____ Phone with built-in answering machine

8. ____ Rebuilt/reconditioned VCRs

a. call Ms. Ling at 298-4133

b. call 898-7297, ask for Rosa

c. go to the VCR Barn any day except Monday

d. go to Ray's Communication Center

e. call 964-2120

f. call 673-0443 on Monday or Tuesday

g. go to the Phone Factory

h. call 595-6021 in the evening

B. Answer the following questions with complete sentences.

1. Which two types of equipment are advertised in section 3204 of these classifieds?

_____

2. Where can you go to buy *both* a VCR on sale *and* a Slimlite telephone?

_____

3. How much does each Slimlite phone cost at Ray's Communication Center?

_____

4. To buy a used VCR with a 60-day money-back guarantee, where could you go?

_____

5. Where could you go or call to learn about the differences between various types of telephone answering machines?

_____

6. How much money would you save by buying the General Electronics VCR from the ad

   rather than buying it at a store? _____

   How would you go about buying this VCR? _____

7. How many ads are there for cordless telephones? _____

   Where would you call or go if the only time you were free to discuss a cordless telephone was after 6 P.M.? How did you make this decision?

_____

_____

8. What is the advantage of the cordless telephone being sold for $45?

_____

9. Who placed a classified ad to help doctors with their phone messages?

_____

   What is this person advertising?

_____

10. How do you know that the VCRs at Ray's Communication Center are now selling for less than usual?

_____

11. Which advertised VCR is the least expensive? Why?

_____

_____

Context Clue Words

The following words are treated as context clue words in the lessons indicated. Lessons that provide instruction in a particular context clue type include an activity requiring students to use context clues to derive word meanings. Context clue words appear in the literature, social studies, and science selections and are underlined or footnoted for ease of location.

Word	Lesson	Word	Lesson	Word	Lesson	Word	Lesson
Aegean Sea	9	devastated	16	irritable	43	royal city	26
amplitude	45	diminishes	37	Laocoön	9	savannas	10
arduous	16	efficient	36	larvae	11	Seb	26
ascends	37	elastic	18	lasers	44	silt	27
bleak	36	electromagnetic	44	machetes	16	skeptically	1
bomas	10	exasperated	16	maimed	36	smidgen	43
briny	35	expanse	28	Menelaus	9	source	26
bypass	1	extraterrestrials	2	mesmerized	43	Sparta	9
cartilage	11	famine	27	migrate	11	spasm	35
chambers	18	feluccas	27	mortar	2	spiral	37
commonwealth	17	frigid	35	Nile	26	taut	35
communal	10	gall	26	Odysseus	9	theories	2
compression	45	gazelles	26	parasites	11	transient	28
concentric	3	germinating	28	phenomenon	3	transmission	44
contraction	18	harrowing	43	prosperity	27	Troy	9
crystalline	1	Helen	9	pulmonary	18	unravel	2
dense	28	hoax	3	quarter	36	vortex	3
descend	37	holography	44	Ra	26	yogurt	10
descent	17	hovering	1	rarefaction	45		
		immigrants	17	resumed	17		

Concept Words

In lessons that feature social studies, science, or mathematics selections, words that are unique to the content and whose meanings are essential to the selection are treated as concept words. Many of these words appear in boldface type and are often followed by a phonetic respelling and a definition.

Word	Lesson	Word	Lesson	Word	Lesson	Word	Lesson
acacias	28	cyclone	37	molecules	45	species	11
acoustics	45	data	38	occluded front	37	square	29
Agnatha	11	decibels	45	orders	11	stationary front	37
air mass	37	difference	12	Osteichthyes	11	storms	37
algebra	46	double bar graphs	38	parallel	29	subphyla	11
Amphibia	11	echo	45	parallelogram	29	succulents	28
anticyclone	37	equation	46	pent-	29	sum	12
aorta	18	equilateral	29	pentagon	29	symmetrical	29
area	29	exponent	4	per	19	tap root	28
arteries	18	factor	4	percent	19	tornadoes	37
atria	18	families	11	pericardium	18	total	12
average	12	Felis catus	11	perimeter	29	trapezoid	29
Aves	11	formula	29	phylum	11	tri-	29
axes	38	frequency	45	pitch	45	triangle	29
bar graph	38	front	37	plasma	18	ultrasound	45
base number	4	genera	11	platelets	18	variable	12
blitzkreig	36	geometry	29	polygons	29	veins	18
capillaries	18	hertz	45	quad-	29	venae cavae	18
Carnivora	11	hex-	29	quadrilaterals	29	ventricles	18
center	29	hexagon	29	rate	19	Vertebrata	11
Cetacea	11	high	37	rect-	29	vertebrate	11
Chondrichthyes	11	horizontal axis	38	rectangle	29	vertical axis	38
Chordata	11	hurricanes	37	red blood cells	18	vibrations	45
circle	29	isosceles	29	regular	29	warm front	37
circle graphs	38	key	38	Reptilia	11	warm-blooded	11
classes	11	kilometers	19	rhombus	29	wavelength	45
cold front	37	line graph	38	right triangle	29	white blood cells	18
cold-blooded	11	low	37	scalene	29		
crop circles	3	Mammalia	11	sectors	38		
		meters	19	sonar	45		